Commodity Market Reforms

WORLD BANK

REGIONAL AND

SECTORAL STUDIES

Commodity Market Reforms

Lessons of Two Decades

EDITED BY

TAKAMASA AKIYAMA

JOHN BAFFES

DONALD F. LARSON

PANOS VARANGIS

THE WORLD BANK
WASHINGTON, D.C.

Cover photograph of a seed market in the Kyrgyz Republic by Tjaart W. Schillhorn-van Veen,
Environmentally and Socially Sustainable Development Unit, Europe and Central Asia Region,
the World Bank.

Library of Congress Cataloging-in-Publication Data

Commodity market reforms : lessons of two decades / edited by Takamasa Akiyama ...
[et al.].
        p. cm. -- (World Bank regional and sectoral studies)
    ISBN 0-8213-4588-5
    1. Produce trade--Government ownership--Africa--Case studies. 2. Produce trade--
Government ownership--Developing countries--Case studies. 3. Privatization--Africa--
Case studies. 4. Privatization--Developing countries--Case studies. 5. Primary
commodities--Government policy--Africa--Case studies. 6. Primary commodities--
Government policy--Developing countries--Case studies. 7. Africa--Economic policy.
8. Developing countries--Economic policy. I. Akiyama, T. (Takamasa), 1944– II. World
Bank. III. Series.

HD9017.A2 C627 2000
380.1'41'096--dc21

                                                                      00-047736

Contents

v

Figures

Tables

Contributors and Acknowledgments

Contributors

Takamasa Akiyama, Lead Economist, Development Research Group, World Bank, Washington, D.C., United States of America.

John Baffes: Senior Economist, Development Prospects Group, World Bank, Washington, D. C., United States of America.

Brent Borrell, Chief Market Economist, Centre for International Economics, Canberra, Australia.

Jonathan Coulter, Principal Economist, Marketing and Enterprise Development, Natural Resources Institute, University of Greenwich, Chatham, United Kingdom.

Donald Larson: Senior Economist, Development Research Group, World Bank, Washington, D.C., United States of America.

Colin Poulton: Research Officer, Research Fellow, Agricultural Economics and Business Management Research Group, Imperial College at Wye, Wye, United Kingdom.

Gotz Schreiber, Lead Economist, Environmentally and Socially Sustainable Development Unit, Europe and Central Asia Region, World Bank, Washington, D.C., United States of America.

Panos Varangis: Senior Economist, Development Research Group, World Bank, Washington, D.C., United States of America.

Acknowledgments

The authors would like to thank Dr. Ron Duncan, Dr. Bruce Gardner, Dr. Yujiro Hayami, and Dr. John McIntire for improving earlier drafts.

Foreword

Structural reform of the economies of developing countries has been in the forefront of development interest since the early 1980s. This interest stems from a recognition within the development community that the structures and institutions of these countries are critical to any enhancement of economic and social development.

One of the key reforms has been that of primary commodity markets, especially agricultural commodity markets, because many developing countries, including the poorest, depend heavily on these for foreign exchange earnings and employment, and hence for poverty reduction.

This book focuses on the political economy and institutional aspects of agricultural commodity market reform. In order to explore in detail factors that are critical to the processes, consequences, and substance of reform, the authors have focused the analysis and evaluation on five commodities important in many developing countries, specifically cocoa, coffee, sugar, cotton, and cereal. In doing so, they highlight important lessons on how agricultural sector reform can be launched and implemented. Some of the factors identified in the book as being key to successful reform include the recognition that commodity markets often affect communities and even politics, that the initial conditions of markets are critical, and that government intervention can crowd out private sector initiatives, especially when it comes to building the institutions necessary for the development of a healthy agricultural sector.

The discussions in the book highlight the importance to the development process of polities and institutions. In so doing, they supplement a rich literature on structural reforms that has tended to focus primarily on economic consequences. Through these discussions it is clear that structural reforms have profound long-term ramifications for the development processes of developing countries.

The authors come to their analyses and discussions from the perspective of their own direct and extensive involvement in the market reform process. We trust that policymakers and others interested this area will find this book valuable, convincing, and highly relevant to the task of raising living standards of poor people in developing countries.

NICHOLAS H. STERN
SENIOR VICE PRESIDENT
AND CHIEF ECONOMIST
THE WORLD BANK

Introduction

SINCE THE 1980s MANY COUNTRIES have redefined the role of government in their economies. Reforming agricultural commodity markets has been an important part of this effort. The reforms have revamped market structures and eliminated or refashioned the mandates of key institutions, changing the way agricultural markets perform. As a result agricultural commodity markets are in transition, and their transformation has important ramifications for market players and supporting institutions.

Commodity market reforms are intended to boost an economy's efficiency—that is, to enhance the productivity of human talents and physical assets. In practice these reforms rely heavily on markets to allocate resources and to direct future investment. In the context of this book, the term *market reform* refers to the steps that are taken to reduce the state's involvement, open domestic and export markets to competition, and put in place public and private institutions that support free-market activities. Governments generally take a number of steps to achieve these goals in commodity markets. These measures include (but are not limited to) eliminating government marketing agencies and statutory monopolies in output and input markets, replacing prices set by the government with prices determined by markets, reducing explicit and implicit taxes, and privatizing marketing and processing assets.

Despite these similarities, commodity market reforms differ in scope across countries and commodities. The variations are significant, largely because the natures of the commodities and their markets differ, as do the social, political, and economic conditions prevailing at the time of reform. For this reason the outcomes of these liberalization efforts also differ. For example interventionist policies tend to tax export crops such as coffee, cocoa, and cotton. In countries where intervention in these markets has been heavy, reforms have improved the producer's share of world prices. Another example involves cotton and sugar markets, which are particularly difficult to reform because the production process is fragmented, including processors, producers, and publicly owned processing facilities. Further, policies affecting grains and sugar commonly favor urban consumers or promote food self-sufficiency, increasing the number of groups affected by reform. And in the sugar market, ongoing preferential trade arrangements help perpetuate existing interventions.

This book discusses the process of commodity market reform in the specific context of cocoa, coffee, cotton, grain, and sugar markets, drawing on experiences in those markets to provide lessons for policymakers. The book is also designed to provide a more general audience with a discussion of the issues associated with commodity market reform. The chapters focus on market-specific conditions that have facilitated or slowed the pace of reform, including the relationship between changing markets and changing institutions.

The examples illustrate the ramifications of market reform for the institutions that produce, market, and process the specific commodities as well as for the political economy. Many of the chapters look at African countries where agricultural commodities account for a significant share of GDP, export revenues, and employment and where reforms of agricultural commodity markets have become common in recent years.

This book supplements a rich literature on structural adjustment in commodity markets. The particular markets covered in this book warrant special attention, for several reasons. First, these commodities play an especially important role in many developing countries. Reforms—and the process of reform—in these markets can affect communities, entire economies, and even political power structures in significant ways. In these cases lessons from experiences with similar reforms can smooth the process of reform and help limit the costs of adjustment.

Second, these markets demonstrate the importance of taking initial conditions into account when designing reforms. They also show how a commodity's special features (derived in part from the production characteristics of the commodities and in part from historical developments) can affect the reform process. Consequently the experiences reported in this book can assist policymakers as they adapt general approaches to reform to the specific needs of key commodity subsectors.

Third, experience from these commodity markets illustrates how long-standing interventions like marketing boards and public ownership of processing facilities can crowd out private sector activities. The history of these markets shows how policymakers and the private sector cope with missing markets and institutions. And finally a close examination of policies in different commodity subsectors illustrates the practical ways that changes in marketing systems can shift political power away from the government to the private sector. This shift is significant, since it provides players in commodity markets with the autonomy they need to adapt to future events.

The first chapter of the book places the reforms in context by discussing the background against which they took place, including the political events and the economic thinking that drove them. In many cases reforms to agricultural commodity markets were undertaken only after state-run systems had become dysfunctional and international donors made further aid conditional on reform. In other cases new regimes were the agents of change. In still other instances external shocks made existing polices unsustainable.

Chapter 2 evaluates in detail the effects of reform on the marketing systems of four major cocoa-producing countries—Cameroon, Côte d'Ivoire, Ghana, and Nigeria. An examination of producer prices before and after liberalization in these countries (especially Cameroon and Nigeria) convincingly reveals that liberalization benefits producers. And while liberalization in these two countries has had some negative effects, these problems are arguably specific to the country itself and not to the cocoa subsector in general. Reforms in Côte d'Ivoire and Ghana have been gradual, focusing on promoting competition in the internal marketing system while maintaining controls on exports. The experience of these countries demonstrates how systems designed to provide stable incomes and orderly markets can evolve into systems that reduce smallholder incomes.

Chapter 3 examines coffee market liberalization in India, Uganda, and Togo. The chapter argues that the collapse of the export quota system under the International Coffee Agreement, along with conditions attached to World Bank financing, were instrumental in initiating the liberalization process. It also shows that liberalization has affected political institutions as well as institutions in the coffee markets themselves, considerably expanding the power of the private sector in designing and implementing policy.

Chapter 4 illustrates how the physical characteristics of a product affect market structure. For instance, sugar cane is difficult to store, so determining quality is not easy. Milling capacity is fixed, and scheduling deliveries requires cooperative action. The chapter argues that those managing reforms of the sugar subsector must understand these characteristics, which often explain past interventions and suggest potential approaches to reform. Governments have often been required to intervene in sugar markets when the necessary cooperative agreements between sugar growers and mills break down and to maintain the special access to protected markets on which some countries depend. Thus policymakers considering sugar mar-

ket reform may also need to address the institutional and economic consequences of long-standing government interventions. The chapter also examines policies that affect domestic policy regimes and international trade in
sugar and discusses approaches to problems such as trade-related distortions, cane pricing, privatization, and the sequencing of reforms in domestic sugar markets.

Chapter 5 focuses on the liberalization of the cotton subsectors in
Uganda, Tanzania, and Zimbabwe. It discusses recent efforts by West
African cotton-producing countries to reform their cotton subsectors and
looks briefly at reforms in the Arab Republic of Egypt, Mexico, Pakistan,
and the United States. In Uganda and Zimbabwe, where liberalization has
been completed, it has not only raised producer prices but also generated a
considerable supply response. In Tanzania producer prices have risen, but
the supply response has been minimal. Reforms in West Africa have also
been designed to raise producer prices in a sector that is already performing
well in terms of production and yields. Reforms in Egypt and Pakistan have
been less ambitious, mainly because of the governments' unwillingness to
delink reforms in the cotton and textile industries—a move that is essential
to successful reform. In the United States and Mexico, where the governments have traditionally subsidized the subsector, reforms have taken a different path and are intended to compensate producers.

Chapter 6 presents grain market reforms experience for Ghana, Mali,
Tanzania, and Zimbabwe. It discusses the approaches to market liberalization various countries have adopted in light of past government involvement. Grains are particularly important, as they affect economic
development, political stability, and the welfare of the poorest groups (who
also happen to be net buyers). For this reason many countries—including
Mali, Tanzania, and Zimbabwe—have had statutory monopolies in the procurement and distribution of grains, either a marketing board or a stabilization fund. In some countries, like Ghana, the grain-marketing system has
always been relatively open, with the majority of the trade in private hands.

Together the chapters illustrate that the positive and negative lessons
from reform are both heterogeneous. Economic theory remains the best
guide to reform but will not fully illuminate the most successful approaches.
Theory tempered by a careful understanding of the markets, informed by
lessons from earlier experience and blessed by good fortune, fosters the
most successful reforms.

1

Market Reforms:
Lessons from Country and
Commodity Experiences

*Takamasa Akiyama, John Baffes, Donald Larson,
and Panos Varangis*

DURING MOST OF THE 20TH CENTURY, most governments intervened in primary commodity markets. In fact such interventions were an accepted part of the development policy framework. While the instruments of intervention varied across both countries and crops, a dominant architecture emerged. Designed to stabilize producer incomes, this architecture was based on a marketing board that provided a single channel for exports and imports, state ownership of processing centers such as cotton gins and sugar mills, and administered domestic prices that were normally panseasonal, panterritorial, and detached from international prices. International institutions took on the challenge of finding collective instruments to stabilize prices and reverse declining terms of trade.

The prevailing policy recommendations of development economists and institutions encouraged these interventions. But the policies, which had only limited success, soon generated a new set of problems. International commodity agreements failed, and the commodity parastatals found themselves financially strained. At the same time steady productivity gains in agriculture, transportation, and communication began eroding the efficacy of intervention instruments. Economists and policymakers turned increasingly to market-based approaches, which took on institutional form when the World Bank and other international organizations began a series of structural adjustment loans and credits conditional on certain policy reforms. At the same time, a series of political and economic events made reform inevitable.

The pace and consequences of reform varied across commodities and countries. The goals of reform were generally not sector specific; rather, the reforms were intended to boost general economic growth. Nonetheless commodity exports were generally taxed, and for this reason reform generally brought immediate income gains to producers (primarily smallholders) in the sectors covered in this volume. Frequently, the reform process also brought unintended consequences and often initially left public and private institutions poorly equipped to support private markets.

This volume draws lessons from experiences with agricultural commodity market reform. Reform efforts have produced outcomes ranging from success to failure. The chapters that follow address the specific market reform experiences for the following commodities: coffee, cocoa, cotton, sugar, and food grains. These commodities differ in their production processes and market organization, and these differences have directly influenced the rationale for and the pace and consequences of reform. Yet the reforms also share common features, and the outcomes provide us with common lessons. The remainder of this chapter covers these shared themes.

The Rise of Commodity Market Interventions

An examination of the specific factors that contributed to government intervention in commodity markets during the second half of the 20th century shows that governments had a variety of reasons for undertaking these strong measures. Experiences with famine and shortages convinced many governments in Asia and in newly independent Sub-Saharan Africa that control of the food crop sector was necessary in order to maintain food security.[1] Controls were frequently extended to cash crops, which had a strategic value as a source of foreign exchange and tax revenues.

Colonialism had also left unanticipated legacies that postindependence governments sometimes addressed through intervention. In some instances—Kenya's tea and coffee markets, for instance—governments allowed parastatals to continue operating. These governments argued that the parastatals were necessary to encourage smallholder participation in cash crop markets that had been closed to small farmers under colonial rule. Similarly shortly after independence the Indonesian government converted plantations established under Dutch rule into government-owned "people's plantations" in order to ensure that plantation resources would be used to promote national goals. In Latin America many government interventions in the coffee and sugar industries date to the 1930s and were in part a reaction to the uneven distribution of land and wealth that prevailed at that time. Trade relationships established during colonial times were later institutionalized in bilateral and multilateral trade arrangements—for example, the agreements that provide preferential access to protected U.S. and

European Union (EU) domestic sugar markets. These arrangements in turn gave rise to domestic controls and institutions in favored producer countries designed to allocate and administer the benefits of preferential trade.

Development theory and practical political considerations also encouraged continued intervention. Many developing countries in Africa, Asia, Latin America, and the Middle East, influenced by the example of the Soviet Union, believed strongly in state-dominated economic development.[2] Moreover governments frequently pursued policies that taxed agriculture in order to promote industrial development. These approaches received support from many development economists in the 1950s.

In countries where one or two commodities were especially important to employment and export revenue, control of the rest of the commodity markets was linked to the larger goal of economic and sometimes social planning. Gunnar Myrdal (1956) argued for government control in economic management as a means of responding to poorly functioning markets or filling gaps where no markets existed. Arthur Lewis (1954) postulated that the transfer of labor from the farming sector to the industrial sector facilitated economic growth when agricultural labor was always abundant. Policymakers used Lewis's argument to justify policies that favor industrialization and implicitly or explicitly taxed agriculture. Hirschman (1958) reinforced this policy, theorizing that investing in industry rather than agriculture would lead to rapid and broad-based economic growth. Moreover, misguided interpretations of immiserizing growth arguments put forward by Johnson (1953) and Bhagwati (1958)—the so-called adding-up problem— also provided theoretical justification for the practice of taxing commodity exports.[3] Some analysts argued that the terms of trade of export commodities had been declining and would continue to fall (Prebisch 1950; Singer 1950). Together these arguments encouraged a development strategy that encouraged resource transfers through policies that discriminated against agriculture.[4]

Practical and political considerations often provided a further rationale for intervening in commodity markets. Commodities were often useful revenue sources, and some policymakers saw taxing commodity exports as the most convenient and practical way to finance state activities (Bates 1981). Government-controlled systems provided a source of political patronage— for example, politicians could reward supporters with trading licenses or high-level appointments to marketing boards. Further, state management often provided politicians and government officials with funding for discretionary expenditures. Government control of key commodity markets created opportunities for corruption. Indirect taxes on export commodities (including overvalued currencies and parallel exchange rates, which generated a black market in foreign exchange) provided financial benefits to the urban elite, who were important political allies (Lipton 1977; Bates 1981). As a result, interventions continued to generate support, despite the fact that they had failed to achieve their stated goals.

The prevailing thinking, then, was that commodity markets could be controlled and manipulated to the advantage of both producers and consumers. The stated objectives of intervention largely reflected the justifications offered by development economists: stabilizing prices, maintaining food security, protecting farmers from local traders (who were perceived to have certain bargaining advantages), controlling exports in order to influence world prices, and protecting sources of foreign exchange and tax revenue. In practice these efforts took several institutional forms and gave rise to several instruments, but regulated prices were a common and often dominant feature. To make planting decisions easier, prices were frequently fixed for the crop year. To smooth annual price fluctuations, domestic prices were uncoupled from international prices. And to resolve regional disparities, fixed prices were panterritorial so that all producers received the same purchase price.

Most commonly, governments controlled domestic markets by restricting trade, by depending on licensing regulations, or by granting monopolistic marketing powers to parastatals. Often government control extended to key processing and transport facilities. The control of domestic processing markets took several forms. In West African cotton and sugar markets and in some of the plantation systems of Asia, all aspects of production and sale were subject to government control and command. More often, private markets and government coexisted in an uneasy relationship. For coffee, cocoa, and grain markets, where investments in processing were smaller and more easily reversed, governments controlled domestic markets by licensing processors and setting processing margins. In cotton and sugar markets, processing required larger irreversible investments. Moreover, the investments conveyed to processors some measure of monopsony, which government regulations were intended to limit. Often, once government policy and management decisions were linked, private investors were unwilling to make additional investments to maintain existing structures or commit to new investments. Moreover, because local communities were dependent on incomes from the processing facilities, governments were reluctant to allow unprofitable mills to close. These factors often put the cotton and sugar processing sectors on a devolving path toward government ownership that was reactive rather than planned.[5]

Not all policy interventions were decided domestically. At the close of World War II, many economists considered the short-term balance of payment problems caused by volatile commodity prices an especially important component of macroeconomic instability (see, for example, Keynes 1943). According to prevailing thought, since commodity prices were determined largely in international markets, collective interventions were the logical response. Common mechanisms designed to manage international price volatility included quota and buffer stock programs arranged through international commodity groups and compensatory financing schemes supported by the International Monetary Fund (IMF) and later the Lomé Agreement between the EU and the African, Caribbean, and Pacific Group of States. Moreover, the success of the Organization of Petroleum Exporting Countries (OPEC) in 1973 in cutting production and raising prices provided added motivation for collective action among commodity producers and prompted the launch of the Integrated Program for Commodities in 1975.[6] This program attempted not only to stabilize the prices of major commodity exports from developing countries, but also to reverse the declining terms of trade (Prebisch 1950; Singer 1950). The program focused on buffer stock operations under international commodity agreements for cocoa, jute, rubber, and tin (among others), and eventually led to the establishment of the Common Fund for Commodities, which was designed to provide liquidity to the individual stabilization programs.[7]

What Prompted Market Reforms?

Though triggered primarily by sudden and often unexpected political and economic events, the commodity market reforms that began in the late 1980s also reflect a gradual evolution in development economists' views on the importance of agriculture to economic development and the role of government in the development process. The increasingly evident inefficiencies of interventionist policies reinforced (and partly motivated) this change in philosophy. At the same time structural changes in commodity markets generated by new production, transportation, and information technologies brought increasing pressure to bear on interventionist instruments during the 1980s and 1990s and precipitated the decline of world commodity prices. (See the data appendix for historical price, production, and trade data.)

What the Economists Thought

Not all economists agreed with the prevailing views of commodity markets. Johnson (1947) argued that agricultural sectors were highly adaptive and required few interventions. Friedman (1954) disputed the benefits of managing commodity income variability. Early on, in the context of West Africa, Bauer (1954) challenged the notion that output markets were inefficient and argued that marketing boards were largely a mechanism for exploiting small farmers. Johnson and Mellor (1961) were among the first economists to attack the pro-urban policies and subsequent neglect of agriculture prevalent in many developing countries, arguing that development in most poor countries depended largely on the agricultural sector. Schultz (1964) argued that agricultural households in developing countries, while poor, were efficient and responded to economic incentives. Early work by Balassa and Associates (1971) challenged the wisdom of exchange rate regimes that favored the manufacturing sector. Bates (1981) was also influential, examining the political and social roots and consequences of marketing systems in many countries in Sub-Saharan Africa.

In 1983 the World Bank (1983) gave these arguments an institutional voice, concluding that policy interventions slowed growth. Three years later the World Bank (1985) emphasized the welfare losses attributable to agricultural policy interventions in both industrial and developing countries. In 1992 a series of developing country studies (Krueger, Schiff, and Valdés 1992) examined in detail the distortions affecting the agricultural sector in 18 countries—distortions introduced through sector-specific and macroeconomic policies.

International Events That Catalyzed Change

As a preference for market-based policy instruments grew among development economists, a number of political and economic events reinforced the notion that market interventions stifle growth and economic opportunity, creating a foundation for reform. Among these events were China's successful introduction of market-oriented domestic agricultural policies, the failure of several commodity agreements, the collapse of the Soviet Union, accumulated debt burdens in Latin America and Africa, and stepped-up efforts by international financial institutions to bring about policy changes.

Following the failed Great Leap Forward, China adopted an approach to domestic agriculture that de-emphasized central planning in favor of the market. By the 1970s the country was making noticeable progress under the reformed regime.[8] While China's success and the success of agricultural sectors in other East Asian countries were not interpreted strictly as an endorsement of free trade, they did reflect an increased reliance on market mechanisms. By the late 1980s the economic performance of the Asian countries, with their relatively open markets, stood in stark contrast to the performance of the government-controlled systems of Sub-Saharan Africa.[9]

The economic problems of the former Soviet Union and its eventual collapse were a strategic blow to policymakers' faith in government-led and -controlled economic development strategies. At the same time commodity markets began to experience practical problems with internationally sponsored stabilization instruments. The buffer stock programs planned under the Integrated Program for Commodities proved unsuccessful for structural and political reasons, and the Common Fund was never put to its intended use.[10] Other international agreements designed to stabilize or raise commodity prices also faced difficulties, especially financial problems, and eventually collapsed. World petroleum prices fell sharply in 1986 owing to

OPEC's inability to limit oil output among its members. The buffer stock provisions of the International Cocoa Organization (ICCO)and the quota mechanism of the International Coffee Organization (ICO) both failed, and member countries chose to dismantle these long-standing market interventions. Together these events strongly suggested that attempting to alter commodity prices was extremely difficult, if not impossible.[11]

At the same time prices in international markets for most commodities began to fall. For some commodities, especially coffee, the declines resulted in part from the release of inventories following the collapse of the commodity agreements; the dissolution of the Soviet Union accelerated the trend.[12] The price declines caused significant fiscal and balance of payments problems for commodity-dependent countries and serious financial problems for the respective parastatals. The problems were especially severe for a number of Sub-Saharan African economies dependent on coffee and cocoa as sources of export and government revenues. International programs designed to provide financial assistance to such countries (for instance, the compensatory financing programs of the EU and IMF) had a limited effect. The parastatals charged with stabilizing domestic prices came under increasing pressure as commodity prices continued to fall.[13]

A significant push for market reform came from the World Bank, which introduced Structural Adjustment Loans in 1980. Initially the objective of structural lending was to provide financial assistance to developing countries with debt problems. Such problems were particularly severe in Latin America and Africa, largely because of poor fiscal management and the sharp oil price increases of 1979. With time, however, structural adjustment policies became synonymous with market reform. Mosley (1991, p. 24) characterizes the policies as the "retreat of the state from economic life and the opening up of economic activity, especially in agriculture."[14] Yet as Meerman (1997) documents, reliance on domestic markets was not a systematic component of adjustment lending until the late 1980s. Early structural lending packages were more likely to restructure marketing boards than to recommend eliminating them.[15]

But the Bank's early experiments in parastatal reform revealed problems of the types Bauer (1954), Bates (1981), and other development economists had anticipated, including mismanagement, the use of political power to influence business decisions, and a lack of transparency in the use of parastatal funds (see, for example, Cleaver [1987]).

By the late 1980s the World Bank, the IMF, and other multilateral and bilateral development institutions were recommending policies that typically included a macroeconomic component characterized by fiscal austerity, exchange rate revaluations, and increased market activity. Countries seeking to follow these recommendations would need to undertake privatization, reduce barriers to trade, and open their domestic markets. Policy recommendations were often conditions of adjustment loans, which were dispersed in tranches. Conditions commonly applied to agricultural commodity subsectors included eliminating or significantly reducing government intervention in determining prices, dissolving parastatals or stripping them of some powers, and eliminating some agricultural import subsidies (Mosley 1987).

By the late 1980s and early 1990s, many of the Sub-Saharan African commodity parastatals had become insolvent. Many governments—either convinced of the merits of reform or forced into it by events—began to revamp their agricultural commodity marketing systems and policies.

Domestic Events That Shaped Reform

In many instances commodity market reforms were part of a larger set of economic reforms undertaken because of economic crises or prolonged periods of poor economic performance.[16] Sometimes the crises precipitated regime changes that facilitated reform, as the new regimes tended to be less vested in the old systems and could take advantage of the incentives structural adjustment programs offered. New leaders frequently took the initiative in carrying out reforms.[17]

The commodities and the markets for them differed widely from country to country. As a result the political dynamics engendered by interventions also varied. Policies were frequently designed to protect producers of food crops such as grain staples or sugar, although this objective was often at odds with efforts to assist urban consumers. Similarly policies designed to promote food self-sufficiency differed from policies covering export crops such as coffee and cocoa. These varied policies resulted in equally varied outcomes across crops and countries. In the most extreme cases price fluctuations in international markets caused changes in the prevailing regimes (see for example the examination of the link between coffee prices and regime changes in Africa in Deaton [1992]).

COFFEE AND COCOA. Governments' fiscal problems and parastatals' financial difficulties combined to prompt market reforms in many coffee- and cocoa-producing countries. In several countries in Sub-Saharan Africa (Cameroon, Côte d'Ivoire, Madagascar, and Uganda), reforms followed closely on the collapse of the quota scheme of the International Coffee Agreement. International prices declined as inventories accumulated under the quota scheme reached market, and the demand for fresh funds to prop up domestic producer prices grew while coffee-generated tax revenues to government fell. Budgetary shortfalls made it impossible for many of the parastatals to carry out their core function—maintaining fixed producer prices. The collapse of the international agreements changed the political economy of domestic interventions as well. For example during the ICO's quota operation the allocation of export quotas under the International Coffee Agreement became a major source of rents and was used to sustain government marketing agencies (Bohman and Jarvis 1996).

Ironically cocoa prices and cocoa-producing countries were relatively unaffected by the collapse of ICCO's buffer scheme because the stock program itself had not been effective in stabilizing cocoa prices. Nonetheless fiscal crises of other sorts frequently motivated the reform of cocoa marketing boards. For example reforms in Togo followed fiscal problems brought on by a prolonged general strike that lasted from late 1993 until mid-1994. Ghana undertook limited reforms of its cocoa subsector in the early 1980s to raise the incomes of cocoa farmers facing a lingering economic crisis. And in 1987, faced with the prospect of continuing to finance the cocoa marketing board's substantial (and increasing) costs, the Nigerian government dismantled it overnight.

India is an unusual case in that producers initiated the reform process. The country's producers had become increasingly skeptical of the coffee board's marketing functions after domestic prices fell along with world prices in the late 1980s and early 1990s. Well-organized producer associations successfully demanded market reforms and trade liberalization. Advances in communication played an important role in these events, helping producers realize their political power and develop the capacity to initiate change.

GRAINS. Postindependence marketing systems for grains in Africa were developed largely along the lines of the controlled marketing systems inherited from the colonial period. But these systems also sought to redress the neglect of smallholder agriculture and provide cheap food for urban dwellers. Unlike coffee, however, grains had a relatively low value relative to transportation costs, making one aspect of the systems—panterritorial pricing—costly to implement. The programs gradually became an unsustainable fiscal burden. Official monopolies could not be maintained, and a flourishing but illegal private trade in grains emerged. To limit budget outlays governments increasingly pushed the costs of the program back onto producers by lowering prices, adversely affecting production and further undermining the programs.

COTTON. In East Africa the cotton parastatals in Uganda, Tanzania, and Zimbabwe were insolvent by the early 1990s, largely because of poor management. The monopolies could no longer carry out their responsibilities in terms of trade and producer financing, and their capacity to invest in or maintain publicly financed gins was severely limited. Unable to finance the industry through budget subsidies, the governments had little choice but to reform the subsector. In West Africa a number of countries, including Benin,

Chad, Côte d'Ivoire, and Togo, also faced financial difficulties, but financial restructuring and a significant devaluation of the common currency partially mitigated the problems. But these countries also began the reform process (although in a somewhat less sweeping form) in the late 1990s. The reforms were in part spurred by analyses conducted by multilateral lending institutions showing that farmers were receiving very low prices (less than 40 percent of the world price) and that by controlling the cotton input and credit markets, government activities discouraged the production of other commodities.

SUGAR. Many sugar-producing countries initiated domestic reforms in the 1990s. These reforms generally had as their centerpiece the privatization of state-owned sugar estates and mills. Three factors contributed to reforms in sugar markets:

- The dissolution of the Soviet Union, an event that ended the oil-for-sugar deals with Bulgaria, Latvia, and Romania;
- The poor performance of publicly owned mills and estates in countries such as Côte d'Ivoire, Kenya, and Peru; and
- General reforms of state-owned enterprises in countries such as Brazil and Mexico.

The financial crisis of 1998 accelerated reforms in Brazil and sparked trade liberalization in Indonesia. But sugar trade policy remains largely unreformed in many countries, and most countries protect their domestic industry. Local communities depend on an industry that itself depends on the government, making the political cost of reform high. Because sugar programs often finance themselves through an indirect tax on consumers, they do not face the budgetary pressures most policy interventions generate.

The lack of extensive trade reform is also in part the result of the policies of several large producer-consumers, especially the EU and the United States. The results of the Uruguay Round of the General Agreement on Tariffs and Trade (GATT), which made little progress toward reducing sugar-related trade restrictions, reflect this fact. Policies set by these large producer-consumers also directly influence the policies of the handful of countries that enjoy special access to protected U.S. and EU markets, since the need to distribute the gains from these preferential arrangement encourages central management in the sugar sector.

The Consequences of Market Reforms

Regardless of what sparked the reforms, most focused on putting in place a new set of incentives that encouraged economic efficiency. By changing the implicit or explicit costs and benefits associated with existing systems, the reforms redistributed income and, because of changing price signals, had long-term cumulative effects on investment and human capital formation. Some of the most immediate consequences of these reforms related to domestic prices, the supply response, private sector activities and institutions, and financing for public goods. The capacity of the public and private institutions on which efficient markets depend profoundly affected the response to reform.

Market reforms that eliminated single-channel marketing systems often changed the relationship between the government and private industry significantly. When these reforms were successful, they resulted in a more open and consultative policymaking environment as well as a more competitive market.

Policies

Several of the studies in this volume demonstrate the growing influence of the private sector in formulating policy and providing services. Because of the lack of transparency in the management of government-controlled systems (especially with regard to financial matters), they usually did not collaborate with the private sector and in some cases displaced it. The new mechanisms for creating and implementing policies suggest a significant shift of political power from the government to the private sector. One manifestation of this shift is the inclusion of private sector stakeholders in bodies that formulate and implement policy. For example, as discussed in chapter 3, private sector representatives play a key role in the Coffee Development Agency in Uganda and the Coordination Committee in Togo.

Although in many countries reforms resulted in a significant shift of political power to the private sector, they did not benefit all private players. Those private organizations able to influence government policies were often traders and producer associations rather than farmer groups. Organizing farmers into marketing associations or pressure groups is generally difficult (see Bates 1981). And marketing cooperatives in several countries developed problems coping with the competitive situation introduced by liberalization.[18] (See, for example, the discussions of cotton reforms in Uganda, or sugar reforms in Peru.)

Domestic Prices

Many commodity market interventions were designed to protect smallholders from predatory pricing and to stabilize incomes. This section summarizes country experiences reported in later chapters in light of these objectives.[19]

PRICE LEVELS. In most coffee- and cocoa-producing countries, the increased competition and lower taxes (both implicit and explicit) resulting from reform raised the ratio of farm prices to export prices substantially. For example following reforms, cocoa producers in Cameroon and Nigeria saw prices for their products increase to well over 70 percent of the f.o.b. (free on board) price, up from 40 and 20 percent before the reforms. Following reforms that began in 1991, Ugandan coffee producers saw prices increase from 30 percent of the f.o.b. price to over 60 percent. Cotton producers in Zimbabwe were receiving close to 80 percent of the f.o.b. price two years after reforms, and cotton producers in Tanzania and Uganda also saw their prices increase following reforms. The devaluations that often accompanied market reforms (a condition of the structural adjustment programs) contributed to these increases.

Often the reforms brought an end to panterritorial pricing, which in effect had forced producers located close to markets to subsidize producers located further away. With the elimination of panterritorial pricing, producer prices began to reflect transportation costs. In countries with an underdeveloped infrastructure, producer prices in relatively remote areas declined relative to producer prices in the more accessible locations favored by traders and exporters. For example coffee farmers in remote areas of Madagascar have been receiving around 40–50 percent of the f.o.b price since the reforms, while farmers in more accessible areas receive between 60 and 70 percent (chapter 3). In multi-ethnic countries, attempts to eliminate panterritorial pricing brought with them tensions among ethnic groups in different locations (chapter 6).

By and large, consumers gained from market liberalization. Marketing and processing costs fell, in many cases wholly offsetting the negative effects of eliminating consumer subsidies. Many beneficiaries of these changes were small farm households that are typically net buyers of grains. In Ghana the average retail price for maize declined after liberalization because trading margins fell and price spreads narrowed. Tanzania had a similar experience with the liberalization of the maize market (chapter 6). In the case of sugar, reforms were successfully forestalled in instances were consumers would have benefited most (chapter 4).

VOLATILITY. Reforms established a link between domestic and world prices, so that producers faced increased price volatility, especially in several important grain markets (chapter 6). Prior to reform parastatals and governments had internalized the price risk, in part through panseasonal pricing. But when parastatals had some success stabilizing prices for a year, they were rarely able to stabilize price across seasons—and in many cases, they exhausted all their resources in the attempt. Moreover in periods of low world prices when the need was greatest, parastatals were often unable to compensate producers, having failed to save enough during periods of high prices (Deaton 1992). Thus producers were effectively trading market risks for risks involving policy and the performance of the parastatal, as Larson (1993) found for Mexican maize.

Market reforms potentially offered some producers, especially coffee, cocoa, and sugar growers, the opportunity to access futures, options, and related price risk markets to insure against volatile prices. But with few exceptions such risk mitigation devices have not emerged in the domestic markets of the countries reviewed here.[20] And the existing exchanges in industrial countries may not be useful because of the high basis and exchange rate risk.[21] Gilbert (1997) found that the cost of price stabilization was high relative to the benefits of stable but lower producer prices in African cocoa-producing countries, a result confirmed by McIntire and Varangis (1999) for Côte d'Ivoire. Hazell (1994) found only modest potential gains from reduced price uncertainty for Costa Rican coffee farmers.

The Supply Response

In some instances market reforms were offered not only as a solution to poor overall economic performance but also as a way to revive poorly performing commodity sectors. However, the evidence regarding the effects of reforms on the commodity supply response is mixed. For the coffee, cocoa, and cotton subsectors, which were heavily taxed before market reforms, policy reforms were expected to evoke a positive supply response. In some instances they have. In both Uganda and Zimbabwe, cotton reforms raised producer prices and induced a relatively strong positive response. Uganda's coffee production increased sharply after liberalization. But cotton production also increased in West Africa, where producer prices remained low. Cocoa production in Côte d'Ivoire and Ghana—two countries where relatively little progress was made in cocoa market reforms and producer prices remained low—also increased substantially.

Per capita income grain production in Africa as a whole remained relatively static in the 1980s and 1990s, with no evidence of a change in supply response. The immediate impact of the reforms was most adverse in eastern and southern Africa, where marketing boards and other state services had promoted smallholder production of high-yielding varieties. In Ghana, where reforms were mildest, per capita production rose significantly. Production stayed fairly constant in Mali and declined in Tanzania and Zimbabwe. Some of the declines in grain production can be attributed to the severe droughts of 1992 and 1995, the contradictory approaches that were adopted, and the fact that the reforms were rarely fully implemented (chapter 6).

Finally several countries experienced a weak supply response, for several reasons. In some countries, including Madagascar and several West

African economies, more than one commodity subsector was reformed at the same time, and given that agriculture's aggregate supply elasticity tends to be much lower than elasticity for individual crops, the supply response was minimal. Weak marketing institutions and poor physical infrastructure also hindered the supply response. These outcomes indicate that market reforms can eliminate one of the key factors constraining supply. But if other constraining factors exist, the supply response to price changes will be slow (Krueger, Schiff, and Valdés 1992). This result is consonant with the argument put forth by Timmer (1991, p. 14) , who states, "Getting prices right in the agricultural and marketing sectors will not by itself induce the necessary private investment of competitive market structure." Removing inappropriate policies may be necessary, but without supporting institutional and legal reforms, it is often not enough to generate increased private investment.

Private Investment and Credit

Private investment is the primary mechanism for reallocating resources following reform. In markets where interventions resulted in heavy taxation, reforms were expected to increase long-term investment by producers and processors. In addition the elimination of government monopolies on output markets would create demand for working capital to finance trade, storage, and processing.

When countries are open to direct foreign investment, private investment (both domestic and foreign) can increase considerably after liberalization. Direct investment in processing facilities was largely responsible for the successful privatization of sugar mills in Mexico, Peru, and Poland. In Uganda a South African company began rehabilitating two cotton gins shortly after liberalization in the cotton sector, and both domestic and foreign private firms invested heavily in coffee-processing equipment following reform. In Zimbabwe a multinational corporation purchased almost one-quarter of the country's 1997–98 cotton output. In Côte d'Ivoire a number of gins were sold to a foreign company, and a joint venture handled one-third of domestic cocoa processing.

Providing adequate levels of working capital is frequently a concern following reforms. Market participants may be new and inexperienced and may not be perceived as creditworthy. In Mexico's sugar sector a combination of debt accrued during privatization and a sharp unexpected hike in interest rates following the peso crises of 1994 severely hampered newly privatized firms' ability to raise working capital.

Financial institutions that have traditionally lent to a single government parastatal may be equally inexperienced, much like the institutions that had lent to the coffee sector in India and Uganda. Ironically because commodity market reform is often part of a larger package of economic reforms, domestic credit can become more expensive and less available immediately after the reforms are implemented. One unintended consequence of reform in Uganda and Tanzania was that producers and traders found their already limited access to credit reduced still further as governments tightened monetary policy—a condition of structural adjustment. In India the elimination of parastatals that could draw on government treasuries for crop financing exacerbated the credit crunch. Reforms to financial institutions aimed at increasing the efficiency and profitability of financial organizations in countries like Uganda sometimes required banks to close unprofitable rural branches. And concerns about the effects of open marketing systems on recovery rates for input financing are an obstacle to further reform of the cotton subsector in West Africa.

Deriving the benefits of competitive marketing may involve trade-offs in terms of credit delivery, as policies that limit marketing to a single channel facilitate certain forms of credit recovery. Zoning restrictions allow cotton gins to extend crop financing to small farmers and to recover it. Mandatory auctions also allow creditors to recover loans. Opening other marketing channels hinders these methods of recovery. This issue is particularly important to cotton production, which tends to require high levels of chemical inputs.

Prefinancing arrangements with off-shore importers is a common solution to the problem of financing export crops. In these arrangements an offshore buyer contracts with a local trader for a delivery of a certain volume of the crop and lends the trader the money to cover the cost of local purchases, plus a profit margin. The loan serves as working capital, and the local trader delivers the crop as payment. These arrangements require only one currency conversion (foreign to local), reducing transaction costs and sometimes convertibility problems. The arrangement also allows domestic traders to access credit at lower rates of interest through the offshore trader.

The development of inventory financing systems in countries such as Cameroon, Ghana, India, and Uganda is another response to the increased demand for credit.[22] These systems have helped mobilize credit for some commodities. In India, for example, a futures exchange and a privately run auction market have been established for coffee. While many such private institutions were successful, established cooperatives often lagged behind. In several countries, including Côte d'Ivoire and Uganda, cooperatives were expected to assume a greater role after the reforms. And cooperatives' failure in Tanzania to gain crop financing prompted market liberalization for coffee, cotton, and cashews.

The development of strong and viable producer associations has often remained a weak point. For export crops such as cocoa, coffee, and cotton, prefinancing arrangements with foreign partners (buyers) frequently fill the need for working capital.[23] But these arrangements may not be optimal, as they can constrain efforts to market crops and obtain independent financing. They can also create a barrier to entry, as the thinking may be that only exporters with links to foreign buyers are viable businesses.

Other Factor Markets

Land policies and markets are often important to the sugar and grain industries. In Fiji future sugar policies are important in determining the value and duration of long-standing lease agreements. In the Philippines difficulties surrounding land reform complicate leasing and investment arrangements. In Senegal and Chad water resources and sugar policies are linked (chapter 4). Benefits and costs are not evenly distributed during the reform process, and simultaneous reforms can generate political trade-offs (and standoffs). In Zimbabwe the politics of reform meant that the government compensated farmers for the lack of progress on land reform by maintaining price supports for grains (chapter 6).[24]

The Transition of the State from Marketer to Regulator

Marketing boards often perform a variety of functions in addition to marketing. Typically they are responsible for quality control, the collection and dissemination of market information, and research and extension. Reform requires not only the privatization of marketing functions but also the continued provision of public goods and services. Because boards are typically long-standing monopolies, the private marketing firms and associations that can potentially provide public goods and services are usually not present when reforms are initiated. Entrepreneurs are generally available to fill the gap in marketing functions, however. For instance after the governments of Cameroon and Uganda initiated reforms of the coffee subsectors, hundreds of entrepreneurs joined the newly created export sector (chapter 3).

Because financial crises frequently precipitate reform, budgetary considerations drive the pace of implementation. Thus state trading may continue after the reforms, although considerably fewer statutory monopolies and dominant market players remain. In rare cases marketing boards are simply abolished (for example, Nigeria's Cocoa Board) and the commodity market receives no oversight (chapter 2). In other countries parastatals are transformed into institutions with regulatory responsibilities—for example the National Coffee and Cocoa Office (ONCC) in Cameroon and the Uganda Coffee Development Authority (UCDA) (chapter 3).

MARKET FUNCTIONS. In general marketing boards retain their regulatory functions and continue to register and license new traders. Striking the right balance between proper regulation and free entry is a difficult task, however, in emerging and newly reformed markets. The appropriate standards for entry are not clearly defined, and the voluntary associations that can promote self-regulation are largely missing. From the perspective of international buyers, then, new entrants are unknown quantities, and counterparty risks increase dramatically. In Uganda three-quarters of new entrants were bankrupt within 2 years, and of the remaining 50, just 10 accounted for 80 percent of exports. Uganda subsequently introduced registration criteria and began requiring exporters to obtain bank performance guarantees. Côte d'Ivoire followed suit. But in Nigeria's cocoa subsector, a number of traders with questionable qualifications and motivations continued to control much of the market, raising questions about counterparty risk for the entire sector.

THE PROVISION OF PUBLIC GOODS. In many countries market reforms that abolished marketing boards also eliminated key public goods that largely benefited smallholders. In Cameroon market reforms meant the end of rural road maintenance; in Mexico they eliminated extension and research services for sugar; and Brazil and Togo lost similar services for coffee. In some cases, however, governments were more forward thinking. For example following the liberalization of the coffee sector in the Congo, Ghana, and India, marketing agencies became regulatory agencies and continued to provide the same public services (chapter 3). And in Peru the government specifically addressed the transfer of schools and health services from government-run plantations during sugar market reform (chapter 4).

Well-organized producer organizations and industry associations can provide public goods, as they do in several Latin American coffee-producing countries. In Colombia and Guatemala research, extension services, market information, and rural road maintenance are among the services producer associations provide. The associations are financed by a small ad valorem tax on coffee exports. The Coffee Institute in Costa Rica, a public-private sector partnership involved in research, extension, and market information, is also financed by an ad valorem tax on coffee exports (chapter 3). Mauritius has a long history of privately financed and publicly organized institutes that support sugar research (chapter 4).

Public goods can be publicly financed and privately delivered as well. In Togo a private firm is providing various services, including research, extension, and the provision of agricultural inputs, to the coffee sector under a technical agreement with the government (chapter 3). Importers also frequently employ private companies to guarantee quality when public quality controls fail are questioned.

Before the reforms parastatals often maintained fixed or average producer prices. When finances were adequate such arrangements resulted in prices that were panseasonal and sometimes panterritorial. In the liberalized environment producers must seek price information and judge the adequacy of prices traders offer. In some countries producers have difficulty acquiring information on market prices, and this price uncertainty contributes to income uncertainty. Some governments continue to assist with price discovery by collecting and publishing statistics and disseminating the information through the radio and newspapers—for example, for Ugandan coffee and cotton. In some countries formal spot and forward markets emerge (like those for coffee in India) that facilitate both price discovery and the dissemination price information.

What Leads to Successful Reform

The experiences discussed in this volume suggest that there is no single recipe for successful market reforms. The design and pace of reforms depend on the initial conditions policymakers face—conditions that are largely beyond the control of national governments. These conditions also define obstacles to reforms and dictate the types of instruments that will be used. But policymakers can increase the potential for success by taking into consideration the experiences (some general, some commodity specific) of earlier reformers.

Initial Conditions

As discussed, a number of factors, both international and domestic, affect the design and implementation of commodity market reforms. These include international and regional markets, the macroeconomic environment, factor markets, current government policies and services, and the state of the private sector. By comparing the starting point for market reform, policymakers can build a comprehensive strategy.

TRADE MARKETS. The conditions of the commodity trade market are important to the reform process in several ways. When domestic and international markets are well integrated, international markets can help with price discovery and provide instruments for managing price volatility. This situation generally prevails for the sugar, coffee, and cocoa industries in developing countries. Because of differences in quality, however, basis risk can be high for cotton. And while some grain markets, such as those for yellow maize and wheat, are well integrated, markets for white maize and even rice are fragmented.

Trade markets are subject to interventions as well. The sugar market in particular is subject to trade restrictions and preferential arrangements. As mentioned, preferential access to sugar markets gives rise to domestic interventions and to agencies that distribute the benefits of special access—for instance in Mauritius, the Philippines, and Zimbabwe. For grains and sugar, policy interventions by large industrial countries, including export subsidies and guarantees, can influence the political process of reform—and provide political arguments against reform.

Border trade policies are another important consideration during the liberalization process, since commodity market reforms have contagion effects. For example when a country reforms its coffee subsector by removing a tax, producer prices usually rise, prompting coffee smuggling from neighboring (unreformed) countries. Neighboring countries that have not liberalized their markets suffer a decline in export and government revenues, encouraging governments to consider adopting policies consistent with liberalized marketing systems. This situation affected Uganda before liberalization, when coffee was smuggled out of the country to Kenya, which had a relatively open economy. After liberalization the flows were reversed, and coffee was smuggled into Uganda from neighboring Burundi, Congo, Zaire, Rwanda, and Tanzania. Informal cocoa trade in Côte d'Ivoire, Ghana, and Togo and cotton trade in West Africa also indicate that commodities flow to countries where prices are highest.[25]

THE MACROECONOMIC ENVIRONMENT. Macroeconomic policies, especially exchange rate policy, have a huge impact on the success of reforms. Overvalued exchange rates, which often lead to sudden devaluations, undermine competitiveness and delay responses to market signals following reforms. Exports from West Africa suffered prior to the 1994 CFA franc devaluation. Conversely devaluation in Uganda and India in the early 1990s contributed to increases in coffee producer prices during liberalization. In Mexico the sugar industry was privatized largely through highly leveraged buyouts backed by variable-rate loans. Because of the peso crises in 1994 and subsequent interest rate hikes, the government had to intervene to refinance the industry. And in Nigeria exchange rate distortions were partly responsible for the deteriorating quality of cocoa following liberalization, when traders were using cocoa to obtain scarce foreign exchange.

Budget deficits and inflation often negatively impact reform efforts. Deficits like those in Zimbabwe tend to crowd out bank lending to private traders, and inflationary fears increase governments' reluctance to relinquish price controls, as happened in Zimbabwe with maize and Indonesia with sugar. Policies aiming at macroeconomic stability contributed to the success of the reforms in Uganda's cotton sector, however. Stable macroeconomic conditions and an unrestricted capital market encouraged many private firms from South Africa and Europe to invest directly in cotton mills during privatization. Similarly, private firms—some with foreign partners—invested heavily in coffee processing.

GOVERNMENTS AND PARASTATALS. Policymakers need to have a good understanding of how policy interventions affect markets in order to anticipate the consequences of reform.[26] Policymakers planning commodity market reforms also need to examine the roles of both the government and parastatals prior to reforms. Instruments and institutions appropriate to one role are generally not well suited to others. Some public services—for example, research, the collection and analysis of statistics, and quality control—need to continue uninterrupted during and immediately after the reform process. Governments need to ensure the continued provision of key services during reform either directly or by encouraging private provision.

THE CAPACITY OF PRIVATE MARKETS. The efficiency of commodity markets depends on well-functioning factor markets. As already discussed the presence of inexperienced private traders and poor performance in land, input, and credit markets can limit the potential benefits of commodity market reforms. Before implementing reforms governments need to ensure that credit markets are functioning properly, as the availability of credit can worsen with reforms. In several countries the systems of providing directed credit through state marketing agencies became unworkable, constraining access to private credit during the reforms. As marketing agencies withdrew, financial institutions with little experience lending to new private traders were left as the primary source of credit.

THE CAPACITY OF VOLUNTARY ASSOCIATIONS. The private sector's ability to provide many of the services that parastatals had been providing can affect the success of market reforms, especially during the initial stages. Voluntary associations can often help fill the gap, but inadequate institutions are found in the private as well as the public sector. In some countries private sector actors—especially farmers—are not well organized to participate in the reform process. Farmers, usually among the key beneficiaries of liberalization, lack the organization and the means to participate in the reform process. In Uganda traders, processors, and farmers were all given seats on the UCDA and the Cotton Development Organization. Exporters and processors quickly organized themselves to participate in policy debates. But the farmers were represented by their legislators or government officials.[27]

In countries where farmers are organized into effective associations or cooperatives, they can help facilitate privatization. In Zimbabwe around one-third of the shares of the government-run cotton company were sold to farmers (20 percent to smallholders and 10 percent to large-scale farmers, chapter 5). Government policy encouraged the distribution of cotton-related assets in Uganda and sugar mills in Peru to cooperative members. In both cases members were ill prepared to assume managerial tasks, and the governments responded by providing targeted business management services.

Implementing Process

An understanding of initial conditions is essential to formulating an effective reform strategy. But experience suggests that additional factors are involved in a successful reform experience.

GOVERNMENT COMMITMENT. Because policy reforms often result in income redistribution, groups that will be adversely affected have opposed them, making the government's commitment to liberalization all the more important to the success of reforms (World Bank 1998). All the studies in this volume demonstrate the need for strong government commitment to reform. Government commitment was a key factor in advancing liberalization in Uganda's cotton and coffee subsectors, India's coffee subsectors, and the sugar industry in Mexico and Peru. The most effective grain market liberalization process in Africa took place in the Republic of South Africa. The one factor distinguishing it from similar reform efforts in other countries was the absence of equivocation and backtracking at the policy level. Mali and Togo also addressed these issues successfully, largely because they had consensus-building mechanisms in place.[28]

THE GOVERNMENT'S ROLE. Governments play an important role during the reform process. Some priorities for government action include:

- Modernizing the legal and regulatory framework;
- Encouraging competition;
- Strengthening organizations such as farmers' associations for collective action;
- Facilitating the dissemination of market information (including price signals and new technology); and
- Implementing and coordinating targeted programs to enhance food security, especially for vulnerable groups that lose as a result of reforms.

In Uganda and Togo the governments assumed an appropriate role in creating an enabling legal and regulatory environment, ensuring that services previously offered by the marketing board (such as quality control) continued and monitoring the newly reformed coffee subsector.

PRIVATIZATION. Government or government-sponsored cooperatives often own a significant part of the physical capital required to process and trade commodities, including warehouses, sugar and flour mills, and gins. While some governments have used trade policy to enhance the value of state-owned enterprises, others have successfully used debt relief to facilitate privatization, including Peru (the sugar industry) and Uganda (cotton).

Poor performance frequently motivates the privatization of state enterprises, but a history of poor management makes privatization difficult. Equipment is often out of date, titles may be missing, and relevant information about the enterprise is often poorly organized or simply nonexistent. The governments of Peru and Uganda provided direct assistance and partial debt relief to cooperatives to help develop information systems and strategic plans.

THE LEGAL STRUCTURE. Governments often need to modify legislation and regulations. In Togo an important element in the success of reforms in the coffee subsector was the formalization of decisions in legal texts that became the regulatory framework. Legal and regulatory provisions covered the criteria for exporting and marketing, the level of bank guarantees, quality controls, and the price information system. In Uganda regulations on the coffee sector were modified and monitored during the process of liberalization. The lack of an appropriate regulatory framework following liberalization was one of the main problems in Nigeria. And in Cameroon regulatory enforcement was weak, creating uncertainty in the new system, particularly from the point of view of foreign buyers.

STAKEHOLDER PARTICIPATION. Coordinating with as many stakeholders as possible facilitates a smooth liberalization process. In Mali close coordination between the government and donors during the liberalization of the cereals subsector not only prevented donors from duplicating efforts and giving the government contradictory signals but also helped ensure that food aid was properly used. Similarly coordination among donors, international financial institutions, and the government was a key factor in the market reform process in Côte d'Ivoire. And consultations with growers' associations resulted in a smooth liberalization process in India's coffee subsector.

Involving private sector stakeholders in the reform process often contributes significantly to successful liberalization. These stakeholders are likely to benefit from liberalization but may be handicapped by a lack of information on the policies governing the subsector and the potential effects of liberalization. In Uganda the government institutionalized private sector participation in the liberalization of the coffee subsector by including representatives of private organizations on the board of the UCDA. In Togo representatives of the private sector served on the Coordination Committee during the reform process for the coffee and cocoa subsectors.

MARKET INFORMATION. Information plays a key role in the market reform process. The fact that producers and their associations had access to information on prices helped triggered liberalization in India's coffee subsector. Similarly sugar mills have often been privatized only after information on their operations became widely available.

Providing mechanisms for the dissemination of market information—particularly on prices—is an essential part of the reform process. Growers and small traders will not benefit from market reforms if this service is not available. Governments often continue providing it, as they did in India with the coffee subsector and in Togo with the coffee and cocoa subsectors. In some countries—Uganda, for instance—private sector organizations have assumed responsibility for disseminating market information. But an attempt to establish a price information system in Cameroon following the reforms failed when the system became politicized.

SEQUENCING AND PACING. The pace of reform is a key element in the liberalization strategy. Dialogue among key actors in the reform process can help determine the order of specific reform measures and the speed with which they are implemented. Other considerations, such as the ownership of essential assets mills and gins, food security, and the state of input markets, also affect the sequencing and pace of reforms.

Governments give a number of reasons for implementing reforms gradually, often listing the political, economic, and food security risks. Reforms affecting commodities that are important exports or sources of revenue and employment are often delayed.[29] In Côte d'Ivoire and Ghana the government liberalized the coffee subsector first. Cocoa market reforms came one year later in Côte d'Ivoire, but the cocoa subsector in Ghana was not liberalized. Similarly Cameroon instituted reforms affecting arabica coffee before those affecting robusta coffee and cocoa.

Market reforms in the sugar subsector were generally implemented gradually because of the risk that sugar mills would go bankrupt, costing sugar growers the processing facilities their product requires. Governments often establish the pace of reform in this industry by setting high tariff protection. Few countries have been able to move forward after setting high tariffs, however, as the protection provided is incorporated into the value of the enterprises. The firms remain dependent on continued support, as happened in Côte d'Ivoire and Mexico (chapter 4).

In Africa, the process of reforming grain markets has been stressful because of the large numbers of producers and consumers affected and political sensitivities over food security and related matters. Governments have tended to be overtaken by events, with the emergence of parallel markets and the massive budgetary costs of supporting loss-making parastatals, and reform has been unavoidable. A review of 13 countries showed

that liberalization had occurred in all of them, but in only three were public policies unambiguously proliberalization. Given the underlying political sensitivities, governments often engaged to varying degrees in
"second-generation controls"—ad hoc interventions that sent contradictory
signals to the private sector and tended to discourage investment in storage and trade (chapter 6).

Governments frequently choose to hold off on trade reform while they
liberalize domestic markets. When governments do choose to open domestic markets to trade, they often set the pace of reform by controlling entry.
As noted, in Cameroon, Côte d'Ivoire, and Ghana, coffee and cocoa market
reforms began with increased competition in the internal market, though
export monopolies and some domestic price controls were retained. In
Uganda the government chose to eliminate the coffee board's export
monopoly gradually by phasing in the process of licensing private exporters
who competed with the parastatal for business. But failure to privatize expe-
ditiously has its costs. In Uganda the government neglected to sell the marketing board's well-functioning coffee-processing facility promptly, leading
private investors to build their own facility and significantly eroding the
value of the government's plant (chapter 3). Taking too long to implement
reforms can reduce their effectiveness, however, especially when important
decisions are postponed, as the experience of the cereals subsector in Kenya
and Zimbabwe suggests (chapter 6).

MONITORING AND EVALUATION. Monitoring, evaluation, and analysis of the
subsector before and during liberalization can make a vital contribution to
the reform effort. Valuable research was conducted on Mali's cereal subsector before the reforms. Initial reforms to Uganda's coffee subsector were
evaluated twice to determine the need for additional measures. The detailed
studies conducted before and during Togo's liberalization of its coffee and
cocoa subsectors helped win support for the reforms, especially from the
private sector, as did an evaluation of the 1994–95 reforms to Côte d'Ivoire's
coffee and cocoa industries. During the privatization of sugar mills in Peru,
financial regulators helped standardize financial reports as information-
related problems emerged.

Summary and Conclusions

In designing reforms policymakers were often motivated by common
events and guided by common objectives. Yet actual experiences with
reforms varied significantly, largely because of differences in the conditions under which the reforms were begun. For example the state of land
and other input markets, the government's role in processing and financing, and the policies of other countries all affected the potential pace of

reform. The initial conditions also helped define the groups that would incur the costs and reap the benefits of reform, as well as what policy-makers viewed as the politically feasible pace of reform. And outcomes were often affected by events in related output and currency markets—a fortuitous boom in international markets or an ill-timed currency crisis, for example.

Clearly many factors contribute to the reform process. How then can commodity reforms be successfully managed? This volume seeks to provide some useful answers to this question. We know, for example, that success-fully managing commodity market reform requires an understanding of how global markets influence local markets; how well domestic markets for information, capital, land, storage, and other factors work; and how past interventions may have displaced or distorted private markets and crowded out the voluntary associations that support markets. Successful commodity market reform also requires an understanding of the role of public and private institutions and of how best to modify them and foster new ones. Policymakers must be able to manage the economic, political, and human consequences of reform, plus the risks associated with events outside the government's control. Finally, understanding these factors requires an understanding of commodity-specific production, market characteristics, and policy approaches.

The market reforms discussed in this volume often share objectives, and many were triggered by similar events. However, because reform processes have different starting points, because production and market characteristics differ among commodities, because reforms may affect land and water resources in differing ways, and because of differing consequences among reforms, the pace and path of reforms will differ.

Notes

1. See for example the discussion of the 1955 Essential Commodities Act in India in chapter 4 and the experience from the grain markets of Africa in chapter 7.

2. The World Bank (1997) examined the rise of central planning and the beliefs of policymakers in many developing countries after independence. The assessment notes that "(the) state would mobilize resources and people and direct them toward rapid growth . . . State control of the economy, following the example of the Soviet Union, was central to this strategy. Many [Asian], Latin American, Middle Eastern, and African countries followed this state-dominated [industrialization path]" (p. 23).

3. This argument implies that an increase in the supply of commodities in the face of low price elasticity of demand reduces revenues. In this case the decline in prices resulting from the oversupply of commodities overwhelms the value of the supply increase. For details see Akiyama and Larson (1994).

4. See Eicher and Staatz (1998) for a discussion of agriculture, development, and economic thought. See Stern (1989) for a review of development economists' view of peasant economies.

5. For more on systems of cotton production, see the discussion of the cotton producer structure of West Africa (chapter 5).

6. The program was launched by the United Nations Conference on Trade and Development (UNCTAD).

7. Larson, Varangis, and Yabuki (1998) provide an brief history of international price stabilization efforts.

8. With regard to China's agricultural productivity and production growth, the World Bank (1993) noted, "Reforms giving farmers greater control over the land they tilled, together with a 25 percent real increase in crop prices, boosted agricultural productivity" (p. 59).

9. See, for example, Wallace (1997) and Lindauer and Roemer (1994).

10. In the 1990s UNCTAD began actively promoting the use of market-based risk management instruments to alleviate problems stemming from fluctuating world commodity prices.

11. The difficulty or even impossibility of controlling prices becomes clear when we consider the impossibility of predicting medium- to long-term commodity price trends. Commodity prices also tend to stay low for many years, with occasional spike-like increases—a situation that makes price stabilization difficult or impossible at a reasonable cost. For details, see Williams and Wright (1991), Deaton (1992), Larson and Coleman (1993), and Gilbert (1996).

12. For an analysis of commodity price declines in the 1980s, see Reinhart and Wickham (1994).

13. Farm support programs in developing countries were not immune. Both the United States and the EU accumulated large and expensive stockpiles of agricultural products during the 1980s, and Australia's scheme to stabilize wool prices was restructured.

14. Engberg-Pedersen (1996, p. 3) states, "Structural adjustment involves measures to reduce the spending and direct economic involvement by the state, to move toward market allocation of resources and provide an 'enabling environment' for private enterprise."

15. See Meerman (1997) for a survey of conditionality in Bank lending for agriculture. See Krueger and Rajapatirana (1998) for a survey of trade reform conditionalities. For a case study of structural adjument lending and commodity market board reform, see the discussion of cocoa reforms in Ghana in Pearce (1992).

16. This volume treats four countries that exemplify this situation: Ghana, India, Mexico, and Uganda. See also the review of trade reform experiences in developing countries in Dean and Riedel (1994)

17. Discussions on the political economy of market reform can be found in Widner (1994).

18. In many countries governments established cooperatives for political reasons, and consequently most of these groups lacked commercial and entrepreneurial experience.

19. See World Bank (1994), Meerman 1997, and Krueger and Rajapatirana (1999) for reviews of studies that quantify the short-run costs and benefits of market reform.

20. Countries that have successfully launched domestic futures exchanges include Argentina, Brazil, India, and Malaysia. Access to risk management markets (the relevant measure) is harder to gauge, but direct participation in formal markets is limited in developing countries (World Bank 1999).

21. Basis risk refers to the degree of linkage between futures prices and spot prices in commodity-producing countries.

22. With inventory financing stored commodities are used as collateral. Using warehouse receipts greatly reduces transaction costs.

23. See Varangis and Larson (1996) for a discussion of commodity prefinancing.

24. See Migot-Adholla (1999) for lessons from and suggested approaches to land reform and titling.

25. Recognizing the role of smuggling is also important when food security issues are at stake. Lessons from chapter 6 on grain marketing show that smuggling undermined nontargeted pricing policies designed to ensure domestic availability in Tanzania. Similarly trade restrictions designed to cap consumer sugar prices following the devaluation of the Thai baht in 1998 largely failed because of smuggling and hoarding. Excessive smuggling was also reported more recently in Indonesia after the 1997 financial crisis, when the government imposed a ban that was subsequently replaced by a 60 percent export tax on palm oil exports.

26. Informal markets such as black markets for currency or smuggled goods are sometimes as significant as formal markets in countries with high levels of intervention. See Bauer and Yamey (1957).

27. The interested reader can visit the Ugandan Coffee Trade Federation at http://www.uganda.co.ug/coffee/.

28. Some governments were reluctant to liberalize their coffee and cocoa subsectors, fearing the problems liberalization might bring. Some of these problems, such as the lack of private sector response, did not materialize. Others, such as declining quality, depended on the way liberalization proceeded. Some opposition to reforms in the cocoa subsector in Côte d'Ivoire and Ghana was attributed to problems associated with marketing reforms in Cameroon and Nigeria. Similar problems plagued reforms of the cotton subsector in West Africa.

29. One reason for commodity market reforms in Australia and New Zealand was the government's realization that the agricultural commodity sector was important enough to the economy to warrant an overhaul that would increase the sector's efficiency.

References

Akiyama, T., and D. Larson. 1994. "The Adding-Up Problem; Strategies for Primary Commodity Exports in Sub-Saharan Africa." Policy Research Paper 1245. Washington, D.C.: World Bank.

Balassa, B., and Associates. 1971. *The Structure of Protection in Developing Countries.* Baltimore: Johns Hopkins Press.

Bates, R. H. 1981. *Markets and States in Tropical Africa: The Political Basis of Agricultural Policies.* Berkley: University of California Press.

————. 1989. "Structural Adjustment and Agriculture." In Simon Commander, ed., *Structural Adjustment and Agriculture: Theory and Practice in Africa and Latin America.* London: Overseas Development Institute.

Bauer, P. T. 1954. *West African Trade: a Study of Competition, Oligopoly, and Monopoly in a Changing Economy.* Cambridge: University Press.

————. 1976. *Dissent on Development.* Revised edition. Cambridge, Mass.: Harvard University Press.

Bauer, P. T., and B. S. Yamey. 1957. *The Economics of Under-developed Countries.* London: James Nisbet.

Bhagwati, J. 1958. "Immiserizing Growth: A Geometrical Note." *Review of Economic Studies* 25, pp. 201–205.

Binswanger, H., and K. Deininger. 1997. "Explaining Agricultural and Agrarian Policies in Developing Countries." *Journal of Economic Literature* 35(4):1958–2005.

Bohman M., L. Jarvis, and R. Barticello. 1996. "Rent Seeking and International Commodity Agreements: the Case of Coffee." *Economic Development and Cultural Exchange* 44.

Cleaver, K. 1987. "The Impact of Price and Exchange Rate Policies on Agriculture in Sub-Saharan Africa." Staff Working Paper 723. Washington, D.C.: World Bank.

Dean, J. S. D., and J. Reidel. 1994. *Trade Policy Reform in Developing Countries Since 1985: A Review of Evidence.* Discussion Paper 267. Washington, D.C.: World Bank.

Deaton, A. S. 1992. "Commodity Prices, Stabilization, and Growth in Africa." Discussion Paper 166. Center for International Studies, Woodrow Wilson School, Princeton University.

Eicher, C. K., and J. M. Staatz. 1998. "Agricultural Development Ideas in Historical Perspective." In C. K. Eicher and J. M. Staatz, eds., *International Agricultural Development.* Baltimore: Johns Hopkins University Press.

Friedman, M. 1954. "The Reduction of Fluctuations in the Incomes of Primary Producers: a Critical Comment." *Economic Journal* 64:698–703.

Gilbert, C. L. 1996. "International Commodity Agreements: An Obituary Notice." *World Development* 24(1):1–19.

————. 1997. "Cocoa Market Liberalization: Its Effects on Quality, Futures Trading, and Prices." The Cocoa Association of London. Draft.

Hazell, P. 1994. "Potential Benefits to Farmers of Using Futures Markets for Managing Coffee Price Risks in Costa Rica." Working Paper. Washington, D.C.: International Food Policy Research Institute.

Hirschman, A. O. 1958. *The Strategy of Economic Development.* New Haven, Conn.: Yale University Press.

Johnson, D. G. 1947. *Forward Prices for Agriculture.* Chicago, University of Chicago Press.

Johnson, H. 1953. "Equilibrium Growth in an Expanding Economy." *The Canadian Journal of Economics and Political Science* 19(4):478–500.

Johnston, B. F., and J. W. Mellor. 1961. "The Role of Agriculture in Economic Development." *American Economic Review* 51(4):566–593.

Keynes, J. M. 1943. "The International Regulation of Primary Products." Reprinted in D. Moggridge ed., *Collected Writing of John Maynard Keynes.* London: MacMillan and Cambridge University Press, 1980.

Krueger, A. 1998. "Whither the World Bank and IMF?" *Journal of Economic Literature* 36(4):1983–2020.

Krueger, A., and S. Rajapatirana. 1999. "The World Bank Policies towards Trade and Trade Policy Reform." *World Economy* 22(6):717–40.

Krueger, A., M. Schiff, and A. Valdés, eds. 1992. *The Political Economy of Agricultural Pricing Policy.* Baltimore: Johns Hopkins University Press.

Lal, D. 1985. *The Poverty of Development Economics.* Cambridge, Mass.: Harvard University Press.

Larson, D. 1993. "Policies for Coping with Price Uncertainty for Mexican Maize: Policies for Maize Price Variability in Mexico." Working Paper 1120. Washington, D.C.: World Bank.

Larson, D., and J. Coleman. 1994. "The Effects of Option Hedging on the Costs of Domestic Price Stabilization Schemes." In R. Duncan and S. Claessens, eds., *Commodity Risk Management and Finance,* Vol. 2. Oxford, UK: Oxford University Press.

Larson, D., P. Varangis, and N. Yabuki. 1998. "Commodity Risk Management and Development." Policy Research Working Paper 1963. Washington, D.C.: World Bank.

Lewis, W. A. 1954. "Economic Development with Unlimited Supply of Labor." *Manchester School of Economic and Social Studies* 22(2):139–91

Lindauer, D. L., and M. Roemer. 1994. *Asia and Africa: Legacies and Opportunities in Development.* San Francisco: International Center for Economic Research and Harvard Institute for International Development.

Lipton, M. 1977. *Why Poor People Stay Poor: Urban Bias in World Development.* Canberra: Australian National University Press.

McIntire, J., and P. Varangis. 1999. "Reforming Côte d'Ivoire's Cocoa Marketing and Pricing Systems." Policy Research Working Paper 2081. Washington, D.C.: World Bank.

Meerman, J. 1997. *Reforming Agriculture: The World Bank Goes to Market.* Washington, D.C.: World Bank.

Migot-Adholla, S. 1999. *Land Policy and Administration: Summary of Bank Experience since 1975 and Best Practices.* Washington, D.C.: World Bank.

Mosley, P. 1987. "Conditionality as Bargaining Process: Structural Adjustment Lending 1980–86." *Princeton Essays in International Finance* 168. Princeton: Princeton University.

Mosley, P., J. Harringan, and J. Toye. 1991. *Aid and Power: The World Bank and Policy-Based Lending.* London: Routledge.

Myrdal, Gunnar. 1956. *An International Economy: Problems and Prospects.* New York: Harper.

Prebisch, R. 1950. *The Economic Development of Latin America and its Principal Problems.* New York: UN Economic Commission for Latin America.

Reinhart, C. M., and P. Wickham. 1994. "Commodity Prices: Cyclical Weakness or Secular Decline?" *IMF Staff Papers* 41. Washington, D.C.: International Monetary Fund.

Singer, H. 1950. "The Distribution of Gains between Investing and Borrowing Countries." *American Economic Review* 40 (May) 473–85.

Schultz, T. W. 1964. *Transforming Traditional Agriculture.* New Haven, Conn.: Yale University Press.

Stern, N. 1989. "Peasant Economy," in J. Eatwell, M. Milgate, and P. Newman, eds., *The New Palgrave: Economic Development.* New York: Norton.

Timmer, C. P. 1991. *Agriculture and the State: Growth, Employment and Poverty in Developing Countries.* Ithaca: Cornell University Press.

Varangis, P., and D. Larson. 1996. "Dealing with Commodity Price Uncertainty." Working Paper 1667. Washington, D.C: World Bank.

Wallace, L., ed. 1997. *Deepening Structural Reform in Africa; Lessons from East Asia.* Washington, D.C.: International Monetary Fund and Ministry of Finance of Japan.

Widner, J. A., ed. 1994. *Economic Change and Political Liberalization in Sub-Saharan Africa.* Baltimore: Johns Hopkins University Press.

Williams, J., and B. Wright. 1991. *Storage and Commodity Markets.* Cambridge, UK: Cambridge University Press.

World Bank. 1983. *World Development Report 1983.* New York: Oxford University Press.

———. 1985. *World Development Report 1985.* New York: Oxford University Press.

———. 1993. *The East Asian Miracle: Economic Growth and Public Policy.* New York: Oxford University Press.

———. 1994. *Adjustment in Africa.* New York: Oxford University Press.

———. 1997. *World Development Report 1997.* Washington.

———. 1998. *Assessing Aid: What Works, What Doesn't, and Why.* New York: Oxford University Press.

———. 1999 *Dealing with Commodity Price Volatility in Developing Countries: A Proposal for a Market-based Approach.* Washington, D.C.

2

Cocoa Market Reforms in West Africa

Panos Varangis and Gotz Schreiber

WEST AFRICA ACCOUNTS FOR ABOUT TWO-THIRDS of the world's cocoa production. Until the 1980s the region's cocoa was produced and marketed under state-controlled systems, but in the mid-1980s and 1990s several West African cocoa-producing countries began reforming their cocoa-marketing and -pricing systems. These reforms aimed to improve efficiency and reduce costs in the presence of historically low cocoa prices. In addition the reforms aimed to increase producer prices, which under the previous systems had been low both as a percentage of the f.o.b. (free on board) price and in absolute terms.

All four of West Africa's largest cocoa-producing countries—Cameroon, Ghana, Nigeria, and Côte d'Ivoire—plus Togo (a smaller cocoa producer) undertook such reforms. Cameroon, Nigeria, and Togo initiated drastic reforms to completely liberalize their marketing and pricing systems, while Côte d'Ivoire began with much more gradual measures (complete market liberalization was introduced in August 1999, prior to the beginning of the 1999–2000 crop year). Ghana's cocoa market has seen only modest changes thus far, but the government took steps to accelerate market reforms in 1999 and 2000. Overall these diverse approaches to liberalizing cocoa markets have generated economic benefits, but in some countries the too-rapid reforms have weakened functions that were the responsibility of government-run institutions before liberalization. This chapter looks at the experiences with liberalization in West Africa and draws some lessons from them.

The World Cocoa Market

Global cocoa production, which in the late 1990s stood at around 2.7 million tons per year, is concentrated in only a few countries. Eight producers—Brazil, Cameroon, Côte d'Ivoire, Ecuador, Ghana, Indonesia, Malaysia, and Nigeria—account for 90 percent of world production and 92 percent of global cocoa bean exports (figure 2.1). The four West African countries produce about two-thirds of the world's processed cocoa. Côte d'Ivoire alone contributes over 40 percent. Ghana, which dominated world markets in the 1960s, provides about 15 percent, and Indonesia produces around 13 percent. These four countries also account for more than 70 percent of global exports of cocoa beans, in part because Brazil and Malaysia process a significant share of their production domestically and then export the processed products. Côte d'Ivoire and Ghana furnish well over half the world's cocoa bean exports each year.

In Côte d'Ivoire cocoa production virtually doubled during the 1980s because of high producer prices, strong incentives to plant new crops, the ready availability of immigrant labor, easy access to forest land for new plantings, and the widespread use of hybrids in plantings established during the 1970s and early 1980s. Output stagnated during the first half of the 1990s, a period when the overvalued exchange rate and a sharp decline in farmgate prices eroded grower incentives. But new plantings in the late

Figure 2.1 Market Shares of Cocoa-Producing Countries During 1997/98

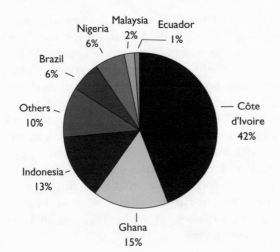

Source: E. D. & F. Man, Cocoa Market Report, January 1999.

1980s boosted output after the mid-1990s. Production in Ghana, which had fallen dramatically in the 1970s and early 1980s owing to overtaxation and severe economic policy distortions, began recovering after 1986, in large measure because of policy reforms designed to restore macroeconomic stability and farmers' incentives. Production in Nigeria followed a similar pattern. Following the abrupt liberalization of cocoa marketing in 1986 and the subsequent brief upheaval in the country's cocoa economy, production began steadily recovering. Production in Cameroon remained stagnant for more than 20 years but has started to show some increase since market liberalization in 1994–95.

Production in Brazil increased after the cocoa price boom of the late 1970s, when the government began providing incentives (mainly subsidized credit) for planting cocoa. This program ended in the mid-1980s, and new plantings declined significantly. Unstable macroeconomic conditions, the high cost of credit and production, declining world cocoa prices, and serious problems with witches' broom disease caused a significant drop in production in the 1990s.

Production in Indonesia and Malaysia, where cocoa is produced both by smallholders and on plantations, rose significantly after 1980 with the adoption of high-yielding varieties. Vigorous competition and the virtual absence of taxation also kept production and marketing costs low and producer prices attractive. Producers received a very high share of the f.o.b. price (around 85–90 percent in Indonesia and more than 90 percent in Malaysia). While Indonesia continues to expand its output, Malaysian production has been declining since 1992–93, primarily because production costs on plantations have been rising in response to rising wage rates.

The International Cocoa Trade

Cocoa producers usually sell their unprocessed cocoa beans to an international dealer or trader, who subsequently sells them to final users (generally chocolate companies) or processes them for sale. (Processed products include cocoa liquor, paste, butter, powder, and cake). The international cocoa trade is markedly concentrated, with a few large traders accounting for over two-thirds of worldwide cocoa purchases. This concentration is the result of economies of scale, improvements in supply management technology (such as bulk shipments), and the globalization of world commodity markets. Final users such as chocolate manufacturers prefer to purchase through traders, because traders provide a variety of services at competitive prices. Traders deliver the cocoa to a port close to the buyer and shepherd it through customs. Buyers can inspect the shipment and refuse to purchase it if the quality of the cocoa is not acceptable to them. Traders can sell rejected shipments elsewhere or blend them with other cocoas, process the new batch, and sell that.

There are two types of transactions in the international cocoa trade: physical trade and transactions in the terminal market. Physical trade involves the actual delivery of cocoa as a commodity. Transactions are carried out either for immediate (spot) delivery or for delivery in the future as a forward sale. Forward sales are an important instrument in the cocoa market. Because they hedge against the uncertainty of future prices, countries such as Côte d'Ivoire (until 1999) and Ghana have used forward contracts to sell cocoa before the new crop year begins. Prices in forward sales reflect the costs of storing the crop until the delivery date (discounted for the risk of nondelivery) and expectations concerning future supply and demand.[1] Thus exporters with assured access to supplies (for instance those that directly control exports, such as the marketing board in Ghana and, until 1999, the Stabilization Fund in Côte d'Ivoire) are able to sell forward. For buyers forward sales involve a counterparty risk—the risk of nondelivery because spot prices have risen in the interim or because the seller cannot obtain the amount specified in the contract.

The terminal market in cocoa has two key functions—price discovery and the provision of hedging instruments. Operations in the terminal market for cocoa primarily involve futures and options, which are paper transactions that do not involve the physical exchange of goods. Traders use these instruments to lock in profit margins, and processors use them to hedge against price risk. Some cocoa exporters, particularly in Asia and Latin America, also use futures and options to hedge their price risks. In the terminal market a purchase is almost always canceled by an offsetting sale (and vice versa) before the delivery date, and only a small proportion of cocoa is delivered under futures contracts. The futures and physical markets for cocoa are closely linked through the price mechanism. Almost all the cocoa traded in the world is sold at prices that reflect the futures prices set at the commodity exchanges in London (LIFFE) and New York (New York Board of Trade).

Prices and Stocks

During the last 20 years, world cocoa prices have exhibited a pronounced downtrend interrupted by brief periods of price recovery (figure 2.2).[2] This trend is largely the result of producers' response to attractive prices in the late 1970s and early 1980s. During this period farmers increased their cocoa plantings, supplies and stocks of cocoa grew (especially after 1985), and prices subsequently fell.[3]

Following the unprecedented boom of 1976–79, prices fell sharply through 1982, recovered slightly for a brief period in the mid-1980s, and then continued to decline through 1993. Despite a modest recovery during 1995–98, world cocoa prices remained relatively stable at very low levels throughout the 1990s, particularly in real terms.

Figure 2.2 Constant and Current Cocoa Prices, 1950–98

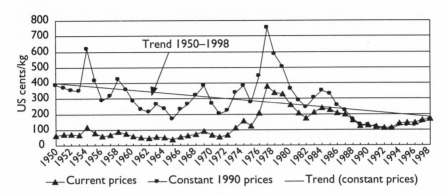

Not surprisingly an inverse relationship exists between the ratio of global cocoa stocks to grindings and real world cocoa prices. Global end-of-season (end-September) stocks rose steadily throughout the 1980s but began declining from their peak of 1.48 million tons in September 1991. In September 1999 they totaled around 1.2 million tons, an amount equal to 41 percent of worldwide grindings in 1998–99, still ahead of the ratios recorded in the mid-1980s (around 31 percent).

There are no distortions in the world cocoa market. The International Cocoa Agreement (ICA) of the International Cocoa Organization (ICCO) operated a buffer stock program aimed at defending world cocoa prices (represented by the ICCO's daily price) within a certain price range, or band. [4] During the late 1980s the decline in world cocoa prices forced the buffer stock to its limit (it reached 250,000 tons in 1988), and efforts at price stabilization were effectively abandoned. Recent renewals of the ICA do not contain economic clauses (that is, there is no price support or price stabilization) and in 1997 the buffer stock held by the ICCO was liquidated.

In the Northern Hemisphere cocoa stocks can be stored for several years, as storage conditions tend to be good in cold climates. Storing cocoa at its point of origin in warmer climates can be difficult, but the degree of difficulty varies across countries. In Ghana properly prepared cocoa is reportedly very resilient and can be stored for some time despite the humidity and heat. In general cocoa needs to be moved from its point of origin as soon as possible because of the effects of heat and moisture. Cocoa that is delivered to a port wet can rapidly develop mold and problems with free fatty acids and ochratoxin. Much cocoa is dried at port in order to prevent mold from forming. This process is delicate: exporters want parcels to arrive at their final destination with no less than 5.5 percent moisture (in order to keep the cocoa from becoming brittle) and no more than 7.5–8.0 percent (since buyers do not want to pay for water).

Cocoa Marketing and Pricing Systems

Cocoa marketing systems generally fall into three main categories: free market systems, marketing board systems, and price stabilization funds. These systems differ in a number of important aspects (Varangis, Akiyama, and Thigpen 1990) (table 2.1).In a free market system, the marketing chain comprises many private agents, the government is not directly involved in marketing the crop, and market forces determine prices. Commonly local traders or cooperatives buy from primary producers at the point of origin or at village markets, transport the cocoa to secondary or assembly markets or to a port, and sell it to private exporters either directly or through intermediaries. Exporters may also employ agents who buy directly from farmers. The pass-through of international to domestic prices is high, and producers usually receive a much higher percentage of the f.o.b. export price than in other marketing systems. At the same time any volatility in international cocoa prices is transmitted more readily to farmers.

A free market system is not a completely laissez-faire approach. The government may retain the right to intervene if it sees a need to coordinate or regulate the actions of agents in the system. In practice, however, government involvement is usually limited to quality control, taxation, and general monitoring and supervision. Countries with cocoa-marketing and -pricing systems of this type are Brazil, Cameroon (since 1994–95), Côte d'Ivoire (since 1999), Indonesia, Malaysia, and Nigeria (since 1986). Other relatively important cocoa producers with free market systems are Colombia, the Dominican Republic, Ecuador, and Mexico.

The marketing board system is at the other end of the spectrum. A parastatal with a monopoly over internal and external crop marketing dominates the system from the moment the crop is purchased from the grower to the moment it is exported. Ghana has such a system, and Nigeria did until 1986. The marketing board or its agents handle the crop at every step along the marketing chain. In some cases a few closely controlled private agents are involved, usually handling a small part of the crop at certain stages of the marketing chain. Producer prices are administratively determined by the marketing board (usually in conjunction with government authorities) and are fixed for the entire crop year or for several years. Farmers receive a uniform price irrespective of their location and often of the quality of their crop. The producer price the marketing board sets generally seeks to provide some degree of insulation against fluctuations in world market prices.

A stabilization fund resembles a marketing board system in that internal prices are administratively determined. Cameroon had such a system until 1993–94, as did Côte d'Ivoire until August 1999. The fund, or *caisse*, is a government-controlled marketing agency that regulates only the internal market and exports. Unlike the marketing board it does not handle the physical

Table 2.1 Key Characteristics of Different Cocoa-Marketing and -Pricing Systems

Characteristic	Free market	Stabilization fund	Marketing board
Legal ownership of crop	Traders, exporters	Traders, exporters	Marketing board
Physical handling of crop	Traders, exporters	Licensed private agents	Marketing board
Domestic price setting	Market forces	Stabilization fund	Marketing board and government institutions
Price stabilization	None	Yes	Yes, but not explicit
Taxation	Absent or very low	Mainly explicit	Implicit
Marketing costs and margins	Low	Medium to high	High
Producer prices	High	Medium to low	Low

crop, although it licenses agents to do so and determines how much they will be paid. A schedule of prices (purchasing and selling), costs, and profit margins at each stage of internal commercialization and exporting is administratively established and fixed for the entire crop year or a number of years. Adherence to the schedule is mandatory.

Like a marketing board, a stabilization fund sets producer prices in order to provide a degree of price stability in the face of international price volatility. Thus a stabilization fund is designed to accumulate reserves when prices are high and support producer prices when prices decline. Unlike the marketing board system, the stabilization fund is not officially linked to the government for administrative purposes. Private exporters operate under terms and conditions approved by the fund.

Marketing costs and margins tend to be significantly higher in countries with marketing boards or stabilization funds, for several reasons. In the absence of competition, there is no pressure to operate efficiently. Costs are further inflated by the excessive number of staff on the administrative payroll, which tends to be bloated not only because of the proliferation of administrative functions but also because of patronage and featherbedding. The budgeting and accounting systems of the parastatals are suitable for government departments but not for business enterprises, making it difficult to assess actual operating costs and functions and easy to disguise inefficiencies and waste.

A comparison of major cocoa-producing countries in 1989 (figure 2.3) shows that in free market systems (for example Brazil, Indonesia, Malaysia, and Nigeria) marketing costs and taxes are lower. Costs and taxes in free market systems ranged from 13 to 28 percent of the selling price, compared with 43 to 59 percent in countries with stabilization funds or marketing boards (Cameroon, Côte d'Ivoire, and Ghana). A similar comparison for 1995 shows that marketing costs and taxes declined dramatically in Cameroon and Nigeria following market liberalization, while cocoa growers in Côte d'Ivoire and Ghana continued to face very unfavorable conditions (figure 2.4). The differences in costs and taxes reflect the differences in the systems themselves. Where farmgate prices are determined by fiat and farmers have no alternative outlets for their product, the monopsony buyer's high marketing and other costs are easily transmitted to growers. (Growers may, of course, seek recourse by arranging unauthorized sales across the border, as happened between 1960 and 1990 in Ghana and neighboring Côte d'Ivoire).

The effect of the high costs of stabilization funds and marketing boards is most evident in the f.o.b. price cocoa growers receive. In countries with these systems (Côte d'Ivoire until 1999 and Ghana), growers receive substantially less than growers in countries with effective competition among buyers (figure 2.5).

Under the stabilization fund and marketing board systems, purchasing prices are set in relation to a long-term trend. Any windfall export revenues realized when international prices are above the trend level are meant to cover shortfalls or losses in anticipated export earnings when world prices fall below the trend level.[5] As we have seen stabilization funds administer

Figure 2.3 Marketing Costs and Taxes as a Percentage of the Selling Price, 1989

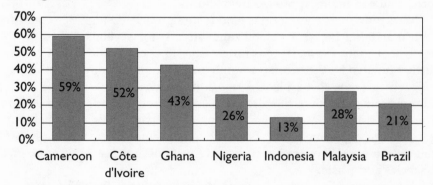

Source: Based on Ruf and de Milly 1990.

Figure 2.4 Marketing Costs and Taxes as a Percentage of the Export Price, 1995

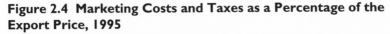

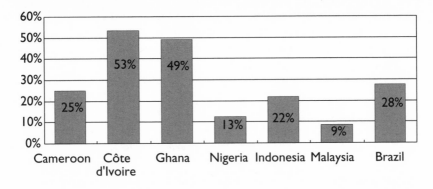

Figure 2.5 Farmgate Prices as a Percentage of f.o.b. Prices in Early 1994–95

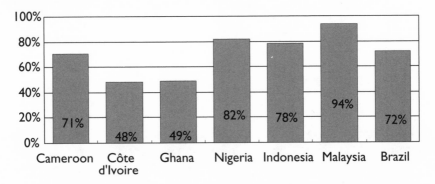

their own finances in agreement with the government. In the case of marketing boards, there is no explicit fund, and the government (usually the Ministry of Finance) manages the difference between the producer and f.o.b. prices, minus the marketing board's operating costs.

Theoretically the funds are self-financing. In practice, however, the funds have not been used for their intended purpose (see, for example, Deaton 1992). Instead, many governments and governmental agencies have used resources accumulated during international price booms for a variety of purposes, so that there has not been enough money to support internal prices when world prices are low. Moreover it has been very difficult to determine long-term equilibrium price trends and levels and to distinguish between temporary and permanent deviations from these trends. The parastatals have also had problems resisting political pressure both to raise administered producer prices when world prices increase significantly and to maintain high domestic prices when an international price boom subsides. The stabilization funds in Cameroon and Côte d'Ivoire faced enormous financial difficulties after the mid-1980s, when world prices fell precipitously and governments were unable or unwilling to adjust domestic purchasing prices to these reduced levels.

Getting the price right is a major problem when prices are administered, regardless of the commodity in question (see, for example, Singh, Squire, and Kirchner 1985). Administered pricing systems usually go awry not because their objectives are unclear (although the objectives may indeed be opaque), but because the quantitative effects of the system are inadequately understood and measured. In addition administrative pricing systems do not transmit market signals to producers, creating distorted incentives and inducing misallocation of resources. Administered pricing schemes that aim to ensure high producer prices also tend to be unsustainable when world prices are low. Governments (or government agencies) that are obliged to finance the difference between the guaranteed producer price and the actual export price soon face fiscal constraints. They encounter these constraints more quickly when revenues accrued during periods of high world prices have been used to augment fiscal revenues rather than set aside for periods when prices are low. Reviewing the experience of pricing reforms in Africa, Duncan and Jones (1993) note that administered pricing systems provide few incentives for a monopolistic marketing organization to be efficient. Unless scrutiny is extremely tight, costs are likely to rise over time.

Experience in West Africa has clearly shown that cocoa farmers in countries with stabilization funds and marketing boards have been poorly remunerated, as parastatal marketing agencies and governments have appropriated a substantial part of the export price. Ghanaian farmers have been treated particularly harshly, rarely receiving more than 50 percent of the export price and taking in less than 30 percent in 1984–87. Growers in Cameroon and Côte d'Ivoire have fared only slightly better, except in 1986–89, when their governments maintained high domestic producer prices while world market prices declined. In both countries this policy resulted in substantial financial difficulties for the systems and soon proved unsustainable. Figure 2.6 shows the relation of West African producer prices to the world price; figure 2.7 shows the percentage of the world price going to producers in the same countries.

The Nigerian data require special explanation. Until 1987 they are distorted by an overvalued currency. From 1987 onward growers benefited considerably from the vigorous competition among buyers in the liberalized marketing system. Between 1988 and 1990 exporters bought cocoa from farmers at prices above world market prices, because substantial profits

Figure 2.6 Cocoa Producer Prices in West Africa, 1983–84 to 1997–98

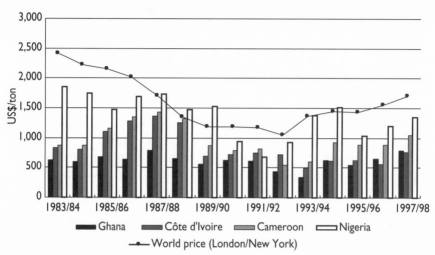

Note: World prices are represented by ICCO daily prices.

Figure 2.7 Producer Prices in West Africa as a Percentage of the World Price, 1983–84 to 1997–98

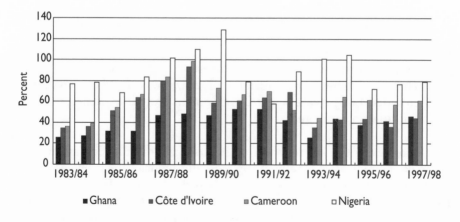

could be made through currency transactions in the parallel foreign exchange market. The Nigerian cocoa economy has begun to stabilize, confidence in the trading system is returning, and farmers are receiving very attractive prices.

In Côte d'Ivoire, despite the relatively low producer prices, cocoa production increased from around 400,000 metric tons in the early 1980s to 1.2

million in 1999. Two factors contributed to this increase. First, although overall producer prices in Côte d'Ivoire were low, they were high in the second half of 1980s, encouraging new plantings that came to maturity in the 1990s. Second, the cost of producing cocoa in Côte d'Ivoire is low, so that even the low producer prices were enough to make cocoa production profitable.

The Case for Market Liberalization

Both marketing boards and stabilization funds came under significant pressure in the 1990s, particularly from major donors of financial assistance to African cocoa-producing countries. Although critics of reforms claim that the pressure was ideologically motivated, other factors were more important (Gilbert 1997).

- Cocoa prices were at historically low levels in the late 1980s and early 1990s, and stabilization agencies that attempted to maintain high producer prices found themselves facing serious financial difficulties.
- The operations of marketing boards and stabilization funds were not considered transparent. Accounts were opaque and difficult to audit.
- Both marketing boards and stabilization funds became large organizations (often with a great deal of political power) that absorbed a significant share of export earnings as operating costs.
- The administrative pricing systems employed by marketing boards and stabilization funds imposed high marketing costs. Along with the operational costs and falling world cocoa prices, these costs exerted significant pressures on farm incomes.
- The involvement of parastatal organizations in cocoa marketing crowded out private sector development and stifled entrepreneurial activities in rural areas.

Donors grew tired of refinancing the insolvent stabilization agencies, as the major beneficiaries of refinancing were the agencies themselves (and the political causes they espoused) rather than the farmers. The lack of transparency made it difficult to account for the funds the agencies provided. Liberalization was seen as a way to reduce high marketing costs, raise farmers' incomes by increasing farmgate prices, and open up the cocoa subsector to private operators. This last point has often been overlooked. Private sector activity in commodity marketing and high farm incomes that create surpluses in rural areas unleash entrepreneurial forces and contribute to rural development. Arguing that cocoa market liberalization was imposed without local support is too simplistic. Liberalization has benefited both farmers and private sector operators, particularly new entrants. On several occasions these new entrepreneurs have voiced their support for and participated in the design of reforms (for example in Togo). And in Nigeria, the first West African country to liberalize its cocoa-marketing system, liberalization took place without any encouragement from donors.

Cameroon

Until 1990 the parastatal National Marketing Office for Primary Commodities (*Office National de Commercialisation des Produits de Base,* or ONCPB), a stabilization fund, controlled the marketing of cocoa. The system:

- Fixed purchase prices as well as prices and margins along the marketing chain;
- Allocated geographical areas where buyers were allowed to purchase cocoa;
- Determined the days on which purchases could take place (providing growers with a planning horizon so that they could properly ferment and dry their beans);
- Verified the quality and grading of the crop at the time of purchase; and
- Sometimes arranged transportation for crops.

The ONCPB was directly responsible for quality control and grading as well as for licensing and controlling domestic marketing and transportation. It also arranged all overseas cocoa sales, with exporters acting as agents. The ONCPB operated a fund that aimed to stabilize producer prices intra-annually and interannually. When world prices declined after 1984, the ONCPB sought to maintain high producer prices, but this approach created severe financial difficulties, which the increasingly overvalued exchange rate compounded. Trapped by declining international cocoa prices and the overvalued exchange rate, the ONCPB cut producer prices for grade I and grade II cocoa from CFAF 420/kg in 1988 to CFAF 250/kg in 1989 and to CFAF 220/kg in 1990.[6] But these measures came too late to prevent the financial collapse of the ONCPB under a debt of about CFAF 120 billion.

The Reforms of the Early 1990s

The ongoing difficulties led to a number of institutional and operational changes in the early 1990s. The initial reform efforts included the elimination of the ONCPB and limited attempts to liberalize the internal and external marketing of cocoa. The post-1990 marketing reforms included the following:

- A floor price and marketing margins fixed at levels that would not require subsidies;
- Intra-annual (but not interannual) price stabilization through a stabilization fund;
- A parastatal agency smaller than the ONCPB, the National Coffee and Cocoa Office (*Office National du Café et du Cacao* [ONCC]), which would oversee the stabilization fund and ensure quality control; and
- A professional organization in the private sector, the Interprofessional Council of Coffee and Cocoa (*Conseil Inter-Professionnel du Café et du Cacao* [CICC]); its responsibilities were only vaguely defined.

In practice these changes did not significantly improve matters. At times the stabilization fund was misused, sometimes for activities that were at cross-purposes with the fund's intent. A number of exporters, for example, speculated against the stabilization fund during 1994, and by the end of the year the fund was depleted.[7] The ONCPB had also left substantial arrears with exporters and the banking system. Furthermore producer prices were not differentiated by region to account for variations in access to markets and transportation costs, and although traders did not pay the official price to farmers, they claimed compensation from the stabilization fund as if they had. Finally the ONCC had substantially increased its staff and expenses, with funding guaranteed out of official marketing margins.

The Post-1994 System

By 1994 it had become evident that the situation was once again unsustainable. As a result the government adopted a free market system that became effective with the 1994–95 season. Since the 1994 reforms private traders have been able to procure cocoa directly from farmers and sell it to exporters, who also use their own agents to procure cocoa from farmers. Producer prices, as well as other costs and margins along the domestic marketing chain, are determined entirely by the market, and the stabilization fund has been eliminated, along with restrictions on when and where buyers may purchase cocoa beans. Sales can be effected at any time.

Efforts to control quality at the time beans are purchased from farmers have essentially been abandoned, although in theory responsibility for this function has been vested with the Ministry of Agriculture since 1989. Internal and external trade are open to anyone, and exporters do not need approval from any public agency (they register with the exporters' association). Immediately following the reforms, roughly 200 operators were registered as buyers and exporters of cocoa, but only about a dozen of these operators are considered serious. Together these 12 account for more than 80 percent of total exports. Nevertheless many of the smaller operators and a considerable number of speculators have also been buying cocoa (often without any regard to quality) in an effort to increase their share of the market.

TRADE FINANCING. Cameroon's cocoa subsector faced serious liquidity problems following the insolvency of the ONCPB. Domestic exporters and traders who bought cocoa from farmers and transported it to ports depended on their own resources or bank credit to finance their operations, but most domestic banks were unable (and reluctant) to finance cocoa traders. Initially the Stabex system of the European Union compensated countries in Africa and the Caribbean and Pacific regions when they had shortfalls in their export revenues. Stabex provided financing to three major banks to help ease this constraint. However the majority of financing for cocoa came from foreign banks and a few foreign buyers. The main instrument for financing that has evolved since liberalization is the so-called green clause letter of credit. To obtain such a letter, a trader must first have enough money to transport a truckload of cocoa beans to Douala and store them in a warehouse. The trader then takes the warehouse receipt to a bank, which issues a letter of credit against the stored beans. The letter guarantees that the warehouse receipt is genuine and that the exporter, as custodian of the goods, is a solvent company and has appropriate insurance policies (with the buyer as the beneficiary in case of a claim). The trader takes this letter to the buyer, who then advances 70 percent of the value of the crop the exporter has stored, and the trader returns to purchase more cocoa.

THE ONCC AND QUALITY CONTROL. With the elimination of the stabilization fund, the ONCC was confined to three main functions: maintaining statistics, verifying quality and grade prior to export (that is, verifying that shipments corresponded to the contract), and representing Cameroon in international coffee and cocoa forums. Soon after the reforms the ONCC increased its staff from 60 to 150 and its annual budget to CFAF 2 billion, funded by a levy of CFAF 7,500 per ton on coffee and cocoa exports. However the ONCC has not performed effectively, particularly in terms of its quality control function. Foreign buyers have contracted with a private company to verify quantities and provide quality control at the time shipments are assembled in Cameroon, in effect paying for these services twice. Reportedly the certification documents provided by the ONCC and the private company often show significant discrepancies. Donors have argued for the abolition of the ONCC but have agreed to allow it to stay in business provided that its functions are limited to representing Cameroon's cocoa industry and collecting statistics. Quality control has not yet been privatized, although privatization was scheduled for June 1996.

Effects of the 1994 Reforms

The most recent reforms have had mixed results. They have had a highly positive effect on producer prices in Cameroon but have done little to improve the quality of cocoa. And they have resulted in a high level of concentration in cocoa exporting,

PRODUCER PRICES. The most immediate (and persistent) effect of the 1994 liberalization was a significant increase in prices paid to growers (see figure 2.8). Producer prices doubled after the CFAF devaluation of January 1994, rising from CFAF 150/kg to CFAF 300/kg—a 100 percent pass-through of the devaluation effect to farmers. During the crop year immediately following liberalization (1994–95), producer prices rose to about CFAF 475–525/kg; without export taxes, they would have been around CFAF 600/kg. In late 1995 Cameroon's cocoa was selling at an f.o.b. price of around CFAF 650,000/t. During that period farmers reportedly received about CFAF 475,000/t, or 73 percent of the f.o.b. price. Those who organized themselves to bulk up their sales did even better. With producers receiving 73 percent of the f.o.b. price and export taxes at 15 percent, marketing costs stood at around 12 percent.

QUALITY. The quality of Cameroonian cocoa was problematic even before the reforms.[8] These problems reportedly became particularly severe after

Figure 2.8 Cocoa Producer Prices in Cameroon, 1993/94–1994/95

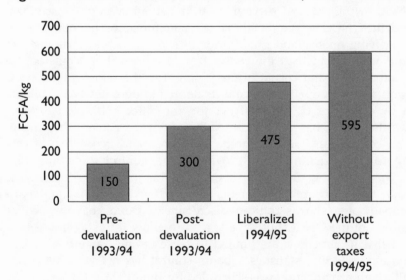

1990, for two reasons. First, many of the new domestic buyers and exporters showed little regard for quality, and second, the quality control provided by the ONCC was both ineffective and unreliable. As buyers and exporters sought to maximize their profits, low- and high-grade beans were increasingly mixed together. Cameroonian farmers paid less attention to drying and fermentation in order to take advantage of the opportunity to sell quickly to local buyers. It has been suggested that even buyers who would like to buy high-quality cocoa bid for low-quality beans for fear of losing out to a competitor. Cameroonian cocoa has always commanded a premium over cocoa from Côte d'Ivoire because of the high fat content and the reddish color (a characteristic of the *Trinitario* variety), which are highly valued by many processors. But the premium declined sharply throughout the early 1990s and by 1994 had virtually disappeared. It recovered slightly during the late 1990s, suggesting a gradual improvement in quality.

Cocoa analysts offer three reasons for the problems with the quality of Cameroonian cocoa and the subsequent reduction in the premium (Gilbert 1997).

- A shift in production to the humid southwest that may have resulted in a higher proportion of relatively low-quality beans;
- Bulk transportation, which makes exporters and buyers less willing to pay a quality premium, causing them to focus on average quality instead (importers are unwilling to pay for good fermented beans when bulk transportation mixes good and fair fermented beans); and
- Production levels that rose from around 100,000 tons in the early 1990s to 130,000–140,000 tons in the late 1990s, putting downward pressure on the Cameroonian premium.

FORWARD SALES. Another consequence of the reforms has been a collapse in forward sales owing to counterparty risk—that is, the risk of one party in the transaction not performing. Before the reform of the marketing system, Cameroon used to sell forward a large part of its cocoa exports prior to the new crop year, with the ONCPB acting as counterparty in international transactions. Since liberalization private exporters act as counterparties in forward transactions, raising the performance risk.

CONCENTRATION OF EXPORTERS. The number of exporters rose immediately following market liberalization, only to drop dramatically during the postliberalization period. Two foreign-linked companies handle an estimated 80 percent of all exports, leaving around 15 percent for the local processing factory and around 5 percent for the remaining 50 or so local exporters. The local exporters have been reduced to traders, selling to either foreign-linked exporters or the local processing factory. Official statistics that list exports according to the company that delivers the beans to port (Douala) show that in 1996–97 the 10 largest domestic traders accounted for 65 percent of the beans brought to the port. Despite this concentration competition has raised producer prices significantly compared with the preliberalization period.

A number of reasons have been put forward for the concentration in cocoa exporting (Gilbert 1997). Among them are the following.

- *The premium attached to red cocoa beans from Cameroon.*
- *The cocoa grinders in Europe that specialize in cocoa powder.* A small number have traditionally dominated the grinding of Cameroonian beans, and competition has reduced their number to two.
- *The bulk shipment method, which has made consolidating shipments of beans for export in Douala more profitable than exporting smaller quantities and consolidating them in Amsterdam.* The bulk shipment method has forged strong relationships between grinders and Cameroonian exporters who can assemble the necessary quantities (in fact, the two major exporting companies in Cameroon are effectively agents of the Dutch grinders).
- *The banking system.* Liberalization in Cameroon took place when the domestic banking system was effectively crippled and traditional exporters were accumulating significant arrears with the ONCPB. The two large exporters managed to establish their market share because of financing arrangements with the Dutch grinders and foreign banks.

Côte d'Ivoire

Prior to liberalization, which began in 1995, private firms and individuals handled cocoa marketing in Côte d'Ivoire. The 1995 reforms were only partial, and the marketing system did not undergo full liberalization until August 1999. Until then the parastatal Fund for Stabilization and Price Support for Agricultural Products (*Caisse de Stabilisation et de Soutien des Prix des Produits Agricoles,* or CAISTAB) set prices within a rigid structure and managed a system of controls and regulations. The ostensible purpose of these controls and regulations was to stabilize prices and returns and reduce risks to market participants.[9] A schedule of costs, prices, and margins known as a *barème* regulated the entire marketing chain from point of purchase to actual export (including the export of processed products). CAISTAB therefore determined the revenues of all participants in the domestic cocoa economy.

PRICING. CAISTAB established the administered prices annually at the beginning of the crop year, beginning with an assessment of the world prices for the coming year. Domestic prices were stabilized intra-annually through a system of regular forward sales on international markets, the Program of Average Forward Sales (*Programme de Ventes Anticipées à la Moyenne*, or PVAM).[10] The schedule itself was based on an estimated export price determined with a formula based on the weighted average of the forward sales prices (approximately 60–70 percent of the next year's export sales) and the anticipated price for the remaining 30–40 percent of the crop.[11]

Prices at different stages of the marketing chain were derived from the PVAM price. However they took into account reasonable costs and returns at each level and responded to the bargaining power of processors and exporters. The schedule also included the return to the government from direct (explicit) export taxes and indirect taxes (minus CAISTAB's administrative costs). The explicit export tax was the Single Export Tax (*Droit Unique de Sortie*, or DUS). The indirect tax, or stabilization margin, was the difference between the world price and the official export price. The indirect tax was in place during 14 of the 16 crop seasons between 1983 and 1999; for the other two, the tax was a subsidy.

Until 1986 adjustments to purchasing prices were sufficient to maintain real producer prices at fairly constant and remunerative levels. Over the subsequent three years, real prices declined modestly but steadily, followed by a drastic reduction in 1989–90. Between 1989–90 and 1996–97 real producer prices remained fairly constant at low levels, with a modest upturn after 1996–97 (figure 2.9).

DOMESTIC MARKETING. The private sector in Côte d'Ivoire consisted of exporters, traders, farmers, and farmer cooperatives. Cocoa moved from

Figure 2.9 Nominal and Real Producer Prices in Côte d'Ivoire, 1975/76–1997/98

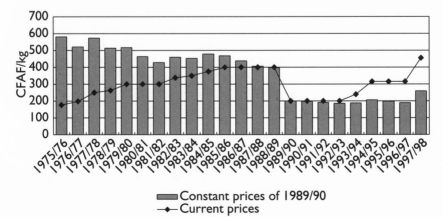

════ Constant prices of 1989/90
─◆─ Current prices

farmers through traders to domestic processors and exporters, and some farmers formed cooperatives to sell directly to exporters or large traders. Exporters commonly utilized traders to obtain cocoa from farmers, but they also bought from cooperatives. Cooperatives often had difficulty mobilizing funds to provide credit and other services to their members. There were some 700 licensed traders, many of them local merchants, who generally provided additional services to farmers, such as credit and agricultural inputs. CAISTAB reimbursed all traders by the amounts set in the schedule, including a profit margin also set by CAISTAB.

EXPORTS. In the 1998–99 crop year (before full liberalization) 5 large operations and around 62 relatively small licensed exporters handled physical trading. The bulk of the annual crop was negotiated and sold directly by individual exporters, who had to obtain CAISTAB's approval on the quantity and price before actually shipping the cocoa. (CAISTAB authorized each individual shipment that left the country.) CAISTAB directly negotiated and sold (but did not physically handle) a portion of all exports and then designated individual shippers and exporters to send the consignments, which had already been purchased from local sources. CAISTAB's criteria for assigning such export rights to individual exporters were not necessarily transparent.

TRANSPORT. Traders provided local transport. Until the 1995–96 reforms CAISTAB applied a system of transport cost equalization to ensure panterritorial producer pricing. The system reimbursed transporters on the basis of both tons carried and kilometers traveled. Collecting reimbursements required transporters to obtain verification at regional CAISTAB offices at collection centers.

QUALITY CONTROL. The quality of Ivorian cocoa shipments began declining around 1990, largely because traders and exporters increasingly took to mixing high- and low-quality beans in order to increase shipment volumes and revenues. Traders did not grade beans, paying basically the same price for all beans regardless of quality, so that growers had no incentive to produce high-quality crops. Most of the mixing took place when exporters cleaned, dried, graded and rebagged beans, although CAISTAB was nominally responsible for controlling the quality of beans at that stage.

Reforming the Cocoa Subsector

In 1995–96 Côte d'Ivoire initiated several reforms of its cocoa marketing system.[12] These changes, which affected both internal and export sales, were intended to increase competition, improve the transparency and accountability of the export allocation system, and increase returns to farmers. In 1997 the government agreed to further reforms designed to completely liberalize the external marketing of coffee (October 1, 1998) and cocoa (October 1, 1999) and to replace CAISTAB with a much smaller entity with a greatly reduced role. Following the liberalization of the coffee subsector, Côte d'Ivoire liberalized its external cocoa marketing system ahead of schedule in August 1999.

The 1995–96 Reforms

As part of the effort to increase transparency, promote competition, and improve the allocation of export rights, the first round of reforms had a number of specific goals. These included reducing marketing costs as a share of f.o.b. prices, increasing producers' income (in line with f.o.b. prices), reducing the fiscal risks of exporting, creating strong and independent producers' organizations, and promoting a strong and efficient financial sector.

INTERNAL MARKETING AND PRICING SYSTEMS. The reforms aimed to eliminate CAISTAB's costly uniform national prices at three points in the marketing chain and at the purchasing centers. These centers were responsible for distributing bags of cocoa beans and certifying the transport allowances designed to preserve the panterritorial policy for producer prices. The centers were eliminated at the beginning of the 1995–96 crop season, and the management of the transport cost allowance system was transferred to the private sector. The reform allowed exporters and processors to manage an allocated amount of beans, with ex-post assessment by the exporters' association.

EXTERNAL MARKETING. These reforms aimed to introduce more transparency and efficiency into CAISTAB's operations. CAISTAB had been regulating the quantities that would be exported and assigning export rights to private exporters at its own discretion. The discretionary assignment of export rights undermined transparency and prices. The reforms included auctions of export rights and limited CAISTAB's direct sales to 15 percent of one season's cocoa production. The rationale for adopting the auction system was to eliminate CAISTAB's involvement in price negotiations and the allocation of export rights. The auction system was adopted in May 1996, and CAISTAB's involvement was reduced to deciding the quantity of export rights that would be offered at each session and setting the opening minimum bid price.

CAISTAB'S EXPENDITURES AND EXPORT TAXES. Prior to the 1995–96 reforms, CAISTAB's operating budget (dubbed "delta") was high enough to constitute an implicit tax on farm income. In light of CAISTAB's withdrawal from internal marketing activities, and in the interest of streamlining its budget, the government reduced the parastatal's expenditures, eliminated subsidies included in the "delta," and transferred all budgetary spending to the state. As a result CAISTAB's expenditures dropped from about CFAF 100 billion in 1994–95 to CFAF 64 billion in 1995–96 and CFAF 53 billion in 1997–98.

The reforms also supported the streamlining of the stabilization fund introduced in 1993–94 to cover price fluctuations below the guaranteed f.o.b. price. To this end the government introduced a cap on the fund of CFAF 35 billion for 1995–96 (that amount was raised to CFAF 50 billion for the 1997–98 season). If the fund was depleted during the season, the guaranteed f.o.b. price was to be lowered so that CAISTAB would not incur any losses. Finally, in order to increase the pass-through rate of international prices to farmers, the government reduced export taxes to around 20 percent of the f.o.b. price (from CFAF 200/kg to CFAF 150/kg).

Evaluating the 1995–96 Reforms

The 1995–96 reforms had three pronounced effects on the cocoa-marketing system. First, they gradually reduced the role of the state in domestic and external marketing so that ultimately the private sector handled all marketing. Second, they lifted zoning and other restrictions that had limited competition in private domestic marketing. Third, they eliminated some of CAISTAB's discretionary powers and improved transparency by instituting auctions of export rights.[13]

Despite some delays and a lack of local ownership of the reforms, initially implementation went well. The major risk was that the government might yield to various vested interests opposed to the reforms. At the time the program was being prepared, government agencies and external donors were deeply concerned about the appropriate pace of liberalization, largely because the public sector was reluctant to relinquish control. Under these circumstances, the challenge was to establish a broad consensus among all partners, local and external. In the end a gradual approach helped to keep all key players on board throughout the reform process.

The prospect of gradual market liberalization was initially met with some skepticism. Numerous fears surfaced: that middlemen would take advantage of farmers, that the quality of cocoa would decline, that international trading houses with easy access to credit would wipe out local competition, and that there would be massive defaults among exporters unable to deliver the cocoa at the price bid for in the auction. But these fears did not materialize. The 1995–96 reforms in internal and external marketing did not result in major changes for farmers. The producer share in international prices remained stable and rather low, usually between 45 and 55 percent.

Eliminating the uniform pricing policy across the country also did not result in significant differences in producer prices. It is not clear whether the reforms had any impact on the quality of the exports of cocoa. The number of buyers and exporters increased and the share of cooperatives in the collection of cocoa climbed from 22 to 29 percent during the 1997–98 crop year. The reforms succeeded in reducing CAISTAB's role in the cocoa (and coffee) trade and introduced more transparency to the cocoa subsector. In effect they set the stage for full liberalization.

Despite initial fears, the auction system worked satisfactorily. Evidence from the auctions shows that shippers often overbid in their efforts to obtain the approval needed to export. Overbidding signified a willingness to pay more than the f.o.b. price, but some feared that it would result in substantial defaults, undermining the reputation of Ivorian cocoa exports. During the operation of the auction system, there were some defaults, and their number increased after the decline in world prices in late 1998 and early 1999. However whether the number of defaults increased compared with the system prior to reform is not clear.

Some defaults occurred because the guarantees exporters were required to put up were very low and because sanctions were difficult to enforce when exporters defaulted. Some analysts attributed the willingness to overbid to the second-price feature, which allocates exports rights to the second-highest bidder if the highest bidder does not want the entire amount put up for auction. But overbidding more likely reflected the high cost allowances in the schedule; by squeezing margins set in the schedule to cover a potential loss on export rights, the shipper could still make a profit. This practice can be viewed as a transfer of rents from the shippers to the marketing agency.[14] Also, contrary to earlier fears, the auction system did not increase—and may even have reduced—the concentration of exports. In 1997–98 the 5 country's largest exporters accounted for around 60 percent of exports and the 10 largest exporters for around 83 percent.

Despite the early reforms, however, the Ivorian cocoa-marketing and -pricing system still had some serious problems.

- First, maintaining fixed producer prices when world prices change created fiscal risk. Because world prices were not transmitted to producers quickly, they caused macroeconomic disruptions through their influence on the government account. For example, high domestic producer prices and declining world prices in the late 1980s bankrupted the marketing system. In 1990 the government was forced to cut the producer price in half and in 1998 was still repaying debts incurred before 1991 to both foreign and domestic private sectors.
- Second, the reforms did not improve producer prices. Producers continued to receive a relatively small share of the f.o.b. price, and Ivorian

cocoa farmers remained among the lowest paid in the world. Producer prices also benefited little from the 100 percent devaluation of the CFA franc in 1994. The real dollar price of cocoa in 1997–98 was about the same as the real dollar price in 1993–94 (the last season before the devaluation), despite rising world cocoa prices. After 1995 low domestic producer prices and rising world prices allowed the government to accumulate substantial parafiscal surpluses that distorted income distribution because they were not rebated to producers. The main reason that farmgate prices did not improve after the reforms was that the system of administrative prices remained in place, leaving few incentives to reduce marketing costs. Both domestic marketing costs (between the farm and the port) and international costs (f.o.b to CIF), were high by world standards—in some seasons by as much as 10–15 percentage points. Years of partial and perhaps at times half-hearted measures to tinker with the pricing system did not achieve much in the way of improving marketing cost competitiveness.

- Third, implicit public contract guarantees granted through the cocoa (and coffee) export systems caused moral hazard in the financial markets. In effect authorization to export constituted a public guarantee that the exporter acquired at a low cost and then used as collateral for export credit. This moral hazard repeatedly expressed itself as poor credit discipline and delayed repayment or default on bank loans for cocoa (and coffee) exports.
- Fourth, the bias of the administered margins in favor of exporters and domestic traders and a long tradition of parastatal domination in cocoa marketing stifled independent producers' organizations, as well as other private sector institutions.

Thus, while the early reforms went some way toward improving transparency (especially in the allocation of export rights), reducing CAISTAB's intervention in cocoa marketing, and promoting competition, much remained to be done. Marketing costs as a share of f.o.b. prices had not fallen significantly, nor had producers' incomes risen. Exporting still involved a degree of fiscal risk, and producers' organizations remained stifled. Significantly, the reforms had not gone far enough in promoting a strong and efficient financial sector.

The government's main strategy for realizing these objectives was to liberalize further, particularly in the export sector. Its key concern in liberalizing exports was the potential loss of benefits from eliminating the (public) forward selling system. Proponents of this system emphasized its two main benefits. First, it allowed the government to offer a fixed annual price to farmers, and second, it improved total export revenues, as forward prices tended to be higher than spot prices. An analysis of the costs and benefits of forward sales found that seasonal cocoa price volatility was relatively low and that therefore the potential gains from market liberalization were significantly higher than the benefits of stable prices. These gains were attributable to lower marketing costs and included the costs of CAISTAB and the stabilization margins (McIntire and Varangis 1999). On the issue of the forward premium, McIntire and Varangis (1999) and Gilbert (1997) conclude that evidence pointing to a positive and statistically significant forward premium is at best inconclusive. But even if the forward premium appeared positive, CAISTAB's operating costs and the inefficiencies in the domestic marketing system rendered it negative.

The 1999 Reforms

The 1999 reforms were designed to completely liberalize Côte d'Ivoire's cocoa marketing system. They focused on two major changes:

- They replaced the "old" CAISTAB with a "new" CAISTAB, reducing it to the role of an advisory and regulatory agency and eliminating its interference in export marketing. The board of the new CAISTAB included private sector participants, although it retained its previous government-appointed management.
- They radically changed the system of export marketing, eliminating the indicative minimum farm price and liberalizing farmgate prices. The schedule of prices and margins disappeared, the public forward sales program ended, and the export authorization became obsolete.

As of this writing it is too early to evaluate the results of the 1999 liberalization. One key issue has been the decline of cocoa producer prices (in absolute terms) that began in the third quarter of 1998. Producer prices fell from CFA 540 per kg during the last year of fixed prices (1998–99) to CFA 280–320 per kg during the first six months after liberalization. This decline is consistent with the significant drop in world cocoa prices (around 40 percent) that began in December 1998. The causes of the decline were primarily weak market fundamentals and large stocks in cocoa-consuming countries.

Ghana

Until the mid-1970s Ghana was the world's largest cocoa producer. But throughout the 1970s and early 1980s, production declined sharply in response to internal and external shocks and poor overall economic management. The cocoa subsector was neglected and overtaxed. In 1982–84 prolonged drought and bush fires took a heavy toll on cocoa trees, particularly in the Brong-Ahafo and Ashanti regions, and producers had few incentives to replant their destroyed farms. The area planted to cocoa was reduced by half, and in 1983–84 production fell to an all-time low of 159,000 tons.

Following the introduction of macroeconomic reforms in 1983, cocoa production recovered to around 400,000 tons per annum. Producer prices increased gradually in both nominal and real terms every year until 1988. After 1988, however, real producer prices began declining, falling sharply until 1993–94 as inflation outpaced price adjustments and world prices declined. Since then nominal farmgate prices have been increased almost fourfold in an effort to keep pace with domestic inflation and to keep the farmers' share of the export price over 50 percent.

PRODUCER PRICING. Producer prices are administratively set and are fixed for the entire crop year by the Producer Price Review Committee, a body consisting of the marketing board (Ghana Cocoa Board, or COCOBOD), government officials, and representatives of private cocoa buyers, the national cocoa farmers' organizations, and haulers and transporters. The committee takes into account expected export prices during the coming year, the operating costs of COCOBOD and its subsidiaries, the explicit tax, and farmers' production costs.[15]

Along with farmers in neighboring Côte d'Ivoire, Ghana's 600,000–800,000 predominantly small cocoa growers receive the lowest share of the export price in the world—roughly half (figure 2.10). At 30 percent the export tax is the highest by far among all the major cocoa-producing countries. Marketing costs are also relatively high (15 percent), and the costs of COCOBOD and its subsidiaries account for around 5 percent. Low farmgate prices have proved a significant disincentive to good crop husbandry and to the adoption of improved technologies. As a result Ghanaian yields are only about two-thirds of those in Côte d'Ivoire.

Ghana's pricing system is designed in part to help stabilize producer prices (and therefore acts as an implicit stabilization fund), but the stabilization margin is not clear. The difference between the producer price and the f.o.b. export price includes domestic marketing costs, all operating and administrative expenses of COCOBOD and its subsidiaries, the explicit export tax, and the stabilization margin (or COCOBOD's profit or loss). Determining the specific size of each item is difficult—the more so since marketing costs and COCOBOD's other expenses are determined a priori in budgetary negotiations with the Ministry of Finance. Moreover a portion of COCOBOD's expenses covers activities unrelated to cocoa marketing that in another country would be performed either privately (plantations and processing plants and input marketing) or as public services funded from fiscal revenues (research, extension, and disease control).[16] COCOBOD's budget thus represents compensation for crop marketing and related services, a subsidy for commercial activities, and an implicit tax that finances public

Figure 2.10 Distribution of Share in the ICCO Daily Price, 1983/84–1997/98

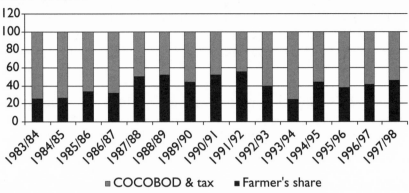

■ COCOBOD & tax ■ Farmer's share

Note: Each day, the International Cocoa Organization (ICCO) publishes a reference price for cocoa based on the prices of cocoa traded at the London and New York exchanges.

goods and other quasi-fiscal activities. Although COCOBOD's staff was cut from over 120,000 in the early 1980s (of which many were "ghost workers") to about 60,000 in 1986 and to fewer than 11,000 in the mid-1990s and input marketing has been sharply curtailed, scope for further economies remains.

Producer price stabilization has proved elusive, and governments have in fact utilized the funds intended for this purpose to augment fiscal revenues. Producer prices declined significantly in real terms from 1986–87 until 1993–94, because nominal increases in official prices failed to keep pace with domestic inflation in all but two of those years. Cocoa farmers received a very low share of the export price during the second half of the 1980s and early 1990s (significantly less than farmers in Côte d'Ivoire). Under agreements negotiated with the World Bank, the share of f.o.b. prices paid to farmers increased after 1993–94, and Ghanian farmers began receiving about the same share as farmers in Côte d'Ivoire. But accelerating inflation and the depreciation of the Cedi mean that farmers effectively receive a lower share of the f.o.b. price as the crop year progresses.

DOMESTIC MARKETING. Until 1992–93 COCOBOD controlled all stages of cocoa marketing through several subsidiaries, beginning with purchases at the farm gate and continuing through exports and sales to domestic processors. The Produce Buying Company (PBC), a COCOBOD subsidiary, was the sole purchaser, buying directly from farmers at over 2,000 buying centers. These centers had regular and convenient operating hours, so farmers could readily sell their cocoa in their own or a nearby village whenever they decided to do so. Until 1992–93 cocoa procured at these centers became the property of the PBC until it was delivered to the COCOBOD's exporting subsidiary. The PBC arranged and paid for transportation and storage along the internal marketing chain. The cocoa takeover price (the price at which the PBC delivers the cocoa to the exporting subsidiary) covered the price paid to producers as well as all the PBC's costs and was administratively established prior to the season. In 1992–93 private domestic buyers began competing with the PBC to purchase cocoa from farmers and sell it for export.

EXPORTS. COCOBOD's exporting subsidiary still has the monopoly on cocoa exports and sales to local processing companies. Over a period of nearly 50 years it has established a reputation for quality produce and reliable service in a market that has at times been very volatile and in which defaults on contracts are not unknown. Ghanaian cocoa has long fetched a small but significant premium in the world market that is generally explained as reflecting high and consistent quality. But a sizable portion of the premium is offset by the costs incurred in shipping cocoa long after it has been harvested, generally after buyers have evacuated the bulk of the annual main crop from Côte d'Ivoire. A significant part (around 60–70 percent) of Ghana's cocoa is usually sold forward, with sales beginning around one year in advance of the harvest.

QUALITY CONTROL. COCOBOD has long operated a very thorough quality control and grading system. At present the system includes three inspections along the marketing chain that are meant to safeguard the high quality of Ghanaian cocoa. The most important quality check takes place at the time of the initial purchase from the farmer at the buying station. COCOBOD's Quality Control Division is responsible for this inspection. The initial checking, grading, and bagging of beans take place at the buying station, and the Quality Control Division seals each bag. Markings on the bag identify the grade of the beans, the inspector who graded the beans, and the village organization that bought the beans from the farmer. In this way each bag can be traced back to its origin. The beans are reinspected and regraded at the exporting subsidiary's takeover points, and cocoa destined for export is checked one more time before being shipped. As a result of this process, and because of the reputation of the exporting subsidiary, buyers of Ghanaian beans perform less quality control on deliveries and thus save on costs. These savings and the superior quality are a large part of the reason for the premium on Ghanaian beans.

Quality control is made much easier by the fact that Ghanaian cocoa farmers are meticulous in their cultivation, fermentation, drying, and sorting practices. They carefully check and sort their beans, removing any that are not top quality in order to ensure a grade I rating at the buying center. Farmers that have enough substandard beans sell them separately at a steep discount. Farmers therefore incur costs by presorting beans and forgo considerable revenue by selling relatively low-grade and substandard beans separately at a significantly lower price. These practices differ markedly from those in neighboring countries, where beans of different quality are often blended. We have no way of knowing the exact percentage of beans Ghanian farmers discard as substandard (that is, with no attempts at marketing). But some trade sources estimate that farmers typically discard as much as 3–3.5 percent of their main crop—an example of further income forgone.

Reforms since 1992–93

In 1992–93 Ghana initiated modest reforms to its domestic cocoa marketing system that were designed to improve marketing efficiency by introducing private sector competition in domestic procurement and transportation. The reforms increased prices for buyers to more than the administrative price, which then served as a floor. The government still determines the minimum producer price and, by fixing the takeover price, the margins within which the private buyers (licensed buying companies) operate. To encourage purchases in remote areas, the government calculates evacuation costs and reimburses them separately on a location-specific basis. The licensed buying companies are free to pay producers more than the official price but rarely if ever do so. High start-up costs, small purchase volumes, and the tight margins allowed in the initial years have placed significant pressure on the companies' finances, and until 1999 only one had made a profit on its cocoa operations.

Several other important reforms were decided on during the 1989–99 crop season, using a participatory process that included the government and the private sector (see annex 2.1). First, in 2000 the government privatized the PBC, floating its shares on the Ghana Stock Exchange. Second, as part of cocoa sector reform, starting in crop year 2000–2001 the government instituted a policy of allowing licensed buying companies to export up to 30 percent of their cocoa purchases. The government published operational guidelines for exporting cocoa and conducted a workshop for stakeholders in July 2000. A company must meet four minimum conditions for obtaining an export license.

- It must have been registered as a licensed buying company and been operating actively for at least two years.
- It must have purchased at least 10,000 tons of cocoa in two consecutive years.
- It must be able to demonstrate the required technical know-how.
- It must be able to prove that it has access to adequate financial resources.

Companies that purchase less than 10,000 tons annually can negotiate with others (including COCOBOD's exporting subsidiary) to export on their behalf. Third, the government decided to raise the farmer's share of the f.o.b. price to 65 percent for the 1999–2000 crop season and for 2000-2001 the government announced the producer price as Cedi 3.48 million per ton which corresponds to about 67 percent of the FOB price.

Finally the government decided to take several measures, described below, that will affect local cocoa processing:[17]

- The price discounts for purchasing cocoa for processing will be discontinued, and local processors will have to buy cocoa at f.o.b. prices.
- Processors will be allowed to import relatively cheap low-quality cocoa for processing only.
- Nonprice incentives and special export processing zones will be used to encourage local processing.

Impact of the Reforms

The share of licensed buying companies (excluding the PBC) increased from around 25 percent in 1993–94 to 32 percent in 1996–97 to 41 percent in 1998–99 and to 56.5 percent in 1999–2000. Initially only one private firm, Cashpro, was a significant player, with a market share of 18 percent (57,000 tons) in 1996–97 (up from 11 percent in 1993–94). The shares of the remaining buying companies in 1996–97 ranged between 0.02 and 5.68 percent. The market concentration has changed somewhat since then. At the end of April 1999, 12 buying companies (including Cashpro) were active. Their cumulative shares for the 1998–99 crop year (main crop only) were 59.4 percent (PBC), 15.5 percent (Cashpro), and 0.1–7.9 percent (other firms). One cooperative captured 4.9 percent of the market share, making it the fifth-largest licensed buying company. (This cooperative has a lean cost structure, since it does not need buying agents.) For 1999–2000, the PBC's share was 43.5 percent and Cashpro's 13.2 percent; the share of the 11 other private licensed buying companies ranged between 0.2 and 9.8 percent. During 1999–2000 all companies (the PBC, Cashpro, and the private licensed buying companies) sold 100 percent of their purchases to COCOBOD's exporting subsidiary.

There has been no indication that the quality of cocoa delivered to or exported by COCOBOD's exporting subsidiary has declined. The PBC and the licensed buying companies pay COCOBOD's Quality Control Division for its services, and the division's staff routinely visit all buying centers and secondary assembly points to carry out inspections and, if needed, treatment. Although the PBC and buying companies pay the same prices as before the reforms, farmers have benefited from the entry of private competitors into the market. Some buying companies, in an attempt to gain farmers' loyalty, have provided farmers and some farming communities with in-kind benefits such as inputs, classrooms, and utility poles. Others have been paying farmers in cash rather than by check, eliminating the need for travel to sometimes distant local banks—another cost savings. Cocoa is being transported from growing areas more quickly because private buyers are keen to reduce their handling and financing costs. Unfortunately the exporting subsidiary's facilities and procedures, along with port and shipping practices, have not yet responded adequately, and port congestion has become a problem. Poor transport infrastructure in many cocoa-producing areas has a significant impact on evacuation costs, and private buyers are reluctant to operate where cocoa must be moved by canoes or tractors rather than by truck and requires headloading.

Nigeria

Nigeria has long been one of the world's leading cocoa producers, but its share of total worldwide production has declined sharply since the mid-1970s. From an all-time high of 317,000 tons in 1970–71, cocoa production fell off sharply during the oil boom years of the 1970s, bottoming out at just over 100,000 tons in 1986–87. This decline in production had three main causes:

- The massive movement of farm labor into the industrial, construction, and service jobs created by the oil boom;
- Unattractive producer prices; and
- Deteriorating productivity due to aging trees, black pod disease, scarce inputs, and diminishing attention to cocoa orchards.

The macroeconomic and sectoral policy reforms initiated in 1986 dramatically improved the incentive system for agriculture generally and for cocoa production in particular. For cocoa growers the abolition of the monopsonistic Nigerian Cocoa Board, complete liberalization of domestic and external cocoa marketing and pricing, and an adjustment of the exchange rate to a more realistic level combined to restore profitability to cocoa farming. Production has increased, fluctuating between 135,000 and 170,000 tons annually (mainly in response to climatic conditions) since the late 1980s.

The Pre-1986 Marketing System

Until 1977 a number of regional marketing boards controlled cocoa marketing. These boards were responsible for purchasing cocoa from farmers and for quality control. Produce inspectors operating at the state level ensured that cocoa entering the marketing chain was of high quality. The cocoa was then sold through the Nigerian Produce Marketing Company (NPMC), a monopolistic parastatal owned by the federal government. In 1977 the Nigerian Cocoa Board (NCB) replaced the regional marketing boards and NPMC. This new national parastatal set producer prices and held the monopoly on domestic procurement, sales, and exports. Its was also responsible for quality inspection at the points where farmers sold their cocoa, for cocoa extension services, and for the procurement and marketing of production inputs.

However Nigeria's macroeconomic environment deteriorated steadily throughout the 1970s and 1980s. Rising domestic inflation, an increasingly overvalued exchange rate, and steadily worsening terms of trade for agricultural producers made cocoa production increasingly less remunerative for farmers and trapped the NCB between falling international prices and rising costs. In real terms the official producer price fell by 100 percent between 1978–79 and 1984–85, and by 1985–86 farmers were receiving less than 20 percent of the world price. The NCB absorbed the remainder in marketing expenses, taxes, and other operating costs.

The 1986 Liberalization

In 1986, as part of overall reforms, the government took a number of steps to reverse the decline in the production of agricultural commodities, including cocoa. Among the most important measures were the adoption of a more appropriate exchange rate and the abolition of the six parastatal agricultural commodity marketing boards, including the NCB. Price controls were abolished, as were licensing requirements for crop buyers and exporters, and the product inspection and quality control procedures employed by the NCB were abandoned. Owing to fierce competition among a multitude of buyers (as many as 400 were active in the trade soon after the abolition of the NCB), the farmgate price for cocoa increased significantly after this liberalization (see figure 2.11).

THE SHORT-TERM EFFECT. Until 1986 the quality of Nigerian cocoa was considered very good, and foreign buyers had confidence in both the quality of the cocoa and the selling arrangements of the NCB. Nigerian cocoa fetched a price premium over Ivorian cocoa, although not as much as Ghanaian cocoa. But this reputation for quality and the mutual trust evaporated very rapidly after the sudden liberalization, which was effected virtually overnight, with little or no advance planning. Large numbers of previously unknown local traders suddenly began offering enormous quantities of cocoa for sale abroad, and many of them were unable (owing to lack of supplies) or unwilling (when they received a higher offer from another buyer) to deliver the contracted shipments to the contracted buyers. As a result

Figure 2.11 Nominal and Real Cocoa Producer Prices in Nigeria, 1975/76–1997/98

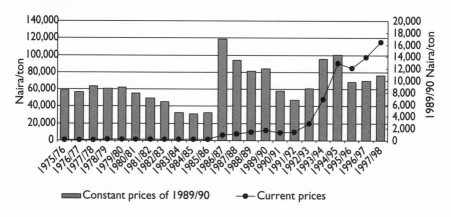

■■■ Constant prices of 1989/90   ●── Current prices

buyers lost confidence in Nigeria's selling arrangements, and most of the country's cocoa was soon being traded on a spot basis only when the cocoa arrived in port stores in Europe or North America, where potential buyers could inspect it. This arrangement, which is still in place, minimizes risks to foreign buyers, many of whom had financially disastrous experiences with unreliable exporters during 1986.

Two major factors lay at the root of these early problems. First, because of the radical nature of the reforms and the suddenness with which they were adopted, no effective arrangements for grading and quality control were in place following the abolition of the NCB. Fiercely competitive buyers purchased beans directly from farmers, often before the beans were fully fermented and dried, and offered these for export without any concern for quality. (The governments of the cocoa-producing states, however, continued to levy grading fees on cocoa at their state borders.). Furthermore there were few established domestic traders with experience in cocoa—a result of the NCB's monopolistic position in the cocoa market.

Second, exchange controls created a high premium for foreign exchange, causing many traders to enter the cocoa export business in order to obtain hard currency that could be exchanged in the parallel market for substantial profits. Cocoa trading thus became a form of trading foreign exchange. Domestic buyers purchased any type of cocoa, regardless of quality. The profits from exchanging foreign currency for naira at the unofficial exchange rate more than compensated for any loss of export revenue because of poor quality. Cocoa trading was also a readily accessible vehicle for capital flight, and many buyers were paying prices for cocoa that were even higher than the f.o.b. equivalent at the parallel exchange rate. Many also significantly understated the unit prices in their export contracts in order to facilitate capital flight. Driven by enormous demand for cocoa, producer prices increased sixfold between 1986 and 1989. Local bean processors complained about the ruinous prices exporters were paying—prices that were sustainable only because of the rent obtained on the unofficial foreign exchange market. Beginning in 1990 the Central Bank of Nigeria liberalized the foreign exchange market and tightened liquidity in the banking system, making it harder for buyers to obtain credit for cocoa purchases.

The Present Situation

Following the trade liberalization of 1986, a number of genuine long-term local traders became involved in buying cocoa, and a number of them remain active in the trade. Several of the serious buyers provide additional services to cocoa growers, notably a reliable supply of quality pesticides on credit, with repayment at the time the crop is sold. Export marketing, which was very fragmented after liberalization, has been consolidated and is better organized. A degree of confidence has returned as the trade has settled down, and fewer than 20 companies now account for virtually all cocoa exports. Some European trade houses have also established operations in Nigeria in order to ensure reliability in both contracting and quality. Nevertheless the quality of Nigerian cocoa, although improving, remains variable. Most shipments undergo a quality control check before foreign buyers pay for them , and much Nigerian cocoa is still traded on a spot basis on arrival in Europe or North America.

THE QUALITY ISSUE. The present marketing system relies exclusively on private traders and exporters. There are no barriers to entry, either in domestic trading or exporting. Exporters are licensed, but these licenses are easy (probably too easy) to obtain. Some unreliable operators are still active in the export trade, with a deleterious effect on the reputation of Nigerian cocoa. Cocoa is still used by some local traders as a means of exporting capital, and these operators pay little attention to quality, although changes in foreign exchange policy have made cocoa less attractive as a means of obtaining foreign exchange. Traders who buy cocoa at the farmgate perform initial quality control and transport shipments themselves. The Federal Produce Inspection Service does carry out an official quality control and fumigation service for exports at the ports, but this service is time-consuming and not necessarily reliable, and officials are reputedly open to bribes.

PRODUCER PRICES. Producer prices are determined by market conditions in both the internal and international cocoa markets. As a result of liberalization, cocoa farmers in Nigeria receive well above 80 percent of the f.o.b.

export price—a much higher percentage of the f.o.b. value than they received before 1986 and considerably more than their counterparts in Ghana and Côte d'Ivoire.[18]

TAXES. Within Nigeria individual states impose taxes on cocoa leaving their territory, inspecting the beans at their borders before the bags are sealed in order to check the quantities (levies and taxes are assessed on the quantities shipped). The federal government does not impose an export tax.

Lessons from Cocoa Market Liberalization

The reforms undertaken in Cameroon, Côte d'Ivoire, Nigeria, and Togo have been profound. Ghana's reforms have been more gradual. In both Cameroon and Nigeria, liberalization encountered problems early on (some analysts even characterized the situation as chaotic), resulting in the perception that such reforms inevitably lead to confusion. However further analysis suggests that the problems following market liberalization in both Cameroon and Nigeria are specific to these countries and that it is unwise to extrapolate from these experiences to argue that every liberalization will have similar results. Furthermore little attention has been paid to the successful and smooth liberalization in Togo (see annex 2.1). West Africa's reforms of cocoa marketing and pricing systems in fact had several important positive effects.

Producer Prices Have Risen

After liberalization in Nigeria—and more recently in Cameroon and Togo— farmers began receiving considerably higher prices (both in absolute terms and as a percentage of the f.o.b. price) than their counterparts in Côte d'Ivoire and Ghana. This increase is the result of growing competition among local traders, relatively low marketing costs and margins, and the abolition of state marketing agencies and thus implicit taxes. In Cameroon and Nigeria producer prices increased from around 45 percent and 20 percent, respectively, before the reforms to over 70 percent and 80 percent afterward. Producer prices in Togo increased from 60 percent of the f.o.b. price prior to reforms to about 80 percent thereafter. But market liberalization has exposed farmers to price volatility from fluctuations in the world market. Seasonal variations in producer prices have increased from almost none prior to reforms to international levels—generally 10 percent or less.

The increase in producer prices in Cameroon and Togo following liberalization was due not only to reductions in marketing costs and margins but also to increasing world cotton prices. In contrast, producer prices in Côte d'Ivoire declined immediately following liberalization because of rapidly declining world cocoa prices that overwhelmed any efficiency gains from liberalization. Thus the timing of liberalization is very important: it always helps to liberalize when prices are not declining.

Marketing Margins, Profit Margins, and Taxes Have Decreased

Liberalization has generated competition that in turn has lowered marketing and profit margins. Margins were high before the reforms because the cocoa-marketing monopolies had few incentives to be more efficient. Governments have also reduced explicit and implicit taxes and abolished the costs associated with the operation of marketing boards and stabilization funds. Stabilization margins have disappeared along with efforts to stabilize prices. Under stabilization funds price stabilization was supposed to be self-financing, with inflows during periods of high prices compensating for outflows when prices were low. In practice, however, self-financing never became a reality, and price stabilization imposed an implicit tax on producers.

The Impact on Cocoa Production Has Been Positive

Market liberalization has had a positive impact on cocoa production, with increased producer prices restoring some profitability to the cocoa subsector. In both Cameroon and Nigeria cocoa production was following a downward trend prior to market liberalization. In Cameroon production increased from a 5-year average of 104,000 tons prior to the 1994–95 reforms to an average of 124,000 tons during the period between 1994–95 and 1998–99. In Nigeria production increased from a 5-year average of 123,000 tons prior to the 1986 reforms to an average of 152,000 tons between 1987–88 and 1991–92 and to an average of 165,000 tons for the period 1994–95 to 1998–99. In Ghana agreements between the World Bank and the government to improve the f.o.b. share of the farmer's price have contributed to the increase in cocoa production. In the mid-1980s average cocoa production in Ghana was around 192,000 tons. It increased to an average of 361,000 tons for the period 1994–95 to 1998–99.

Liberalization Has Almost Eliminated Forward Sales

Following export liberalization the private sector could no longer realize the benefits of public forward sales, since forward sellers usually must put up a crop or some entitlement (for instance, a warehouse receipt) as collateral. In the absence of a margin system, buyers require collateral because sellers have an incentive to renege on the forward contract if prices subsequently rise or if the amount slated for delivery is not available. For this reason forward selling is possible only if the seller has good credit or adequate collateral or if margins are sufficiently large. In the absence of physical inventories, exporters can sell forward only if they have a forward contract with producers. But domestic forward markets do not exist due to performance risk.

Difficulties overcoming performance risk complicate forward selling by private entities in developing countries, particularly if such sales involve smallholder crops or take place in an environment with poorly functioning credit institutions and unreliable contract enforcement—all characteristics of West African cocoa-producing countries. Evidence shows that forward sales decline in volume and period of coverage after liberalization. In Cameroon and Nigeria forward sales have almost disappeared, and the few remaining sales are for short periods.[19] The presence of a monopoly marketing agency such as a marketing board greatly reduces performance risk in forward sales. This agency, by controlling exports through direct sales, granting export rights, or both, can be confident that cocoa beans will be available for sale in the coming crop year (subject to the margin of interyear crop variation). A monopoly also has an established reputation in the market as a reliable counterpart and is therefore able to sell forward even well ahead of harvest time (sometimes 18 months before).

With the virtual elimination of forward sales, the question becomes whether selling forward offers any net benefits. Forward sales offer two presumed benefits. First, they reduce the risk of seasonal price stabilization, and second, they allow producing countries to capture the so-called forward premium (the difference between the forward price and the spot price at the time of the forward sale).

Seasonal price variations in cocoa-producing countries without price stabilization (such as Indonesia and Malaysia) are typically low (less than 7–8 percent, in line with variations of world cocoa prices).[20] Thus the benefits of price stabilization are relatively small compared with the gains from market liberalization, which lowers marketing costs and raises producer prices (McIntire and Varangis 1999). [21] Furthermore Gilbert (1997) finds that the single most important factor behind stable real producer prices in Cameroon and Côte d'Ivoire is the monetary stability provided by membership in the CFA franc zone. Gilbert argues that in Ghana and Nigeria the exchange rate, not the marketing boards, was the main mechanism for real price stabilization.[22] Farmers in general diversify (raising other crops besides cocoa, keeping livestock, and working as laborers, for instance), and high volatility in cocoa prices does not necessarily translate into higher income volatility. In fact in the early 1990s farmers in Nigeria demonstrated when rumors suggested that the government was preparing to return to the previous fixed-price system.

The argument for a forward premium is also questionable. Forward sales can keep prices high when market prices are falling (if the forward price is higher than the spot price at the time of shipment). But in a rising market forward sales can lower prices. Gilbert (1997) and McIntire and Varangis

(1999) have found inconclusive evidence that supports a forward premium. But even with a forward premium, the net benefit of forward sales may be negative when the cost of maintaining the government export monopoly needed to implement such sales and all the attendant inefficiencies are taken into account. Overall, then, eliminating forward sales has not deprived cocoa-producing countries of significant benefits. Increases in producer prices have more than compensated for increased volatility, and no conclusive evidence supports the existence of a forward premium.

Quality Has Deteriorated, but Liberalization Is Only Part of the Explanation

Market liberalization in Nigeria and Cameroon has allegedly lowered the quality of cocoa and thus cost these countries their quality premium. Competition is blamed for this development: buyers fear losing potential shipments to other buyers and so purchase cocoa even if it has not been properly dried or fermented. The reforms also abolished government quality controls, exacerbating the situation. But these developments are only part of the story. As we have seen the quality of Nigerian cocoa declined in the late 1980s primarily because exporting cocoa was an effective way to circumvent exchange controls. Given this fact quality became a secondary consideration. The abolition of quality control and standards following the country's very rapid liberalization did not help matters.

In Cameroon the decline in quality can also be attributed to a shift in production sites to less appropriate areas and to bulk shipping, which has made foreign buyers less willing to pay a premium, and the shifting of production to less appropriate areas. But in Cameroon liberalization per se was not primarily responsible for the deterioration in overall quality; it contributed primarily to the erosion of quality to a fair fermented level. The feared deterioration in quality did not occur in Togo following liberalization, and Togo's cocoa exports continue to command a premium. The postliberalization quality control system in Togo evolved from an agreement between the private sector and the government's quality control service. The government service initiated training for buyers and producer associations wanting to inspect purchases before they reach the port (see annex 2.1).

It is too simplistic to attribute a deterioration in quality entirely to market liberalization or to the advent of a free market system. In fact experience with other crops, such as coffee, suggests that countries with free marketing systems produce very high-quality commodities. What affects production when reforms are introduced is the loss of institutions. During reform institutional arrangements must be in place to deal with quality control issues such as standards and inspection. For example, a public sector institution can continue to set standards of quality while licensed private companies carry out inspections and certification. During a transitional period the government can set minimum export standards, so that cocoa below a certain quality cannot be exported, and continue to control the quality of exports (although this arrangement was not successful in Cameroon). Maintaining such control ensures that foreign buyers receive the quality of cocoa specified in export contracts and that exports do not fall below the minimum standard.

At the same time farmers must have a financial incentive to maintain the quality of their crops. A number of marketing board systems allow farmers to maintain quality regardless of the cost, but in a competitive environment, costs matter. The government and private trade associations have a role to play in educating farmers on improving and maintaining quality. In the end, however, costs and prices determine the quality of the cocoa that is produced.

Institutional Capacity Building Is Essential in a Liberalized Market

As we have seen liberalization raises a number of fears, including concerns about contract performance and quality. These fears are based primarily on the experience in Nigeria, where the government abolished the marketing board suddenly and without making any provisions for an orderly transition to a well-run, market-driven system. Market liberalization is not supposed to engender an environment in which anything goes. While the private sector is in charge of the marketing functions, smooth market operations depend on an appropriate legal, regulatory and institutional environment that provides relevant rules and regulations. The government has a responsibility to provide such an environment and in doing so must address a number of important issues.

- *Quality standards and quality control.* The government can set standards and leave quality control and inspection to licensed private sector companies. The government could also provide training for buyers and farmers interested in carrying out quality control on their own.
- *Rules and regulations.* The private sector needs a transparent and effectively functioning framework (including enforcement) in order to operate using good business practices and codes of conduct. This framework must include penalties for defaulting on contracts, a private system of guarantees, or both.
- *Monitoring.* Public institutions need to be developed to monitor the functioning of the subsector without intervening in cocoa marketing.
- *Private sector professional associations.* Professional associations for cocoa producers, traders, and exporters provide self-regulatory func-

tions; among other things they protect their members against disreputable operators.

- *Licensing.* The government needs to develop a transparent licensing system for private exporters and traders to ensure that they are operating according to standards. However, licensing criteria should not impede competition.
- *Capacity building and training.* Support and training in areas such as risk management and collateralized lending strengthen institutions that support market functions. Two focal points are farmers' associations (and their management) and a market information system.

There Are Ways to Improve Trust in a Newly Liberalized System

In principle a properly functioning market drives unreliable operators out of business fairly quickly. Problems like those in Nigeria after 1986 and Cameroon after 1994 emerge in the presence of significant macroeconomic distortions (for example in the exchange rate), poor institutional arrangements (for instance when quality control procedures are corrupt), and policy failures (such as political interference in licensing). But even a well-functioning market may need some time to weed out untrustworthy agents, so that some form of licensing based on clear and transparent criteria is advisable. Reforms in Uganda require coffee exporters to have a US$25,000 line of credit before they can obtain a license. In Côte d'Ivoire private exporters must have bank guarantees and be well capitalized. In Togo a system based on bank guarantees has been set up to compensate foreign buyers when contracts are not fulfilled.

Forming trade and professional associations helps maintain standards among economic agents. Foreign buyers can also distinguish among exporters and will tend to do business with the more reputable ones. In Nigeria and Cameroon (and in Uganda's coffee subsector), the number of exporters and traders increased dramatically following market liberalization. This number has fallen as less experienced and less reputable exporters and traders have exited, but enough players remain to ensure competition.

Cocoa-producing countries can also consider establishing an organization that licenses and oversees commodity warehouses throughout the country, including in rural locations. This type of organization focuses on handling cocoa stocks according to acceptable trade standards for grading and warehousing procedures. A grading and tendering system such as the London Clearing House system (which supports the LIFFE futures market) tracks stores held for delivery and tests cocoa for quality using an appropriate methodology. Such a system allows buyers elsewhere in the world to trade in warehouse receipts at minimal risk, increases competition in trade, ensures quality, and offers producers maximum benefits.

In this system warehouses must be insured against all risks and bonded or otherwise underwritten against fraud, and an arbitration system is needed to settle disputes. The resulting organization is in effect a physical exchange that attracts buyers with its stock of available goods. Buyers can trade in a secure environment, with warehouse warrants providing a solid guarantee. Banks are able to finance trade in these warrants, and quality is assured by audits.

Some Final Thoughts

Systems that use marketing boards and stabilization funds are designed to provide a fair and stable price to farmers and to maximize government revenues from cocoa. In practice, however, these systems have proved ineffective. They have failed to provide incentives to reduce marketing costs and margins and improve marketing efficiency. Efforts to stabilize producer prices have resulted in a heavy implicit tax on farmers, as farmgate prices are only a small share of the f.o.b. export prices. Price stabilization has also proved costly for government budgets when international cocoa prices decline, as they did after 1985, and governments seek to keep producer prices unchanged (both CAISTAB in Côte d'Ivoire and the ONCPB in Cameroon have been part of such attempts).

Efforts to stabilize producer prices ignore the problems governments face in coping with fluctuating fiscal revenues. In many cases the accumulated funds have been used for purposes other than price stabilization. The activities of many parastatals tend to be discretionary and poorly monitored, leaving substantial room for mismanagement, inefficiencies, and outright corruption. The widespread lack of transparency and accountability has caused significant mismanagement of cocoa revenues. In general these systems lack the flexibility to deal effectively with changes in world commodity markets. The decline in cocoa production in both Ghana and Nigeria during the 1970s and early 1980s was largely the result of inappropriate policies in the cocoa subsector. In Côte d'Ivoire CAISTAB's withdrawal from the cocoa market in 1989 proved disastrous. In general the existence of parastatals has led to policies that have had highly adverse results for the countries themselves and for their many small cocoa farmers.

Administrative pricing systems, such as those in Cameroon and Côte d'Ivoire prior to liberalization, failed because the quantitative effects were not fully understood or measured. Parastatals often became bloated with excessive staff. And because these systems depended on strict regulation of the internal cocoa market, they created opportunities to make large profits and thus encourage rent-seeking activities.

Reforms in cocoa marketing aim to increase the efficiency of both internal and external cocoa trade. Vigorous private sector participation and competition in these activities reduce marketing costs and margins, increase the share of the f.o.b. price farmers receive, and improve transparency. The main beneficiaries of such reforms are the farmers. Increasing the farmers' share of the f.o.b. prices in Ghana and Côte d'Ivoire to the levels prevailing in countries operating with liberalized marketing systems would significantly increase rural incomes in these two countries. The impact of increased prices on rural incomes and living standards could dwarf the combined efforts of governments, external aid agencies, and banking systems to improve rural incomes and living standards.

In countries where market liberalization has already taken place, reforms have improved farmers' incomes significantly. Farmers in these countries (for example, cocoa farmers in Nigeria and arabica coffee farmers in Cameroon) have strongly rejected any suggestion that government-controlled marketing systems be re-established. An efficient and competitive agricultural sector based on private sector participation is an important contribution to economic growth and diversification, as the experiences of many Latin American and Asian economies show.

Annex 2.1
Togo: Liberalizing the Coffee and Cocoa Subsectors[23]

Togo's 1996 reforms were key components of the country's economic recovery and adjustment operation. The reforms entailed the liberalization of coffee and cocoa prices, primary marketing, and exporting—all of which had previously been regulated by the marketing board. The goal was to improve producer incentives and income and develop private participation in marketing and export activities while maintaining the country's reputation as a reliable supplier of quality products in international markets.

The Impact of Liberalization

The reforms had a strong positive impact on exports and on producers' incomes and incentives.

Coffee and cocoa exports reached a record high in 1997 that was more than double the 1996 level. Some of this increase came from cross-border trade, which grew because Togolese traders were able to offer very favorable prices. Cocoa and coffee producers were the big winners from liberalization. The producer's share of the f.o.b. price soared, climbing from below 60 percent to an average of 76 percent for coffee and 80 percent for cocoa for the 1996–97 crop season. Producers have intensified their crop maintenance efforts and expanded their cocoa and coffee plantations. Living conditions have also improved: farmers are renovating their houses and acquiring consumer goods such as radios, bicycles, motorcycles, and sometimes larger vehicles. At the same time access to health services has become easier.

A partnership has developed among the government, the private sector, and producers as a result of liberalization. Potential private exporters were identified early on and invited to participate in the design phase of the reforms. All the key aspects of the reforms were discussed with representatives of various constituencies (the private sector, the banking community, and the administration) in a roundtable format. The results of the discussions were formalized into legal texts that became the regulatory framework for the activity. These texts covered the criteria and administrative requirements for marketing and exporting, including bank guarantees, quality control, and information dissemination.

This participatory process was rapidly institutionalized. A Coordination Committee made up of representatives of the private sector, producer cooperatives, and the government was established to oversee the reform process.

The committee has a legal base, is financed by export proceeds, and is accountable to its constituencies. It monitors developments in the cocoa subsector and operates as a forum to discuss and make decisions on a wide variety of issues. These issues include maintaining competition, determining the responsibilities of the marketing board, stimulating investment in coffee and cocoa plantations, and dealing with the moral hazard associated with crop financing (for large exporters).

Lessons Learned

Togo's liberalization experience offers three lessons. First, including the private sector in the design stage of the reform process facilitates a dialogue with the government and diffuses the tension created by the prospect of radical change. Experts' proposals no longer look arbitrary or dogmatic when they have the support of key economic operators. The experts then become the facilitators in the design process, as they did with Togo's quality control system. The government's quality control team wanted to keep the six controls that were already in place. The private sector wanted to reduce them to two: one check of all bags at the warehouse in Lomé, and one check of a small sample of bags at the port. Ultimately the public and private sectors were able to agree on the experts' proposal: there would be two compulsory checks (at the warehouse and at the port) and one optional check that would become operational at the buyer's request. The government-run quality control service now trains small buyers and producers' cooperatives so they can perform an initial quality control check before transporting commodities to Lomé.

Second, bringing all the actors together around a table (large private firms, small firms, individuals interested in setting up a business, commercial banks, and the administration) allows them all to see clearly each other's sometimes conflicting interests. This approach introduces transparency to the decisionmaking process, promotes consensus, and results in a reform package that from the outset benefits from a broad base of support. A good example is the level of the bank guarantee exporters must have; these guarantees ensure foreign buyers that they will be compensated if contracts are not complete. At stake is the country's reputation as a reliable supplier in international markets. In Togo the large firms favored a complex guarantee system, which the small firms felt would constitute a barrier to entry to the business. The simpler system agreed on—a bank guarantee amounting to the equivalent of 20 percent of the value of each order—is a trade-off. It balances the two important objectives: maintaining the country's reputation and developing the private sector.

Third, information on market conditions is key to fair competition. A system of information on international prices coupled with a reference producer price allows producers to take full advantage of the competitive environment by choosing among buyers and thus increasing the producer share of the f.o.b. price substantially.

Box 2.1: Ghana's Participatory Approach to Designing Market Reforms

Ulrich Hess

(Credit Review and Porfolio Division, the International Finance Corporation)

When Ghana opted to initiate reforms, broad consultations with all stakeholders in the cocoa subsector and a thorough investigation of all the issues facilitated a consensus. In September 1998 the Ministry of Finance set up a task force representing all stakeholders, including farmers, researchers, extension agents, parliamentarians, ministry officials, licensed buyers, haulers, bankers, and processors. The task force members were divided into working groups to analyze issues and recommend reforms in four areas:

- Production, research, and extension;
- Marketing (internal and external), processing, and quality control;
- Infrastructure and finance; and
- Taxation and pricing policy.

The working groups were free to address any issue, aided by specialists (primarily from Ghana), who prepared working papers that formed the basis for the groups' deliberations. The specialists synthesized and updated existing materials and made them available to everybody in the groups.

Prominent stakeholders chaired the groups. A Ministry of Finance official chaired the Marketing Group, for example, and a private licensed cocoa buyer chaired the Taxation and Pricing Policy group. Working groups formulated their recommendations based on the specialists' working papers, and a task force workshop discussed these recommendations in November 1998. Over 70 people participated in the workshop, which was chaired by the Deputy Minister of Finance. On the basis of the workshop discussions a report was written and submitted to a national workshop that include representatives from various ministries and the Parliament, the national and international private sector, and donors such as the World Bank. The Minister of Finance chaired the national workshop, which took place in January 1999. The task force discussed and refined the report, compressing it into a shorter cabinet memo that Ghana's cabinet approved in April 1999. Subsequently the Minister of Finance announced the reforms at a press conference. This participatory process created a better understanding of what was needed and fostered cohesion in the cocoa subsector. Working together and rethinking the future of the subsector forged a spirit of participation and ownership of the marketing reforms.

Notes

1. Forward sales are advantageous for the seller in an environment of declining prices, but when prices are rising, the forward premium may not be sufficient to cover the carrying costs and beat the higher price in the spot market on the delivery date.

2. In real terms world cocoa prices have experienced a secular and pronounced downward trend for the past 45 years (see figure 2.2).

3. Another reason for the low prices was the dramatic and sudden decline in demand in Eastern Europe and the former Soviet Union following the political and economic changes in these countries.

4. The ICCO Daily Price is an average of the first three positions on the terminal markets of New York and London.

5. While stabilization funds are to be used to stabilize prices, resources from these funds often leak to the general government budget.

6. The price premium for good fermented cocoa was eliminated in 1989–90, and in 1989 the quality grading function was transferred to the Ministry of Agriculture, which never undertook this task because of funding shortfalls.

7. Compensation from the stabilization fund was paid based on export contracts and not deliveries (shipments), allowing exporters to choose which export contracts to submit for reimbursement.

8. The reputation of Cameroon's cocoa has suffered for a number of reasons. It is generally prepared poorly (it is often improperly fermented) and may contain a high percentage of damaged beans. It may also be moldy and be substandard in flavor. As a result buyers cannot rely on good-quality cocoa from shipment to shipment.

9. CAISTAB was created in 1962 when the stabilization funds for coffee and cocoa (established in 1955) were merged.

10. Sales under the PVAM system were often quite irregular, however.

11. The expected prices for the remaining 30–40 percent (the crop not sold forward) were based on assessments by CAISTAB and futures prices during the period of calculations.

12. The reforms were supported by a Structural Adjustment Credit from the World Bank.

13. The development of the auction system was supported by a World Bank Agricultural Structural Adjustment Credit.

14. This explanation is also consistent with the experience of other countries. Brazil, for example, had a similar experience when it instituted an auction system to allocate export rights (Bohman and Jarvis 1996).

15. In some years COCOBOD has paid bonuses to producers on top of the announced producer prices.

16. Since 1990, plantation, processing plants, and input marketing have not featured as COCOBOD's cost or as expenditure funded from cocoa revenues.

17. About 20 percent of the cocoa produced is processed locally. Local processors receive discounts ranging from 11 to 20 percent of the price of the beans they process.

18. For 1995–1996 cocoa farmers received an estimated 87.3 percent of the f.o.b. price.

19. Forward sales in coffee, which in almost all coffee-producing countries is handled solely by the private sector (marketing and exports), are also relatively low and cover no more than four to five months ahead.

20. Seasonal volatility is not significantly different for other agricultural commodities that do not have public forward markets (coffee, cotton, and maize, for example).

21. This result is based on the Newberry and Stiglitz (1981) analysis and is consistent with the result obtained by Hazell (1994) for the Costa Rican coffee farmers.

22. Deaton (1992) questions the effectiveness of commodity price stabilization for cocoa, coffee, copper, and cotton in the context of African countries.

23. Togo: coffee and cocoa liberalization (World Bank 1998).

References

Akiyama, T. 1988. "Cocoa and Coffee Pricing Policies in Côte d'Ivoire." Policy, Research, and External Affairs Working Papers Series 64. Washington, D.C.: World Bank.

Bateman, M. J., A. Meeraus, D. M. Newbery, W. A. Okyere, and G. T. O'Mara. 1990. "Ghana's Cocoa Pricing Policy." Policy, Research and External Affairs Working Paper 490. Washington, D.C.: World Bank.

Bates, R. H. 1981. *Markets and States in Tropical Africa: The Political Basis of Agricultural Policies.* Berkley: University of California Press.

Bohman, M., and L. Jarvis. 1996. "The Rise and Decline of Rent-Seeking Activity in the Brazilian Coffee Sector: Lessons from a Study of the Imposition and Removal of International Coffee Agreement Export Quotas." Working Paper, Economics Department, University of British Columbia, Vancouver.

Benjamin, D., and A. Deaton. 1993. "Household Welfare and the Pricing of Cocoa and Coffee in Côte d'Ivoire."*World Bank Economic Review* 3(7): 293318.

Deaton, A. S. 1992. *Commodity Prices, Stabilization, and Growth in Africa.* Discussion Paper 166, Center for International Studies, Woodrow Wilson School, Princeton University.

Duncan, Alex, and Stephen Jones. 1993. "Agricultural Marketing and Pricing Reform: A Review of Experience." *World Development* 21(9): 1495–1514.

Gilbert, Christopher L. 1997. *Cocoa Market Liberalization: Its Effects on Quality, Futures Trading, and Prices.* London: The Cocoa Association of London.

Hanak-Freud, E., and C. Freud. 1996. *Devaluation and Liberalization as Tools for Enhancing Competitiveness? Some Insights from the Recent West African Experience in Cocoa Marketing.* Documents de Travail en Economie des Filières 29. Montpellier, France: Centre de Coopération Internationale en Recherche Agronomique pour le Développement.

Hazell, Peter. 1994. *Potential Benefits to Farmers of Using Futures Markets for Managing Coffee Price Risks in Costa Rica*. Washington, D.C.: International Food Policy Research Institute.

Marchat, J. M. 1994. "Information incomplète et barrières à l'entrée lors de la réforme de la collecte des cultures de rent de Côte d'Ivoire." Centre d'Études et de Recherches de Droit International, Universite d'Auvergne, Clermont-Ferrand, France.

Marquet, Yannick. 1997. *Programme de Ventes Anticipées à la Moyenne et Optimisation des Recettes d'Exportation: Le Cas du Cacao en Côte d'Ivoire, 1978–96*. Brussels: APROMA (Association de Produits à Marché). Draft.

McIntire, J., and P. Varangis. 1999. "Reforming Cocoa Marketing and Pricing in Côte d'Ivoire." Policy Research Working Paper Number 2081. Washington, D.C.: World Bank.

Newbery, D. M. G., and J. Stiglitz. 1981. *The Theory of Commodity Price Stabilization*. Oxford, UK: Oxford University Press.

Ruf, François. 1996. *Booms et Crises du Cacao: Les Vertiges de l'Or Brun*. Paris: Karthala.

Ruf, François, and Hubert de Milly. 1990. *Comparison of Cocoa Production Costs in Seven Producing Countries*. Paper presented at the ICCO's Advisory Group on the World Economy, Seventh Meeting, Accra, Ghana, June 18–22.

Schreiber, Gotz, and Panos Varangis. 1995. *Cocoa Marketing and Pricing Systems in West Africa*. World Bank. Draft.

Singh, I., L. Squire, and J. Kirchner. 1985. "Agricultural Pricing and Marketing Policies in an African Context: A Framework for Analysis." Staff Working Paper Series 743. Washington, D.C.: World Bank.

Trivedi, P. K., and T. Akiyama. 1992. "A Framework for Evaluating the Impact of Pricing Policies for Cocoa and Coffee in Côte d'Ivoire." *World Bank Economic Review* 6(2): 307–30.

Varangis, P., T. Akiyama, and E. Thigpen. 1990. "Recent Developments in Marketing and Pricing Systems for Agricultural Export Commodities in Sub-Saharan Africa." Working Paper Series 431. Washington, D.C.: World Bank.

World Bank. 1998. "Togo: Coffee and Cocoa LIberalization." Findings: Best Practice, Infobrief, Africa Region, Number 29, June.

3

Coffee Market Liberalization since 1990

Takamasa Akiyama

COFFEE-PRODUCING COUNTRIES BEGAN REFORMING their coffee subsectors in the early 1990s. In 1985 only 15 of the world's 51 major coffee-producing countries had private marketing systems.[1] Twenty-five countries sold coffee through state-controlled monopolies, including marketing boards (India and Uganda), stabilization funds (*Caisses de Stabilisation*)[2] (Cameroon, Côte d'Ivoire, Madagascar, and Togo), and *institutos* (Brazil and Mexico). Another 11 countries had mixed state and private sector marketing bodies.

The governments of coffee-producing countries in Sub-Saharan Africa long considered state control of marketing and pricing systems necessary because of coffee's importance as a source of foreign exchange and government revenue. Latin American coffee producers such as Brazil and Colombia controlled prices and exports even before World War II in order to raise world coffee prices. In 1962 the International Coffee Organization (ICO) was created to establish and monitor an international export quota system (see annex 3.1 for details). As we saw in chapter 1, the prevailing development theories of the 1950s and 1960s supported the continuation of these systems, as did the monitoring requirements for export quotas under the ICO. Financial problems in coffee-exporting countries—the result of the sharp decline in coffee prices that followed the collapse of the ICO quota system in 1989—and prodding by international financial institutions were the primary causes of coffee market reform.

In most countries liberalization of the coffee subsector was part of broader macroeconomic reforms. In addition to ending direct government involvement in marketing, these reforms devalued exchange rates and substantially reduced government intervention in the marketing and pricing of traded products. They also introduced commercial principles into public enterprises, many of which have been privatized.

This chapter analyzes the factors that prompted coffee market liberalization and examines the ramifications of liberalization. The analysis seeks to identify the process and institutional arrangements that facilitated successful liberalization and the lessons learned from the reform experiences. Three countries—India, Togo, and Uganda—were chosen for detailed analysis because liberalization has had a significant impact not only on the marketing systems but also on the political institutions of these countries. In all three countries liberalization succeeded in introducing private sector dynamics into the state marketing system, generating important lessons for countries where liberalization has been less successful or further market reforms are needed.

Recent Developments in the World Coffee Market

Coffee is a major export commodity in many developing countries, although its importance has been declining in recent years.[3] In 1998 it was the second most important commodity after petroleum for developing countries in terms of export earnings. Many countries, especially those in Sub-Saharan Africa and Central America, depend heavily on coffee as a source not only of foreign exchange but also of employment in rural areas. Before liberalization heavy taxation also made coffee an important source of government revenue.[4]

The two most important types of traded coffee are arabica and robusta. Arabica, which is grown primarily at high altitudes in Latin America and northeastern Africa, has more aroma, less caffeine, and a less bitter taste than robusta. It is used mainly as roasted coffee, and certain kinds—Jamaican Blue Mountain, Indonesian Toraja, and Kenya AAA—fetch much higher prices than the standard arabicas produced in Latin American countries. Robusta is usually grown in humid areas at low altitudes in Asia and western and southern Sub-Saharan Africa. It is used as filler in roasted blends and instant coffee. Robustas generally sell for less than arabicas; since 1970 prices for robustas have averaged 15 percent less than prices for arabicas.

For years many developing country governments felt compelled to regulate coffee marketing and pricing, not only because coffee was so important as a source of export earnings and foreign exchange but also for institutional and political reasons. For major coffee producers in Latin American (such as Brazil and Colombia), the main objective was to raise world prices (see annex 3.1).[5] In India coffee producers themselves asked the government to take over marketing because of the difficulties Indian marketers encountered during World War II. Controlling foreign exchange was a particularly important factor in countries with overvalued currencies, where there was a high risk of foreign exchange revenues leaking to the black market. Governments also used controls to prevent coffee growers from being cheated by middlemen and to maintain fixed producer prices that shielded farmers from price fluctuations or assured them a minimum price.[6] In Sub-Saharan Africa these policies almost invariably resulted in high taxes and inefficient marketing systems. In most producing countries they generated large stocks of coffee and fiscal deficits that made production and exports less competitive.

In Sub-Saharan Africa political and institutional factors were often paramount. A government-controlled marketing system usually involved a government agency that managed a large amount of money. As Bates (1981) notes, such a system provides politicians with discretionary funds to implement policies and projects that create a political following. Referring to bureaucrats Bates (1990, p. 157) points out that "agencies in charge of markets accumulate political power, and their vested interests in the government's agricultural programs help to perpetuate these policy commitments even in the face of clear evidence that the policies have failed." Under these government-controlled systems taxes were usually heavy, for several reasons. First, price elasticity of supply tended to be low, so the impact of heavy taxation in the short run was not notably adverse.[7] Second, coffee is not a food crop, so the social and political resistance to taxation was usually smaller. Third, as most coffee was exported, collecting taxes was easier than it is with subsistence crops. Finally when the ICO export quota system was in effect, effective heavy taxation was necessary to reduce production and finance government-held stocks.

The International Coffee Organization

The ICO had had a profound impact on the world coffee market until its collapse in 1989. Most coffee-producing countries (accounting for about 90 percent of world production) and most coffee-importing members of the Organisation for Economic Co-operation and Development (OECD) were members. Most developing and Eastern European countries that imported coffee were not. The agreement's main objective was to raise and stabilize world coffee prices through export quotas. The quota system worked relatively well until 1989, keeping world coffee prices within the price range agreed to by members, in part because members policed coffee imports.

The agreement went through several revisions, with the final version lasting from September 1980 until July 1989. The quotas were lifted between February 1986 and September 1987, as world coffee prices were already high owing to a severe drought that curtailed Brazil's coffee production significantly. The agreement collapsed in July 1989 mainly because members could not agree on a way to control exports to nonmembers and to distribute quotas for arabica and robusta.[8] The collapse of the export quota system prompted many coffee-producing countries to export large quantities of coffee from their accumulated stocks. These countries wanted to have large exports on record in case a new agreement was negotiated, since a history of significant exports would make obtaining large export quotas easier. The result of this dumping of coffee on the world market was a sharp decline in world coffee prices that affected the revenue of all coffee-producing countries. By the early 1990s these countries were earning (in real terms) around half the export revenues they had been earning in the early 1980s. The very low world prices, which persisted until early 1994, adversely affected world supply. Prices started to increase in the first half of 1994 as the world supply of coffee fell. Two frosts that hit Brazil in late June and early July of 1994 raised coffee prices throughout the mid-1990s, but by the late 1990s Brazilian production had recovered, once again putting downward pressure on prices.

After the breakup of the agreement, some coffee-producing countries formed the Alliance of Coffee-Producing Countries (ACPC) to regulate coffee exports and raise world coffee prices. The ACPC has had a limited impact on the market, for two reasons. First, the agreement did not have proper policing and punitive clauses. Second, several important exporting countries (Guatemala, Indonesia, Mexico, and Vietnam) did not join. As a result of this competition from nonmembers and lack of punitive clauses, most coffee-producing countries did not withhold exports to raise world prices. Even if the governments of all the major coffee-producing countries had wanted to take some joint market-controlling measures, doing so would have been difficult and costly, given that many had begun liberalizing their coffee subsectors.

The Causes of Liberalization

As we saw in chapter 1, governments had a number of reasons for reforming their commodity markets. Some common influences were changes in the views of development economists, world events since the 1960s, and prodding for market reforms from the World Bank and the International Monetary Fund (IMF). These changes in the political and ideological environment were a factor in the emergence of new political regimes with market-based approaches, such as those in India and Uganda. Overall they made implementing market-oriented policies easier.

The single most important factor behind the liberalization of the coffee subsector was the collapse in July 1989 of the ICO export quota system. The most important factor behind the ICO's demise was undoubtedly Brazil's lack of interest in preserving the ICO—the result of domestic pressure and a more market-oriented economic policy stance (see annex 3.1 for a detailed discussion of Brazil and the ICO).

The collapse of the ICO had a significant impact on marketing and pricing systems in many coffee-producing countries. The elimination of ICO export quotas undermined much of the justification for government marketing agencies. Although most of these agencies had existed before the ICO, the ICO had provided them with a reason to exist—to ensure that exports to member countries did not exceed the quota. Government marketing agencies also facilitated cross-subsidizing (between coffee exports to members and those to nonmembers) and negotiations concerning quotas and other clauses in the ICO agreement. The main reason for the abolition of coffee parastatals in Brazil, El Salvador, and Mexico was the governments' recognition that the suspension of international quotas effectively ended the need to control the coffee market.

In addition the collapse of the quota system resulted in a sharp decline in world coffee prices (figure 3.1.). Once the quotas were lifted, coffee-producing countries exported large portions of their accumulated stocks, bringing prices down. Fixed-price policies are sustainable when world prices are stable (as they were in the 1960s) or in the presence of a stabilizing system such as ICO export quotas. But such policies are difficult if not impossible to maintain when world prices are fluctuating (Deaton 1992). The decline in world coffee prices between 1989 and 1993 caused enormous financial difficulties for the government agencies in charge of marketing coffee in countries with fixed-price policies. Many of these agencies, like those in Cameroon and Uganda, were soon unable to maintain fixed prices. Even in countries such as India that employed average pricing policies, producers became skeptical of the controlled pricing system as prices fell. In addition, as Bohman, Jarvis, and Barichello (1996) argue, the quota system facilitated rent-seeking in some countries, and the government-controlled marketing system simply made these activities easier. The termination of the quota system undoubtedly reduced potential rent in many countries significantly and may even have eliminated it in some, helping to minimize resistance to liberalization.

The Beginnings of Liberalization

Many coffee-producing countries had little choice but to undertake liberalization. In Sub-Saharan Africa the serious fiscal problems resulting from the sharp decline in commodity prices forced many governments to look to international organizations and donor countries for financial assistance. This assistance came with strings attached, in the form of conditionalities requiring market reforms. In some countries (India and Togo, for example)

Figure 3.1 World Coffee Prices

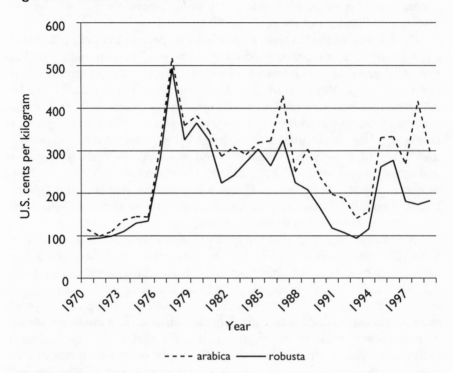

Source: World Bank.

economic shocks gave governments the impetus needed to start the liberalization process (Binswanger and Deininger 1997).

As the liberalization process got under way in some countries, a number of "contagion effects" developed. One such effect was smuggling. When a country liberalizes its coffee subsector, producer prices generally rise, prompting coffee smuggling from neighboring countries. Neighboring countries that have not introduced reforms then suffer declines in export and government revenues. For instance when producer prices in Uganda fell as a result of strict government price controls, large quantities of coffee were smuggled from Uganda to Kenya, which had a liberalized market. Since undertaking liberalization in its own markets, however, Uganda has been the beneficiary of smuggling from neighboring Burundi, Congo, Rwanda, and Tanzania. A second and far more promising contagion effect involved the performance of the subsector. Rwandan policymakers became keenly aware of the sound performance of Uganda's subsector following liberalization and were eager to apply similar policies in their own country.

Initiative by the Producers: India

The gradual liberalization of India's coffee subsector that began in 1992 was prompted by the sharp decline in producer prices following the collapse of the ICO export quota system. India's experience is unusual in that it was initiated by coffee producers who hoped that liberalization would increase producer prices. The timing of liberalization was fortuitous, coinciding with a sharp increase in world coffee prices and the depreciation of the Indian currency. Producer prices rose sharply soon after the liberalization process started, and a flurry of private sector marketing activity followed: an auction system, a futures exchange, and various marketing firms and institutions. India's experience illustrates how market liberalization can induce the private sector to transform a static industry into a dynamic one.

The Marketing and Pricing System before Liberalization

Prior to liberalization, the parastatal Coffee Board controlled the entire marketing chain, from grower to exporter (figure 3.2). This system was created by the Coffee Act of 1942, which established the board under the Ministry of Commerce. The act also mandated the pooling of all coffee for the board to sell at auction. This system was intended to boost the very low prices producers received when they sold coffee soon after the harvest—a situation exacerbated by low demand during World War II (including blockades of some ports). Producers believed the new system would bring order to the market.

Under the pooling system the grower brought harvested and dried coffee (or, in the case of washed coffee, pulped) to a regulated processing factory (known locally as a curing factory) and received an advance on full payment. For a fee registered private operators hulled, cleaned, sorted, and graded the coffee. The Coffee Board set and paid the fee and later deducted the costs from its payments to the grower. The coffee was graded according to a point system that took into account factors such as moisture content and any defects that remained after processing. The board then marketed all coffee for export (70 percent of the total) and domestic consumption (30 percent) through separate auctions. Eastern Europe and Russia received a proportion of exports under a barter agreement. The price of domestic coffee was kept artificially low (15 to 20 percent less than the world price), ostensibly to increase domestic consumption. But the real reason for both this policy and for the significant exports to Russia—which did not belong to the ICO—was India's low export quota under the ICO. India was allowed to export only around 50 percent of its exportable production, making shipments to nonmember countries (such as Russia) and increased domestic consumption important to reducing stocks.

Figure 3.2 India's Preliberalization Marketing Chain

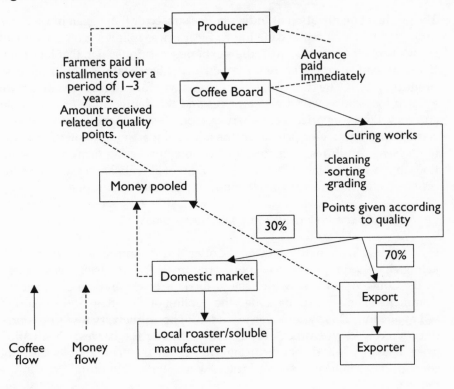

Source: LMC International.

After the auctions the money was pooled. The board paid growers in installments throughout the year according to the number of points awarded at the curing factory. (Similar two-tier payment systems are also employed for tea in several African countries, including Kenya and Uganda.) Growers with the same number of points received the same amount of money. Premiums for high-quality coffee were small, and there were often long delays (up to three years) before growers received their final payment.

The Market Liberalization Process

Producers were generally satisfied with the pooling system as long as they received high prices, and during the 1970s and most of the 1980s the system appeared to be working well for this group. World coffee prices were high in the second half of 1970s because of the heavy frost in Brazil in 1975 and remained high during most of the 1980s because of the ICO quota system. But large producers began pressing for market liberalization because they wanted to export directly to their customers. By exporting directly they could avoid paying the implicit sales tax. (Despite the fact that all exported commodities were exempt from taxation, the board had effectively been paying a sales tax.)

At the same time the decline in world coffee prices that followed the collapse of both the ICO system and the Soviet Union (which had been a major importer of Indian coffee) began adversely affecting producer prices in India. Producers questioned the efficiency of the Coffee Board and the marketing system. To add to their dissatisfaction, the press made public several incidents of corruption by board staff.

These events prompted small and medium-sized producers to join forces with the United Planters' Association of South India, an association of large producers and plantation firms, which the smaller producers rightly believed had more political influence.[9] Together these producers' associations demanded that the market be liberalized. Because they had relatively well-organized associations, Indian producers were able to obtain the information they needed to pursue liberalization and to exert pressure on the government—a sign of their growing political power.

Given the central government's changed policy stance (which occurred when the new regime came to power in the early 1990s), the government was willing to liberalize the coffee market but wanted to proceed cautiously.[10] The board and private sector stakeholders, especially producers' organizations, held a series of consultations to decide on the course liberalization would take.

In 1992 India took the first step toward liberalizing its coffee market by introducing a 30 percent domestic sales quota. The Coffee Board pooled the remaining 70 percent for auction. Initially many growers, both small and large, were hesitant about the plan and did not immediately take advantage of it. Over time, however, most growers and buyers adjusted to the new marketing conditions. In 1994 a 50 percent free sales quota was introduced that allowed producers to market up to 50 percent of their crop themselves on either the internal or external market. With this second step in the liberalization process, the Coffee Board also abolished the auction for domestic sales, eliminating price subsidies for coffee marketed domestically. The system of selling a specified portion of production to the board was difficult to monitor and ultimately proved untenable. After 1994 producers began selling less and less coffee to the Coffee Board, and complete liberalization was put into force in September 1996.

The Effects of Liberalization

Liberalization had a significant impact on the Indian coffee subsector. In addition to changing the marketing and pricing systems, it spurred the

development of a remarkable number of new private sector organizations
and institutions. Immediately following the liberalization of domestic markets, the number of active exporting companies increased from fewer than
10 to as many as 25 before leveling off at around 15.

THE MARKETING SYSTEM. Under the liberalized system, producers have three
ways to market their coffee: they can sell directly to exporters, hold it at a
curing factory before selling it, or sell it at voluntary auction. Currently most
producers market their coffee directly to exporters. The exporters commission agents to buy from the growers, who are paid much more promptly
than they were under the old system. Exporters provide the agents with a
range of acceptable daily prices. Smallholders who market this way prepare
the parchment coffee (or dry cherry) and sell it to the agent. The agent
arranges transportation to take the newly purchased coffee to the curing factory (figure 3.3). The factory checks the quality of the coffee, which must

Figure 3.3 India's Marketing System after Liberalization

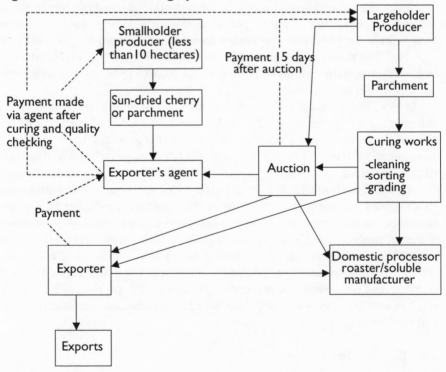

Source: LMC International.

meet the exporters' standards. If it does a banker's draft in the name of the grower is sent from the curing factory to the agent, who then delivers a check to the grower. Under this system the grower receives payment two to three days after the coffee is collected.

A second method allows the grower to store coffee before selling it in order to speculate on price movements. The grower takes the coffee to the curing factory and receives 40–50 percent of the market value as an advance payment. Under the third method the grower sells the coffee at a voluntary auction. Private auctioneers have taken over these auctions, which are organized by the Indian Coffee Traders' Association. Growers using this option tend to be relatively large producers (15 acres and above). They take the coffee to the curing factory and store the green beans in the auction warehouses, sending a sample for auction. The auction is held once a week, and the growers receive payment 15 days after the auction.

PRODUCER PRICES. Liberalization has meant that coffee sold at auction or procured at the farm gate can be resold on both the domestic and export markets, leading to an increase in grower prices, although this is not clear from official statistics (figure 3.4). The declining share of producer prices in export unit values in the period 1993 to 1995 was the result of falling world prices. Most marketing costs remained stable, so the drop in world prices affected only producer prices. The end of subsidized sales to Eastern Europe and the 1993 abolition of the export tax also boosted grower prices. The proportion of the export value growers receive is estimated to have increased from around 65 percent prior to liberalization to over 80 percent afterward. Growers gained another important benefit from liberalization: they are paid for their coffee much more promptly than in the past.

PRODUCTION AND EXPORTS. India's coffee production and exports increased significantly during the 1990s (figure 3.5). Production increased by 40 percent, rising from around 2.5 million bags in the late 1980s to around 3.5 million bags in the late 1990s. This increase is attributable mainly to the maturing of high-yielding, disease-resistant varieties planted in the 1980s and thus is not necessarily the result of liberalization. Some analysts, such as Narayan (1997), are skeptical of claims about the favorable effects of liberalization on production.[11] But to the extent that liberalization caused an increase in producer prices, its affect on production was beneficial. And without the constraints of the international quota system, exports increased along with production.

New Players in the Coffee Market

Possibly the most important impact of market liberalization on the coffee marketing chain in India was the withdrawal of the Coffee Board from cof-

Figure 3.4 Grower Price in India as a Percentage of Export Unit Value

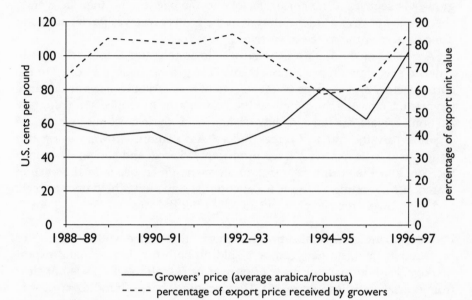

Growers' price (average arabica/robusta)
- - - - percentage of export price received by growers

Source: LMC International.

Figure 3.5 India's Production and Exports

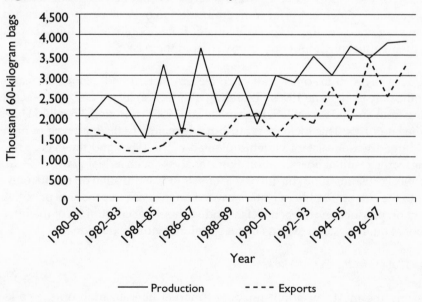

Production   - - - - Exports

Source: ICO.

fee marketing and the emergence of new private sector organizations and institutions. These include not only the numerous traders and middlemen who buy coffee from the producers, but also the privately run auctions, the futures exchange, the private grading firm, and a number of marketing firms. These new players have helped create a more vigorous and dynamic industry.

THE COFFEE BOARD. The board is still the main governmental organization overseeing the industry, but since liberalization its main function has shifted from marketing to research, extension, and promotion. The board represents the Indian coffee industry in the international arena and advises the government on relevant issues. Recognizing the importance of information in a liberalized market, the board is also active in disseminating market information to the industry.

AUCTIONS. The Karnataka Brokers' Association, founded during the initial stages of liberalization, has taken over the Coffee Board's responsibility for the weekly auctions that offer coffee for both export and domestic consumption. The auctions are self-regulated by the Indian Coffee Traders' Association and conducted by tea-brokering companies that hold similar auctions for tea.

FUTURES EXCHANGE. The Coffee Futures Exchange of India established a coffee futures exchange in Bangalore in June 1998. The volume of trading is still low, and it is too early to know if the exchange will be viable. If it is successful, however, it will help reduce the impact of price volatility on Indian coffee producers and traders.

WAREHOUSE-BASED FINANCING. Several different types of warehouse-based financing are emerging. The newly developed futures market, the Coffee Futures Exchange, has designated a number of warehouses, and some banks are designing products for financing. These systems will benefit the entire industry and other commodity subsectors.

Evaluating Liberalization

India's relatively smooth liberalization process was largely the result of careful planning, a gradual approach to reforms, and frequent consultations between the Coffee Board and private stakeholders. Two characteristics of the process in particular stand out. First, the producers themselves initiated it. Second, the private sector was able to take advantage of the business opportunities liberalization offered, resulting in a subsector that is significantly more dynamic than it had been. The private sector response to the reforms was possible only because the sector was already very active and developed in the export business before liberalization. Government regulations and restriction would have made it difficult for the public sector to initiate new marketing institutions.

The Importance of Follow-up Measures: Uganda

Uganda's coffee market reforms, unlike those in India, were initiated by the government, in part because they were a condition of the World Bank Structural Adjustment Program begun in the late 1980s. Until 1991 the parastatal Coffee Marketing Board (CMB) controlled marketing. The board's dominance began to diminish in 1991, when the CMB was turned into a limited liability company and four cooperative unions were allowed to export coffee. Gradually private exporting firms, including the cooperative export unions, were included among those allowed to export and soon began to handle almost all coffee exports. But producer prices have undergone the most significant change since liberalization. They are now linked to world prices and have risen significantly as a share of the border price. Liberalization has also substantially increased the private sector's influence in formulating coffee policies.

Marketing and Pricing before Liberalization

After independence the CMB handled and controlled all Ugandan coffee. The Coffee Act of 1962 gave the board access to all dry-processed robusta coffee for export (around 85 percent of production). Some private exporters operated coffee pulperies, processing and exporting pulped and washed robustas, while the Bugisu Cooperative Union exported wet-processed arabicas. In 1969, under the government of Milton Obote, a new Coffee Act was passed giving the CMB a total monopoly in the coffee export market. In addition to marketing the CMB was responsible for promotion, quality control, and export processing. Apart from some hulling and internal trading, the private sector's activities were extremely limited.

The preliberalization system, with its fixed producer prices and fixed margins for processing, was basically the same as the *caisse* system employed in francophone African countries. Under this system smallholders delivered coffee to cooperatives or private domestic traders. The cooperatives passed the coffee on to cooperative unions for hulling, and private traders hulled and sold the coffee to the CMB (figure 3.6). Payments to cooperatives were often delayed for long periods of time. During the late 1980s and early 1990s, only limited liberalization of the hulling industry took place, and private hulleries competed with the cooperatives. The government administered producer prices with little consideration for world prices. The difference between the producer price and the border price was an important source of revenue for the government—and a heavy tax on coffee producers. One of the major problems with this system (along with the high implicit tax rate) was that it did not reward growers according to the quality of the coffee they produced.

The Beginnings of Liberalization

During the years preceding liberalization, coffee provided over 90 percent of foreign exchange and between 25 and 50 percent of government revenue. The government of Uganda kept producer prices low in order to reduce crop financing requirements (the funds required to pay farmers for coffee),

Figure 3.6 Uganda's Marketing System before Liberalization

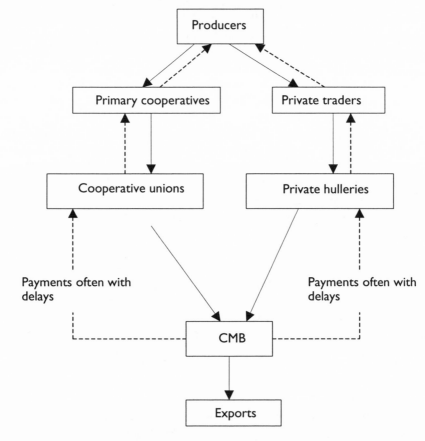

Source: author.

the budget deficit, and inflation. Between 1986 and 1989 the government-controlled producer price fell by more than 50 percent in real terms, dramatically reducing incentives to produce coffee. The sharp price decline in world market prices after 1989 could have reduced real producer prices even further, but at this point Uganda's monopoly marketing system became untenable. The liberalization process started the following year with the support of both the World Bank and Ugandan President Yoweri Musevini.

Cooperative unions emerged as coffee exporters soon after liberalization. They created a joint marketing office, Union Export Services, to function as their agent. In the beginning the unions faced significant obstacles, including the fixed-price margin, the tax system, and the special exchange rate for coffee exports. Meanwhile international prices were falling. Despite this decline the coffee revenue exchange rate was much more unfavorable to exporters than the free market rate (by about 7 to 12 percent).

In January 1991 the CMB was essentially divided in two. A publicly owned corporation, the Coffee Marketing Board, Ltd. (CMBL), was incorporated to assume the trading and processing functions of the CMB. (The government has been trying to divest itself of many of the CMBL's assets, including a very large export processing plant.) The functions of monitoring and regulating the coffee industry and advising the government on policy issues were passed on to the Uganda Coffee Development Authority (UCDA), which was created in July 1991. In November 1991 the Bank of Uganda was relieved of its responsibility for crop financing, and commercial banks began providing financing. In July 1991 the fixed margins that had plagued the exporting unions were dropped, although exports were still prohibited below a floor price calculated by the UCDA (this price, which announced daily, was the lowest at which exporters could sell).

The government took still more actions in 1992, dropping the dual exchange rate system, lifting the export tax, and permitting prefinancing arrangements and the formation of joint ventures. International coffee trading firms considered prefinanced Ugandan coffee a good risk, adding a new dimension to the coffee industry in Uganda by increasing liquidity in the coffee export business and greatly reducing the problems of crop financing. The government also lifted the requirement that all coffee be transported by train (a restriction that had been imposed to prevent smuggling and theft and to save foreign exchange), allowing traders to move coffee by truck.

Other important events occurred after 1992, including amendments to the UCDA statutes (1994) and the abolition of the mandatory floor export price (1995).[12] The new amendments gave the private sector additional freedoms as well as a greater voice in the UCDA's decisionmaking process. The government's powers were reduced and the structure of the UCDA's board was modified to include more private sector representatives.

In 1995 the World Bank recommended removing the mandatory floor export price, which had been intended to keep traders from exporting coffee at prices significantly below world levels. But it presented a major difficulty for exporters, as the floor price often did not reflect market conditions, especially during periods of widely fluctuating world prices. The government resisted dismantling this system, which was an important instrument in monitoring and controlling the coffee market (the government could accept or reject private export deals). Once the system was dismantled, the UCDA had to examine export prices ex post.

The Effects of Liberalization

As it did in India liberalization in Uganda brought significant changes to the coffee subsector. The most important of these were a new marketing system, an increased share of producer prices in border prices, and a dynamism in marketing—the result of growing private sector participation.

THE MARKETING SYSTEM. The primary consequences of the liberalization of the marketing system were the end of the CMB and the introduction of tough competition among exporters trying to purchase coffee from producers (figure 3.7). After liberalization the number of private exporters increased significantly; in 1998 around 50 exporters were registered, many of them joint ventures or companies owned by foreigners. The keen competition caused the CMBL's market share to decline precipitously (it remained close to zero for the last few years of the 1990s). The competition had the effect of raising the share of producer prices in border prices. In some years, however, exporters suffered heavy losses in competing for coffee because of competition and many shortfalls in the market.

PRODUCER PRICES. Probably the single most important effects of liberalization for growers were the jump in producer prices and the end to long waits for payment. Producer prices increased sharply after liberalization, both in absolute terms and in terms of share of border prices (figure 3.8). Devaluation, the elimination of heavy implicit taxes, and increased marketing efficiency resulting from competition contributed to the price hikes. Farmers who before liberalization had been forced to supply coffee on credit to primary cooperatives (the coffee collection points under the government procuring system) began receiving cash payments from both cooperatives and private traders.

PRODUCTION AND EXPORTS. Official statistics show that coffee production and exports increased sharply in the early to mid-1990s (figure 3.5).[13] Liberalization significantly affected two factors that contributed to the pro-

Figure 3.7 Uganda's Marketing System after Liberalization

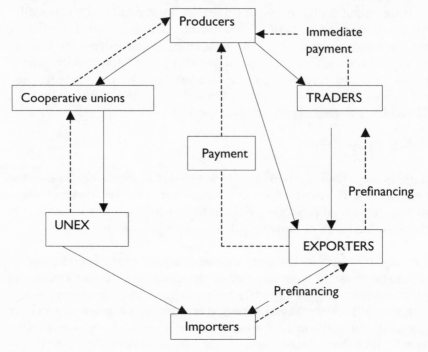

Source: author.

duction increase. The first and more important of these factors was price: because they were receiving higher prices, farmers took more interest in husbandry and in rehabilitating abandoned areas. The second factor was the increased availability of high-yielding varieties of seedlings. Although these varieties had been developed in Uganda around 1970, a very limited number of seedlings had been available to farmers. The situation changed drastically following liberalization, when a large number of private nurseries sprang up. In the new environment of cooperation between the public and private sectors, the UCDA provided the necessary know-how and initial financing to these private nurseries. These nurseries provide high-yielding seedlings that result in increased production and exports. Prompt cash payments and a freely convertible currency have also reversed the flow of smuggling and have attracted coffee from neighboring countries.

ORGANIZATIONS AND INSTITUTIONS. As we have seen the CMB enjoyed a monopoly before liberalization. As liberalization took effect the parastatal's role and power declined bit by bit, beginning with the division of the board into the CMBL and the UCDA in 1991. Most of the staff traders from the for-

Figure 3.8 Development of Producer Prices in Uganda

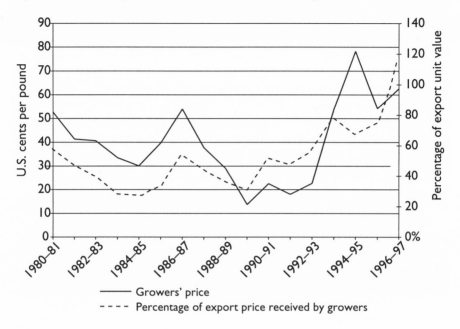

———— Growers' price

– – – – Percentage of export price received by growers

Source: LMC International.

mer CMB were transferred to CMBL.[14] But they found trading difficult in a competitive environment, and the CMBL's market share in exports fell steadily. By 1998 it was almost zero.

After liberalization industry-related groups were permitted to form associations. The most important organizations to emerge were the Uganda Coffee Trade Federation (UCTF)—which began in 1992 as the Uganda Coffee Exporters Association—and the Uganda Coffee Farmers Association. The federation is possibly the most influential private organization within Uganda's coffee industry. In the beginning the organization actively represented coffee exporters' views on various policy issues—including the export floor price, export taxes, and quality control—especially to the government. After the UCDA statute was amended to include more representatives from the private sector on its board, the group's influence increased. It was transformed into a more encompassing trade association that brought together all those concerned with coffee trade in Uganda, and in 1996 it became the UCTF. Exporters dominate this group, and other industry trade groups (such as those for growers) remain weak because the exporters are much better organized and informed.[15] The Uganda Coffee Farmers

Association, for example, was founded in 1995 in response to an amended UCDA statute calling for growers to represent themselves on the board. Unfortunately, apart from existing in order to select UCDA board members, the organization's functions have not been clearly delineated and its activities have been limited.

Apart from being a pressure group for the industry, the UCTF has been active in providing various services to the coffee industry. These include training quality control trainers, promoting Ugandan coffee abroad, conducting training programs for traders, acting as the private sector's contact point for international organizations and donors, and providing market information to the industry. The organization carries out many of these functions in collaboration with the UCDA.

PRIVATE INVESTMENT. Private investment increased substantially after liberalization. Aside from the nurseries discussed earlier, the private sector invested in export-processing facilities and large coffee plantations. The investments, which came not only from domestic entrepreneurs but also from foreign private individuals and firms, substantially improved the production, processing, and marketing efficiency.

Evaluating Liberalization

Because the Ugandan government undertook coffee market liberalization at the World Bank's urging, the process was a top-down affair, especially compared with India's. The reforms were successful mainly because the private sector utilized the opportunities they were offered extremely well, as evidenced by the large number of private firms that entered the coffee export business and the many investments in processing, nurseries, and plantations.

Another important factor that contributed to the success of liberalization in Uganda was the follow-up measures taken by the government. Both government and industry recognized that liberalization could not be completed all at once, so follow-up evaluations were conducted to ensure that the process remained on track.[16] Given the many issues that needed to be addressed (such as the complete privatization of the CMBL and the elimination of the export floor price), these follow-up actions were indispensable to achieving a viable transformation of the coffee industry.

One of the government's main concerns in liberalizing the coffee sector was the private sector's ability to fill the gap in coffee exporting left by the CMB—an issue that led to the establishment of the CMBL. As we have seen this concern was groundless. Domestic processors, merchants trading in other commodities, foreign-owned businesses (including several large international trading firms), and joint ventures entered the coffee export business. Donor countries and former CMBL marketers provided training for the new entrants.

Process in Consultation with Stakeholders

Togo's coffee subsector was liberalized in 1996. Prior to that time its coffee marketing and pricing system closely resembled the *caisse* system. Togo's liberalization program was coordinated with key industry players (businesses, entrepreneurs, and commercial banks). The reforms had an important impact on producer prices and on services previously provided by the government, such as extension, which have been taken over by the private sector.

The Marketing and Pricing System before Liberalization

Before the 1996 liberalization the parastatal Office of Togolese Agricultural Products (*Office de Produits Agricoles Togolais*, or OPAT) enjoyed a monopoly in external marketing, although domestic coffee (and cocoa) marketing was in the hands of the private sector (figure 3.9). Farmers dried red cherry on

Figure 3.9 Togo's Marketing System before Liberalization

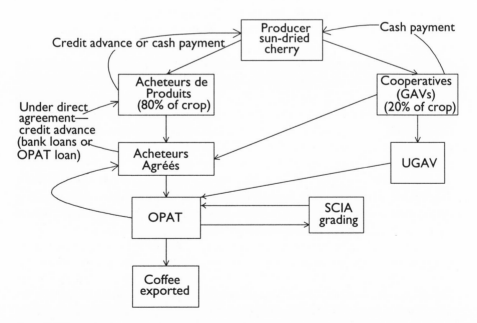

Source: LMC International.

mats in the sun and sold it hulled and sorted to small traders or coopera-tives. Of the 250 hullers operating in 1995, 44 belonged to cooperatives. Farmers paid for this service either in cash or in kind.

Small traders bought dried, hulled, and sorted coffee either directly from the farmer or at one of the 400 marketplaces situated in the coffee-growing areas. The traders stored the coffee in their villages for a short period before selling it to a wholesaler (*acheteur agréé*) with whom they had exclusive supply agreements and who advanced them credit. The whole-salers transported the coffee from the villages to a regional warehouse before moving it to OPAT in Lomé, where it was graded and then exported. These wholesalers supplied OPAT with 70 percent of its coffee; 10 percent came from small traders and the rest from cooperatives. In 1992 some 30 licensed wholesalers handled 60–70 percent of the total coffee and cocoa crop, with cooperatives handling the rest. The cooperatives were encour-aged to become involved in marketing, although the lack of prefinancing made it difficult for them to compete with private traders. Coffee handled by cooperatives was either transported to OPAT by regional cooperative unions or sold to wholesalers.

The Liberalization Process

Togo experienced a major political and economic crisis in 1992 and 1993, when pressure to establish a multiparty system of government caused a general strike that lasted eight months. During this period the international development community suspended aid to the country. When aid resumed, the World Bank made liberalization of the coffee and cocoa markets a con-dition of its Economic Recovery and Adjustment Credit. Negotiations between the Bank and the government were difficult because of the skepti-cism about liberalization that prevailed among government officials and OPAT staff. Some politicians had vested interests in the existing system, and OPAT staff were strongly opposed to liberalization because it meant they would lose their jobs. The Prime Minister was one of the few supporters of liberalization in the government.

The primary sticking point in the negotiations was the government's fear that liberalization would cause the quality of Togo's coffee and cocoa to deteriorate, affecting the country's reputation as a reliable adherent to the terms of its export contracts. The negotiations were also slowed by the gov-ernment's uncertainty about the availability of funds to finance payments to farmers and concern over the possibility of middlemen cheating farmers. The Bank's position was that the existing system made investment in the coffee and cocoa subsectors unattractive by keeping producer prices low, preserved opacity in OPAT's financial dealings and management, and sti-fled private sector initiatives.

Preparatory to and during the liberalization period, an important process took place that involved bringing together key players for consultation, including large firms, small firms interested in commodity trading, commercial banks, and government ministries. To some extent this process eased the skepticism and concern of many government officials. The participatory atmosphere also helped win the support of private sector stakeholders, who came to recognize that they owned the liberalization process. The results of the discussions were formalized into legal texts that became the regulatory framework for the market after liberalization. The texts cover administrative requirements for the conduct of exporting and marketing, quality control, and information dissemination.

In March 1996 OPAT's export monopoly was abolished, and both the coffee and cocoa markets were liberalized. In August 1996 the consultative process was institutionalized in the form of the Coordination Committee, which is made up of representatives of major government and private sector stakeholders. The committee is charged with overseeing and regulating the industry and has been instrumental in identifying and discussing problems, suggesting solutions, and keeping the liberalization process transparent.

The Situation after Liberalization

Liberalization changed the coffee marketing and pricing system in Togo drastically. The most significant development was the shift in government policy, which went from advocating state control to supporting collaboration between the public and private sectors.

MARKETING SYSTEM. Since liberalization the private sector has conducted marketing and exporting activities in the coffee subsector (figure 3.10). The elimination of OPAT has made marketing more efficient, as the parastatal was burdened with high direct and overhead costs and a bloated staff. The old system offered limited incentives for private domestic traders to improve marketing efficiency, as margins were predetermined and profits guaranteed. The new system is far more streamlined and competitive, with many new entries, most of them independent buyers who purchase from farmers and sell to the exporters. In October 1996, 11 private companies were registered as coffee and cocoa exporters.

PRODUCER PRICES. Prior to liberalization the government set grower prices and marketing margins annually based on OPAT's advice. Marketing costs were opaque because of the way government and OPAT revenues were calculated (as the difference between the export price and the sum of the producer price and official domestic marketing costs). An additional margin

Figure 3.10 Togo's Marketing System after Liberalization

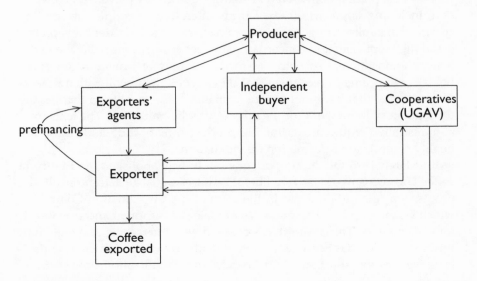

Source: LMC International.

was available to traders operating in remote areas to ensure panterritorial pricing. This system offered farmers few incentives to improve quality.

Producer prices had begun increasing before liberalization, however. In the early 1980s the proportion of the export unit value growers received was less than 30 percent (figure 3.11). But by the early 1990s it had almost doubled, the result of structural adjustment that required the government to reduce the officially set marketing costs. (The sharp increase in the level of producer prices in 1994 was the result of the 50 percent devaluation of the CFA franc.) Following liberalization the market determined prices and margins and competition marketing costs. Since these changes the share of producer prices in export unit value has been more than 80 percent.

PRODUCTION AND EXPORTS. Because Togo is a small country surrounded by countries that also produce coffee, smuggling is rampant, making statistics on production and exports unreliable. Official statistics show a substantial increase in exports in 1996–97 (figure 3.12), suggesting that coffee is being smuggled into the country. If coffee is indeed being smuggled into the country, the situation represents a reversal in coffee smuggling between Togo and its neighbors, especially Ghana. Because coffee is a perennial crop, it is too early to evaluate the effects of liberalization on production. However, higher producer prices should have favorable effects, especially in the long term.

Figure 3.11 Development of Producer Prices in Togo

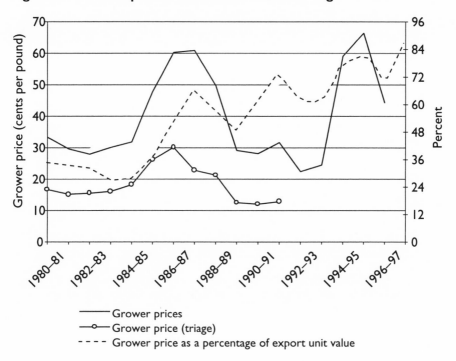

———— Grower prices
—○— Grower price (triage)
— — — Grower price as a percentage of export unit value

Source: ICO and LMC International.

ORGANIZATIONS AND INSTITUTIONS. Since OPAT's demise, the government's only direct involvement in the coffee industry has since been in the area of quality control through the *Service du Conditionnement* (SCOT; "[Export] Packaging Service"), which also controlled documents for exports. Before liberalization a parastatal provided technical assistance in production, processing, and marketing and helped farmers establish interest groups. The parastatal was dissolved in 1996, and its staff (prodded by the Coordination Committee) established a private firm that provides extension services, inputs, and planting materials. Its board members consist of representatives from the government, the private sector (cooperatives, exporters, and input distributors), and the Coordination Committee. Funding comes from the Coordination Committee, cooperatives, a nongovernmental organization (NGO), and a levy on exports under a technical cooperation agreement with the Coordination Committee. Despite this support funding limitations have hampered the firm's activities.

Liberalization has adversely affected one element of the subsector: producers' groups. In Togo around 40,000 farmers produce coffee and cocoa. Of

Figure 3.12 Togo's Production and Exports

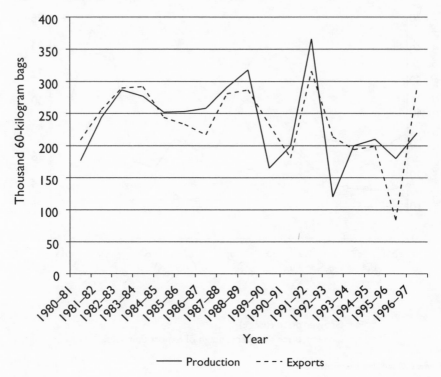

Source: ICO.

these some 9,000 belong to 290 Coffee and Cocoa Producer Groups (*Groupements de Producteurs Café-Cacao*, or GPCCs). These groups belong to 15 apex organizations known as Unions of Producer Groups (*Unions de Groupements de Producteurs*). Before liberalization the GPCCs handled about 20 percent of the produce, but since the reforms that share has declined substantially, as these groups have difficulty competing with private traders. Their costs are also considerably higher than those of private traders, so that farmers increasingly prefer selling to the traders. Experience in other countries supports the finding that such cooperative groups often face difficulty competing with private traders[17].

Exporters have also formed their own association, the Council of Coffee and Cocoa Exporters. The council has established its own regulations and is committed to the principle of fair competition. One of the group's most important rules requires exporters to deposit 20 percent of the f.o.b (free on board) value of each export contract as a bond in case they do not fulfill the contract.

Evaluating Liberalization

While it is still too early to evaluate the full effects of liberalization in Togo, some notable results are already evident. First, producer prices as a share of the f.o.b. price have increased. Second, marketing margins have declined substantially with disappearance of OPAT. Third, contrary to the government's fears, the private sector in Togo has been able to fill the role previously played by the parastatal. Fourth, because of the government's involvement in quality control through SCOT (and despite a considerably reduced budget), quality has not deteriorated and contract noncompliance has not increased. And finally private exporters have replaced OPAT crop financing with prefinancing and cash advances to farmers.

The Lessons of Liberalization

The experiences of the coffee subsectors in the countries examined here and in other countries suggest that liberalization has had positive effects in a number of areas including marketing, producer prices, production, and exports. Among the most prominent changes have been the following:

INCREASED MARKETING EFFICIENCY. Judging from the increased share of producer prices in border prices, the disappearance of inefficient marketing parastatals, and increased competition (the result of private traders entering the coffee market), marketing efficiency has improved substantially in Togo and Uganda. The private sector has introduced a variety of new marketing channels and methods, particularly in India, where private traders have been active since before liberalization. Producer prices as a share of border prices have increased significantly in Togo and Uganda, largely because implicit export taxes were eliminated. But increased marketing efficiency also worked in favor of producers.

INCREASED PRODUCTION AND EXPORTS. The effect of liberalization on production and exports is difficult to determine. It is relatively early to begin assessing the full effects of the reforms, and poor statistics and factors such as smuggling and the weather exacerbate the problem. Also the output response of perennial crops like coffee to price changes is low in the short run. Official statistics do show increases in both production and exports after liberalization in all three countries examined. To the extent that producer prices increase after liberalization, the effects on production should be favorable. However, the effects are likely to be minimal in areas where human and physical infrastructure is weak. Liberalization, in other words, can eliminate one of the key limiting factors in production, but as long as other limiting factors exist, the supply response to prices will be low. The increase in exports is more evident statistically than the increase in production, but again smuggling makes any precise evaluation difficult.

INCREASED PRIVATE SECTOR INVESTMENT. Prior to liberalization private investment in the coffee subsector was almost nonexistent. In Uganda coffee exporters are investing in processing facilities, and firms and individuals are investing in coffee farms. India has seen significant investment in the area of marketing institutions, including an auction, a futures exchange, and innovative marketing and quality inspection firms.

NEW ORGANIZATIONS AND INSTITUTIONS. All three countries have experienced a sea change in the organizations and institutions involved in the coffee subsector. Innovative approaches have emerged from dynamic, unfettered private sector activity, most notably in India. New organizations representing traders, processors, and producers have been established and existing groups strengthened. In all three countries these organizations have been involved in decisionmaking processes in the subsector, and their ability to affect policies is likely to increase.

A SHIFT IN GOVERNMENT POLICY TOWARD COLLABORATION WITH THE PRIVATE SECTOR. As the influence of the private sector in policy formulation and service provision grows, the approaches governments take to these processes have changed significantly. Because of the opaque manner in which preliberalization systems were managed (especially financial matters), government-controlled systems usually did not permit collaboration with the private sector. But both governments and parastatals have learned that carrying out some responsibilities effectively and efficiently requires collaboration with the private sector. In many cases this approach has become the only politically acceptable one.

The new approach is clear in the inclusion of private sector stakeholders in policymaking bodies. Private sector representatives play a key role on the UCDA in Uganda and the Coordination Committee in Togo. Although India's Coffee Board is a parastatal, it consults private stakeholders—especially associations of producers, processors, and exporters—when it is formulating coffee policies and designing its main activities. These bodies serve to institutionalize the process of consultation and collaboration.

The new approach is also evident in the provision of services to the subsector. In Uganda the UCDA has provided technical and financial assistance to fledgling private sector nurseries and collaborated with the UCTF in training quality control personnel, promoting Ugandan coffee abroad, and disseminating market information to the industry. In Togo a private firm is providing various services to the subsector (including research, extension, and farm inputs) under a technical agreement with the government.

Making Liberalization Successful

Successfully liberalizing coffee markets requires a supportive environment. The most important supporting factors are strong government commitment and effective public-private sector collaboration. Promoting private sector activity in countries where there has been none also contributes to a smooth reform process.

GOVERNMENT COMMITMENT. The three country cases we have examined show that once a decision is made to liberalize the coffee market, strong government support facilitates the process. In these three countries each government offered its support, at least at the level of president or prime minister (see the annex for a similar situation in Brazil). This support has been key in setting a broad strategic path toward liberalization. Collaboration with the private sector (and with international donors) helps to ensure that liberalization proceeds, as the process is not a one-time undertaking but rather a set of measures taken in stages.

Government commitment is necessary to counterbalance groups in both the government and the private sector who have a vested interest in either maintaining the old system or rapidly replacing it.[18] In India frequent consultations took place between the Coffee Board and producers' associations during the four years of liberalization—a process that was helped along by the presence of producers' representatives on the Coffee Board itself. In Uganda task forces comprising staff of relevant government agencies, the World Bank, and international consultants undertook two evaluations of the liberalization process. Togo's monitoring and evaluating tasks were institutionalized through the Coordination Committee formed to oversee the liberalization process. The committee included representatives of government agencies and private sector stakeholders.

STAKEHOLDER PARTICIPATION IN PLANNING. A successful liberalization process also requires careful planning and consultations among key stakeholders. Planning and analysis is often necessary to convince the government that liberalization will be beneficial to the development of the subsector. Hasty liberalization often deprives producers of key services that government agencies have been providing. Cocoa producers in Nigeria found themselves in this situation (see chapter 2), as did coffee growers in Brazil and Mexico when liberalization abolished parastatals and with them research and extension functions. These functions, which should have been retained, were subsequently restored. Effective monitoring and evaluation activities such as those undertaken in the three countries examined here must be considered during the planning process. The international development community can provide effective assistance in this area, as it did in Togo and Uganda.

PRIVATE SECTOR ACTIVITY BEFORE LIBERALIZATION. In India and Togo the liberalization process was smooth because, to a significant degree, private traders and exporters were already active before the reforms. Uganda's experience suggests that in countries where private exporters do not exist at the time of liberalization, privatizing the marketing branch of the parastatal and allowing it to compete with private exporters facilitates the liberalization process. If such measures are taken, however, the government must not give favorable treatment to the newly privatized organization—and in fact such an organization is not feasible if the private sector opposes it on the grounds that it will enjoy favorable treatment. (Togo's private exporters strongly objected to the idea of OPAT continuing its marketing operations, for example.) Judging from the liberalization process in Uganda, with time and possibly some training, local private exporters will emerge.

The Challenges of Liberalization

Although liberalization has introduced higher producer prices and more dynamism to the coffee industry in many countries, producers are often faced with new sets of problems after liberalization, including price uncertainty and lack of access to credit. Competition has also created difficulties in some countries.

PRICE UNCERTAINTY. Before liberalization parastatals fixed producer prices or set an average price (as in India's two-tier payment system). These payment systems provided a certain degree of security. In a liberalized environment producers have to acquire price information themselves and decide whether the prices traders offer are adequate. To facilitate access to price and other important market information, governments and private professional associations in a number of countries have established information dissemination systems. In Togo and Uganda these systems take the form of indicative prices, and in Rwanda and Togo coffee prices in major domestic markets are closely monitored. Similarly a number of countries, including Brazil, Mexico, and Togo, need to strengthen their research and extension services, which were significantly weakened with the abolition of parastatals.

A number of governments of commodity-exporting countries and international organizations have raised the issue of price hedging. Some exporters in developing countries use hedging instruments such as options and futures on coffee traded in New York and London. But few small coffee producers have access to these instruments, although some hedging programs are being used for other commodities—for instance maize in Mexico and cattle in Canada.[19]

LACK OF ACCESS TO CREDIT. In many countries parastatals provided credit prior to liberalization. Under systems that gave these parastatals a monopoly over marketing, credit recovery was straightforward because repayments could often be deducted from the sums paid to producers. In a liberalized environment small producers with no collateral often have difficulty obtaining credit from commercial banks. In many countries land is not properly registered and thus is not available as collateral, exacerbating the problem. A system to address this problem is in operation in Guatemala, where the producers' association keeps records of each member's production and sales over several years. The association submits the records to a bank when a member applies for credit, facilitating the provision of credit to coffee growers.

Small local exporters and traders in many coffee-producing countries, including Togo and Uganda, also have difficulty obtaining credit at reasonable interest rates. One of the primary reasons for this situation is the weakness of financial institutions. Foreign-affiliated and large local firms do not face this problem, as they can generally obtain prefinancing from importers in the form of low-interest hard-currency loans.

COMPETITION. Marketing cooperatives in several coffee-producing countries continue to have difficulty coping with the competitive marketing situation introduced by liberalization, although cooperatives in countries such as Mexico and India have enjoyed some success. Under the old system these organizations played key roles in marketing. Efforts by governments and international donors to assist the cooperatives financially have mostly failed.[20] These efforts were usually based on the notion that private traders cheat farmers—a notion that is often unfounded, especially in competitive markets. Providing training and disseminating market information to both cooperatives and farmers can be helpful, but favorable financial assistance or marketing arrangements work against farmers.

Despite the challenges liberalization presents, many countries are well positioned to tackle them, in large part because of private sector participation in the new paradigm. The dynamism and flexibility the private sector has brought to liberalized countries are proving to be indispensable in coping with the changing world economy and markets. Liberalization is a necessary condition for the positive development of commodity subsectors in developing countries. In the new environment it ushers in, governments and the international community can play an important role in the provision of information and training in the areas of innovative marketing, risk management, finance, and production methods.

Our discussion has focused primarily on successfully liberalized countries. Liberalization of the coffee subsector has not generated similar significant benefits in some countries (Madagascar and Tanzania), except for a large increase in producer prices. The major reasons for this lack of success are an underdeveloped legal system to enforce law and order and weak physical infrastructure (such as roads).[21] In Madagascar producer prices did not increase much for farmers in remote areas because of poor transportation infrastructure.[22] This situation underscores the fact that there is more to liberalization than simply getting prices right and removing ineffective policies (Timmer 1991). Liberalization also requires institutional and legal reforms that foster private investment and a competitive market structure.

Annex 3.1
Brazil and the Collapse of the International Coffee Organization

The stories of Brazil's coffee markets and the fall of the International Coffee Organization are inextricably intertwined. We present a shortened version of them here.[23]

State intervention in Brazil's coffee market began in 1906 in the face of an anticipated bumper crop and consequent sharp fall in prices. Led by São Paulo, governments of the major Brazilian coffee-growing states decided to purchase surplus coffee at minimum prices to protect the interest of coffee growers, who constituted the main political base in those states. An export tax was imposed and the currency fixed at a relatively undervalued level. Under pressure from these state governments, the federal government soon afterward agreed to implement national coffee policies. Several stockholding schemes (*valorizations*) were also implemented. In the 1930s governments used coffee destruction programs to raise prices, but World War II depressed world coffee prices

During the 1950s world coffee production increased sharply, and with it Brazil's accumulated stocks. To conduct national coffee policies effectively, the government created a parastatal, the Brazilian Institute of Coffee (IBC), in 1953. The government then decided to seek the cooperation of other countries in forming an international coffee agreement with international export quotas to raise prices. The International Coffee Organization (ICO) was created in 1962. The agreement received important support in the form of U.S. participation, which was spurred by the revolution in Cuba. Unlike oil-consuming countries subject to the market control system of the Organization of Petroleum-Exporting Countries (OPEC), coffee-consuming countries had political reasons for supporting the ICO.[24] The United States felt that high coffee prices would reduce the threat of communism, and Western European countries had the political will to provide aid to their ex-colonies, many of which produced coffee.

Owing to disagreements about the size of the quotas, the quota system became ineffective in December 1972. With the collapse of the ICO quota system, Brazil took the initiative in setting up an international supply-withholding program in the form of a trading company financed by Brazil, Colombia, Côte d'Ivoire, and Portugal (on behalf of Angola). Another company, Otros Suaves S.A., started up with the support of Mexico. The Vigilance Committee, managed by the Inter-African Coffee Organization, was created to monitor trade in robusta coffee. A coordinating committee was set up to implement a voluntary agreement to restrict exports. However, because a few countries, including Colombia, were trying to expand their production using high-yielding varieties, these producers' programs did not work.

In 1975 the world coffee market was jolted by a deadly frost in Brazil that effectively reduced Brazil's output by more than one-half and world coffee outputs by 17 percent in 1976. As a result world prices more than tripled between 1975 and 1977. Along with raising prices the frost affected the world coffee market for years to come by encouraging significant expansion of coffee-growing areas in many countries, including Colombia. Prices started to fall sharply after 1977, prompting Brazil to cooperate with other Latin American producers (the Bogota Group) to intervene in the futures market to prop up prices—an exercise that did not work.

World coffee prices continued to fall, mainly because of increased production, and coffee-producing countries succeeded in reactivating the ICO quota system in October 1980. The United States was still concerned that low coffee prices would raise poverty levels in Latin America, strengthening the power of the Communists and increasing cocaine production. In addition the U.S. coffee industry, which was having difficulty coping with widely fluctuating world prices, urged the government to support the agreement. The European Community (EC) was concerned about the adverse effect of low coffee prices on coffee-producing countries, primarily in Africa. The EC had a program to compensate Asian, Caribbean, and Pacific countries for lost revenues when commodity prices fell but considered the ICO a more economical and efficient way to provide aid. Japan lent its support mainly because of its distaste for widely fluctuating commodity prices.

The ICO succeeded in stabilizing world coffee prices from October 1980 until July 1989, when the quota system collapsed (see Akiyama and Varangis 1992 and Bates 1997). Disagreement among members on the economic clauses of the agreement precipitated the collapse. The main point of disagreement was the two-tier world market that had developed under the quota system. A number of coffee-importing countries remained outside the agreement, including almost all the developing and centrally planned coffee importers in Eastern Europe (Hermann 1986). Because production exceeded the allocated quotas, many exporting countries effectively dumped their coffee in those nonmember importing countries, causing coffee-importing ICO members to question why they were having to pay so much more for coffee than nonmembers.[25] Another point of disagreement was the allocation of quotas among types of coffee and countries. These allocations were essentially fixed during the effective period of the agreement—an unsatisfactory arrangement for countries where relative demand for imported arabicas was increasing.

Another and perhaps more fundamental cause of the collapse of ICO was the Brazilian coffee industry's dissatisfaction with the IBC and by default the ICO. Over the years the IBC gained a reputation as an inefficient and bloated bureaucracy. Brazilian coffee stakeholders began to question whether they needed such an organization when none existed for other agricultural commodities, raising a related question of about the ICO. Was it beneficial to the coffee industry? Coffee producers were unhappy because the government was reluctant to offer high enough minimum prices during bumper crop years and periods when it was trying to keep inflation low. A program called Operation Patricia caused exporters to push for abolishing the IBC. Under this program the IBC contracted with exporters to buy 1.5 million bags of robusta to prop up declining world prices. This exercise proved to be ineffective in raising prices and, as the government did not pay the exporters, the exporters sued.

The new IBC president, who took charge in January 1987, was determined to change coffee policies in a fundamental way and to restructure the IBC. He implemented a number of key policy changes. The most important of these involved auctioning off export quotas instead of allocating them based on previous export levels.[26] With the aim of financing the 1987–88 bumper crop, he also introduced a retention program under which exporters were to retain one bag of coffee for each bag exported. The auction system and the new retention program compelled exporters, who by then had formed an association, to demand the abolition of the IBC.

Given the lack of domestic support for the ICO and the difficulty of resolving the differences in the system of quotas and allocations, Brazil decided to abandon the agreement in July 1989. In March 1990 the government liberalized the coffee trade and abolished the IBC, noting that official intervention would only exacerbate the problems.

The rise and fall of Brazil's interventionist policies for the coffee market were strongly influenced by domestic and international politics and the economic stance of key decisionmakers.[27] The influence of prevailing world economic thinking on development was particularly strong (see chapter 1). The direct causes of the collapse of IBC are similar to the direct causes of market liberalization in Sub-Saharan Africa: an inefficient parastatal and an insupportable fiscal burden. But it was the change in government policy that finally liberalized the coffee subsector in Brazil.

The prima facie reasons for the collapse of the ICO were disagreement among members on technical issues related to the quota system and quota allocation. But as the prevailing economic thinking on the world stage and in Brazil shifted toward market-oriented policies, the ICO had few chances of survival. Most of the parastatals that had controlled the coffee subsector in Latin America (in Mexico and Brazil, among others) collapsed along with it. The associations of private producers that play a similar role (in countries such as Colombia, Costa Rica, and Guatemala) survived the ICO's collapse.

Notes

1. These 51 countries were responsible for more than 99 percent of world coffee output.

2. See Varangis and others (1990) and chapter 3 of this volume for a description of the various marketing systems. Under the *caisse* system, the government controls marketing and sets prices. *Institutos*, which are used in Latin America, are similar to stabilization funds, but producer prices and marketing fees are less rigid.

3. The primary coffee-producing countries are Brazil, Colombia, Côte d'Ivoire, Ethiopia, Indonesia, Uganda, and Vietnam. Domestic consumption is limited in most of these countries (the exceptions are Brazil, Colombia, and Ethiopia), so most production is exported.

4. Most countries reduced or eliminated taxes on coffee. See annex 3.1 for a discussion of the development of coffee policies in Brazil and their impact on the ICO.

5. In a move that reflected coffee growers' strong political strength, politicians and growers in several Latin American countries pressed the government to provide minimum prices (see annex 3.1). Meeting this demand of course required a controlled system.

6. Hayami (1996) argues that the stereotypical notion of middlemen cheating farmers has not stood up to empirical examination. He believes that middlemen have important roles to play in the marketing systems of developing countries.

7. However, long-run price elasticity of supply for perennials is high (see Akiyama and Trivedi 1988).

8. Annex 3.1 discusses the collapse of the ICO. For more details see Gilbert (1996). For the effects of the quota system on coffee-producing countries, see Akiyama and Varangis (1990).

9. According to the Coffee Board, large producers (more than 10 hectares) own 35 percent of the total land planted to coffee but constitute only 2 percent of coffee growers (ICO 1997)

10. The new government was committed to liberalizing the economy after accepting the terms imposed by the IMF to correct the balance of payment crisis.

11. Narayan argues that most of the producer price increase was due to devaluation and high world prices.

12. Although the UCDA's board was composed of representatives from industry as well as government ministries, until 1994 the majority of the board members were from the government, and the UCDA was considered a government body.

13. These statistics need to be interpreted with caution, however, because they are often significantly distorted by coffee smuggling.

14. Many others went to work for newly established private coffee-exporting firms.

15. See Olson (1965) for discussions on the organizational dynamics.

16. The World Bank responded to the private sector's actions by monitoring and assisting the industry during the liberalization process.

17. See, for example, Lele and Christiansen (1989).

18. Bohman and others (1996) suggest that the groups that benefit from controlled markets are often politicians, government officials, and traders.

19. Varangis and Larson (1996) provide examples of commodity risk management programs in several countries.

20. See, for example, Lele and Christiansen (1989).

21. In Madagascar the theft of coffee cherries is so prevalent that coffee trees receive inadequate care and investors are wary of putting money into the subsector.

22. Most coffee farmers in Madagascar and many in Mexico do not apply fertilizer because high transportation costs make it too expensive..

23. The annex, especially on Brazil's coffee policies, is drawn heavily from Bacha (1992).

24. Provision of aid through this mechanism does not require government expenditure. Coffee consumers effectively pay taxes through high coffee prices.

25. Bohman and Jarvis (1990) point out that the export price for members was sometimes twice what it was for nonmembers.

26. According to Jarvis (2000), the old system created enormous rent for exporters and IBC officials.

27. The same can be said of Colombia. See Bates (1997).

References

Akiyama, T., and P. N. Varangis. 1990. "Impact of the International Coffee Agreement on Producing Countries." *The World Bank Economic Review* 4(2):157–73.

Akiyama, T., and P. Trivedi. 1988. "Vintage Production Approach to Perennial Crop supply." *Journal of Econometrics* 36:133–61.

Bacha, E. L. 1992. "Brazilian Coffee Policy: A Centennial Evaluation." In Marcellino Martins and E. Johnston, eds., *150 Years of Coffee*. Rio de Janiero: Exportadores Ltda.

Bates, R. H. 1981. *Markets and States in Tropical Africa: The Political Basis of Agricultural Policies*. Berkeley, Calif.: University of California Press.

_____. 1990. "The Political Framework for Agricultural Policy Decisions." In C. K. Eicher and J. M. Staatz, eds., *Agricultural Development in the Third World*. Baltimore: Johns Hopkins University Press.

_____. 1997. *Open-economy Politics: The Political Economy of the World Coffee Trade*. Princeton, N.J.: Princeton University Press.

Binswanger, H., and K. Deininger. 1997. "Explaining Agricultural and Agrarian Policies in Developing Countries." *Journal of Economic Literature* 35: 1958–2005.

Bohman, M., and L. Jarvis. 1990. "The International Coffee Agreement: Economics of the Nonmember Market." *European Review of Agricultural Economics* 17(1): 99–118.

Bohman, M., L. Jarvis, and R. Barichello. 1996. "Rent Seeking and International Commodity Agreements: The Case of Coffee." *Economic Development and Cultural Change*, 44(2): 379–402.

Deaton, A. S. 1992. *Commodity Prices, Stabilization, and Growth in Africa.* Discussion Paper 166. Woodrow Wilson Center for International Studies, Princeton University, Princeton, N.J.

Gilbert, C. L. 1996. "International Commodity Agreements: An Obituary Notice." *World Development* 15: 1–19.

Hayami, Y. 1996. "The Peasant in Economic Modernization." *American Journal of Agricultural Economics* 78(5), 1157--67.

Herrmann, R. 1986. "Free Riders and Redistributive Effects of International Commodity Agreements: The Case of Coffee." *Journal of Policy Modeling* 8(4): 597–621.

ICO (International Coffee Organization). 1997. *Coffee Profile: India.* London.

Jarvis, L. 2000. "The Rise and Decline of Rent-Seeking Activity in the Brazilian Coffee Sector." Working paper, Department of Agricultural and Resource Economics, University of California, Davis.

Lele, U., and R. E. Christiansen. 1989. *Markets, Marketing Boards, and Cooperatives in Africa: Issues in Adjustment Policy.* Managing Agricultural Development in Africa (MADIA) Discussion Paper 2. Washington, D.C.: World Bank.

Narayan, M. R. 1997. "Impact of Liberalization Measures on India's Coffee Sector: An Economic Analysis." *Journal of Indian School of Political Economy* 9(3):490–514.

Olson, M. 1965. *The Logic of Collective Action.* Cambridge, Mass.: Harvard University Press.

Timmer. P. 1991. *Agriculture and the State.* Ithaca, N.Y.: Cornell University Press.

Varangis, P., T. Akiyama, and E. Thigpen. 1990 "Recent Developments in Marketing and Pricing Systems for Agricultural Export Commodities in Sub-Saharan Africa." World Bank Working Paper 431. Washington, D.C: World Bank.

Varangis, P., and D. Larson. 1996. *Dealing with Commodity Price Uncertainty.* Policy Research Working Paper 1667. Washington, D.C.: World Bank.

World Bank. 1993. *The East Asian Miracle: Economic Growth and Public Policy.* New York: Oxford University Press.

4

Sugar Policy and Reform

Donald Larson and Brent Borrell

THIS CHAPTER PROVIDES LESSONS ABOUT SUGAR POLICIES and the process of sugar policy reform by drawing selectively on cross-country experiences. One general conclusion is that long-standing government interventions frequently displace both the markets and the institutions required to produce efficient outcomes. In addition, households and firms make decisions, based on long-standing policies, that are costly to reverse, so that the outcomes of earlier policies and events affect the pace and process of reform. This view of markets may apply generally and is particularly relevant to the commodity markets covered in other chapters of this book. But the political economy, trade structures, and production characteristics of sugar are different enough from those found in most agricultural markets to warrant special consideration. Chief among these differences are:

- The degree to which international markets are dominated by policy interventions and the effects of preferential trade arrangements;
- The inherent tension between mills and growers that are created by sugar's joint-production characteristics;
- The local monopoly-monopsony relationship between growers and mills; and
- The effect of that relationship on community incomes, assets, and profitability.

Because of these factors governments commonly intervene in sugar markets. The result is a legacy of path-dependent policies, with approaches and instruments that are greatly influenced by past agreements and previous interventions. The accumulated effects of these interventions are embodied in livelihoods, political institutions, capital stocks, and factor markets—elements that not only dictate the starting point for reform but also determine which reform paths are feasible.

To an exceptional level domestic sugar policies in many countries are shaped by the policies of a few large countries. The policies of these countries have their roots in historic events. This chapter discusses the history and current characteristics of these policies, related trade arrangements, and the way the policies of large countries shape those of smaller economies. It also reviews literature that quantifies the benefits of policy reform, but the emphasis is on describing those characteristics of sugar policy, markets, and production that shape the reform process. We draw lessons from domestically driven reforms and from reforms forced by historic events. The emphasis on reform is perhaps surprising, since few countries have completely opened their domestic sugar markets to free trade. However, many countries began the process of domestic reform in the 1990s, including privatizing mills and estates, and a number of developments on the international scene are likely catalysts for further reforms. These developments include the anticipated expansion of the European Union (EU), the effects of the North American Free Trade Agreement (NAFTA) on U.S. and Mexican policy, the regional effects of reform on Brazil's sugar industry, and discussions under the auspices of the World Trade Organization (WTO).

Global Markets

Protected markets, special trade arrangements, and prices that are remarkably volatile characterize the sugar trade. At the same time the market for freely traded sugar is large and deep compared with markets for other agricultural commodities. Sophisticated and liquid financial markets (forward, futures, and derivatives) supplement the physical trade. Understanding this unusual blend of free and protected markets is important for policymakers during the process of domestic market reform, for several reasons. First, producer groups often base their successful arguments for government protection on the policies of other countries.

Second, many market interventions are long-lived, and the accumulated results of these interventions can complicate the reform process. Accumulated investments in land, capital, and human resources are often premised on domestic policy interventions or special access to protected markets in the EU or the United States. In a few countries, such as Fiji and Mauritius, export earnings from sales to protected markets are important to the economy as a whole. These earnings contribute significantly to national incomes, currency reserves, and government revenues. For these countries, policy changes in destination markets can have macroeconomic consequences.

Third, understanding the variability in the sugar market and the secondary and derivative markets for sugar is important. Government interventions to stabilize sugar prices can crowd out international markets as risk management instruments and inhibit the development of domestic risk management practices. Conversely, international markets for risk management offer an opportunity to mitigate the consequences of volatility introduced by domestic reforms.

Government Interventions around the World

Sugar is a basic food consumed in all countries. The Food and Agricultural Organization (FAO) reports that 133 countries produce it. Sugar is traded widely, with annual trade constituting around 26 percent of annual production. However, a handful of large countries produce and consume most of the world's sugar (figure 4.1.) In addition, most large producers—China, the EU, India, and the United States—intervene in the sugar trade in ways that affect international prices.[1] Many other countries intervene in one form or another in domestic markets, and only the smaller market share of these countries keeps their individual interventions from significantly affecting global markets.

In preparation for the Uruguay Round of negotiations under the General Agreement on Tariffs and Trade (GATT) in 1986–94, participants agreed on a common method of analyzing the effects of policy interventions. Although the method has acknowledged limits, it allows comparisons of policy effects across diverse interventions such as quotas, export subsidies, and interventions in input markets.[2] Quantitative estimates of the positive and negative effects of policy elements on producers are summed and divided by output to calculate an estimated producer subsidy equivalent (PSE) per ton. A similar process produces a consumer subsidy equivalent (CSE) that measures the effects of agricultural policy on domestic consumers. The Organisation for Economic Co-operation and Development (OECD) has institutionalized these calculations for industrial countries and now calculates these measures annually.

Between 1982 and 1992 all sugar-producing industrial countries protected domestic sugar at the expense of consumers. Most countries did so at significant levels. On average from 1993 to 1995 producer subsidies in OECD countries were equal to around 49 percent of the world price (OECD 1997). The CSE measure for the same period was 46 percent—that is, the implicit tax on consumers was equal to 46 percent of the average world price (table 4.1). Among industrial countries, only Australia has chosen to dismantle its trade barriers since 1995.

**Figure 4.1 Average Share of World Sugar Production for
Selected Countries, 1994–98**

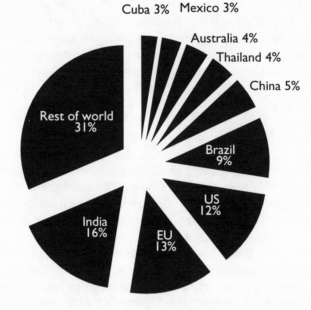

Cuba 3%   Mexico 3%

Australia 4%

Thailand 4%

China 5%

Rest of world
31%

Brazil
9%

US
12%

India
16%

EU
13%

Source: FAO.

The motivations and objectives of sugar policies in developing countries
are more diverse than those in industrial economies and are often contradictory. Some countries, such as Zimbabwe, have attempted to keep consumer prices low, and until recently Brazil used export restrictions to foster
its domestic ethanol industry. Generally, however, governments in most
developing countries, in pursuit of self-sufficiency, attempt to protect
domestic industries, including some state-owned enterprises. Often this
protectionism results in higher prices for consumers, as it does in Chad and
Ukraine. But some countries, including China and India, use input subsidies
from central or state budgets as well.

The Effects of Policies on the World Market and Domestic Welfare

What are the effects of different types of policies on international markets?
The prevailing opinion is that market interventions lower international
prices significantly while increasing price volatility. A GATT panel ruled
that the regime of the late 1970s in the European Community had depressed
world prices (Harris, Swinbank, and Wilkinson 1983). Table 4.2 reports estimates of the effects of various policies on world sugar prices. Valdés (1987)

Table 4.1 Producer and Consumer Subsidy Equivalents for Sugar, 1982–92 (U.S. dollars per metric ton)

Producer subsidy equivalents	1982	1983	1984	1985	1986	1987	1988	1989	1990	1991	1992
Australia		16	18	20	17	22	19	26	27		
Canada			13	10	5	20	7	8	7	9	9
Chile						150	113	12	106	127	118
Colombia			98	91	88	86	25	–26	–27	–21	–19
Czechoslovakia		–38	–59	–39	–96	–79	–17	–29			
Egypt				–77	–55	–176	–205	–332			
EC	43	50	89	110	164	181	55	14	–27	–33	55
Hungary			34	32	201	141	–40				
Jamaica	–110	–133	–14	28	–21	–31	–72	–94			
Japan	604	713	714	719	986	966	912	748	795		
Kenya		15	–8	97	96	63	63	–9			
Nigeria	–264	–379	–403	–262	–221	73	73	106			
Poland	–310	–132	–39	16	–31	–91	–136	331			
South Africa	–112	59	20	21	51	48	12	–62			
Taiwan, China	0	178	214	281	292	196	292	396			
United States			241	200	217	183	153	133	178	170	163
USSR						248	152	74	73		
Yugoslavia		52	119	139	222	69	–126				
Consumer subsidy equivalents											
Canada		–25	–24	–23	–22	–23	–24	–22	–20	–18	
China			–452	–335	–216	–180	–319	–264	–137	–226	
European Union	–338	–317	–350	–454	–570	–605	–398	–322			–150

(Table continues on the following page.)

125

Table 4.1 (continued)

Producer subsidy equivalents	1982	1983	1984	1985	1986	1987	1988	1989	1990	1991	1992
Jamaica	-55	-13	-78	-85	-54	-91	-4	77			
Japan	-611	-521	-546	-523	-709	-831	-719	-491	-589		
Nigeria	323	397	421	269	235	-66	-69	-118			
Poland		-49	-89	-67	-64	-92	-71	-17			
South Africa	70	-125	-47	-66	-53	-68	-99	-17			
Korea, Rep. of		-642	-575	-427	-393	-406	-461	-256	-268	-306	
Taiwan, China			-448	-533	-529	-366	-478	-604	-504	-551	-612
United States			-371	-303	-328	-275	-219	-186	-262	-252	-231
USSR					-138	-147	-81	-19	-20		
Yugoslavia		-61	-44	-44	-80	-55	-30				

Source: Earley and Westfall (1996).

Table 4.2 Results of Selected Studies on Sugar Trade Liberalization

Authors	Study period	Price effect		Change in price volatility	Scenario
		Percentage of change	Cents/lb. US$ 1990	Percentage of change	
Snape (1963)	1959	16	3.04	n.a.	Subsidy through deficiency payments
Valdés and Zietz (1980)	1975–77	6–8	2–3	n.a.	Liberalization by industrial countries
Koester and Schmitz (1982)	1975–77	12	4.18	n.a.	Liberalization by industrial countries
Roberts and others (1982)	1968–81	7–11	2–3.5	n.a.	EU liberalization
Matthews (1985)	1981	11	3.31	n.a.	EU liberalization
Zietz and Valdés (1986)	1979–81	13–29	4–9	n.a.	Multicommodity trade liberalization for 17 industrial countries
Tyers and Anderson (1986)	1987	10	0.78	–22	Liberalization by East Asia and Western Europe
OECD (1987)	1979–81	1	0.31	n.a.	Ten percent reduction in assistance to OECD sugar producers
Webb, Ronigen, and Dixit (1987)	1984	53	4.45	n.a.	Complete trade liberalization, 12 commodities
Huff and Moreddu (1990)	1982–85	25	4.5	n.a.	Multilateral trade liberalization
Martin and others (1990)	1980–83	60	9.1	n.a.	Multilateral trade liberalization
Lord and Barry (1990)	1990	10–30	1–4	n.a.	Multilateral trade liberalization
ABARE (1993)	2000 baseline	5.30	n.a.	n.a.	Implementation of Uruguay Round agreement
USDA (1994)	2000 baseline	2–5	n.a.	n.a.	Implementation of Uruguay Round agreement
UNCTAD (1995)	2000 baseline	5	n.a.	n.a.	Implementation of Uruguay Round agreement
Wong, Sturgis, and Borrell (1989)	1985–2004 simulation	8	n.a.	–33	OECD price liberalization
Wong, Sturgis, and Borrell (1989)	1985–2004 simulation	33	n.a.	–28	Liberalization of EU, Japanese, and U.S. markets

n.a. Not applicable.
Sources: Borrell and Duncan (1992); Gardner (1993); Harris and Tangerman (1993); UNCTAD (1994); Jabara and Valdés (1993).

and Borrell and Duncan (1992), among others, point out that sugar liberalization studies are generally not comparable. Some of the studies in table 4.2
cover a range of commodities, while others focus only on sugar. In addition
the effects are measured against a baseline that differs from study to study.
Yet once the effects are converted into a common measure (cents per pound,
1990 terms), average estimates from 1960 of the effects on prices do not differ significantly from more recent estimates. These similarities persist
despite methodological differences and the significant policy and market
changes that took place in the interim.

The EU and the United States use international markets to manage
domestic sugar surpluses and shortfalls, as do other large sugar-consuming
and -producing countries. In doing so these countries pass their production
and demand uncertainties on to the international market, and international
prices are thus more volatile than they would be under free trade agreements. In addition to the EU and the United States, Brazil, China, and India
have pursued domestic policy regimes in which shortfalls or surpluses in
domestic supply were managed through adjustments in trade (figure 4.2).
The few studies that measure the effects of policy on market volatility sug-

Figure 4.2 Net Trade in Sugar for Brazil, China, and India, 1976–96

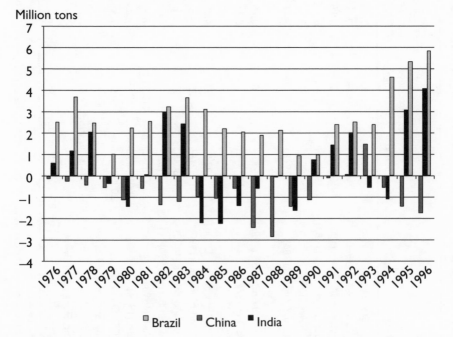

Million tons

□ Brazil   ■ China   ■ India

Source: FAO.

gest that the effects of policy on short-term price volatility are considerable (table 4.2).

The EU uses import substitution and export subsidies to protect domestic markets. The EU has the largest export subsidy program, but this program is not unique: Colombia, Mexico, Poland, and South Africa, among others, subsidize sugar exports. As part of the Uruguay Round of the GATT, several countries pledged to reduce subsidized exports of sugar. The promised reductions, which are to be in place by 2004, equal 1.3 million tons—approximately the same amount as exports from the African, Caribbean, and Pacific Group of States (ACP) to the EU. Nonetheless these same countries retain the right to subsidize nearly 5.4 million tons of sugar (table 4.3)

Many of the studies on sugar polices also measure the distribution benefits. Included are measures of transfers between producers and consumers, between rich and poor countries, and among firms.[3] For example Jabara and Valdés (1993) report that protection in industrial nations reduced the foreign exchange earnings of poor exporters by $2.2 billion to $5.1 billion per year in 1980 dollars. Moreover, studies that measure welfare transfers do not attempt to measure the effects of policy on factor allocation. Since many of these factors are fixed—for example, investments in milling and improvements to land—policies become embedded in capital and other factor stock, and their effects are long lived. By 1990 (prior to recent reforms) interventions put in place during the first International Sugar Agreement in the 1930s had cost the Australian sugar industry over $200 million a year (Borrell, Quirke, and Vincent 1991). Similarly, before reforms commenced in

Table 4.3 Reductions in Sugar Export Subsidies Pledged during the Uruguay Round

Country	Base 1,000 tons	Reduction	Percent
Brazil	1,714	240	14
China	250	35	14
Colombia	257	36	14
EU	1,619	340	21
Hungary	165	134	81
Mexico	1,500	270	18
Poland	170	68	40
Romania	179	25	14
Slovak Republic	5	1	20
South Africa	890	187	21
Total	6,750	1,336	20

Source: Earley and Westfall (1996)

Brazil, policy interventions were costing the country an estimated $2.5 billion a year (Borrell, Bianco, and Bale, 1994.) Estimates for India suggest that allowing existing policies to continue unchanged could cost the economy around the same amount ($2 billion a year) by 2004 (World Bank 1996).

How the Policies of Large Countries Affect Those of Small Economies

The policies of countries that dominate the sugar market influence those of less important players in two significant ways. First, the pervasive interventions of the larger countries encourage others to institute protectionist policies. The influence can be indirect (through unilateral trade policy) or more explicit, especially during the negotiation of regional trade arrangements such as the Association of Southeast Asian Nations (ASEAN), NAFTA, the planned EU expansion, MERCOSUR (the Latin American Southern Cone trade bloc), and proposed regional agreements in Africa. Second, special access agreements often create domestic sugar industries that are dependent on externally determined policies and give rise to domestic policies designed to allocate rents from the agreements, as happened in Cuba, Fiji, the Philippines, and Zimbabwe.

Protection and Trade Agreements

Because interventions by large countries depress world prices, international prices undervalue the domestic resources employed in sugar production. To address this imbalance countries generally choose to ignore the ongoing opportunity to consume cheap sugar and instead erect protective tariffs that more than compensate domestic producers for the effects of the policies of large economies. In trade negotiations countries tend to aggressively defend their capacity to increase protection further. During the Uruguay Round of the GATT, the EU, Japan, and the United States were able to preserve their protective sugar trade policies through special annex provisions to the general agreement, while most developing countries sought to bind tariffs well in excess of applied levels.[4] For 1995, sugar exporters on average bound their tariffs at 92 percent; sugar importers' tariff bindings averaged 117 percent. By 2004 the tariff bindings will average 79 percent for sugar exporters and 98 percent for sugar importers (tables 4.4 and 4.5).

Regional trade agreements frequently must address differences in sugar policies. The entry of the United Kingdom into the European Community in 1973, as well as the United Kingdom's commitments under the 1951 Commonwealth Sugar Agreement, significantly changed European sugar policy. The Commonwealth Agreement formalized traditional colonial sugar imports and gave Commonwealth countries preferential access to the United Kingdom and Canadian sugar markets. The United Kingdom nego-

Table 4.4 Tariff Bindings for Raw Sugar Pledged under WTO Agreements (importing countries)

Country	Ad valorem equivalents (%)[a]	
	1995	2000 (2004)
Algeria	35	—
Canada	C$24.12/T	8.24
Cyprus	25	25
Egypt, Arab Rep. of	20	20
Finland	—	316
Indonesia	110	95
Iceland	350	175
Japan	337	287
Kenya	100	100
Korea, Rep. of	23.7	18
Kuwait	100	100
Macao	100	100
Malaysia	17	15
Mexico	120	96
Morocco	221	168
New Zealand	0	0
Niger	200	200
Nigeria	150	150
Norway	6	2
Pakistan	150	150
Romania	200	180
Senegal	30	30
Singapore	27	27
Suriname	20	20
Sweden	132	112
Switzerland	211	184
Tanzania	120	120
Tunisia	190	100
Uganda	80	80
United States	176	151
Uruguay	60	35
Venezuela	50	40
Average (percent)	117	98

— Not available.

a. All figures are percentages unless otherwise indicated.

Table 4.5. Tariff Bindings for Raw Sugar Pledged under WTO Agreements (exporting countries)

Country	Ad valorem equivalents (%)[a]	
	1995	2000 (2004)
Antigua and Barbuda	100	100
Argentina	35	35
Australia	43	21.6
Austria	38	32
Barbados	160	122
Belize	60	60
Brazil	85	35
China	100	78
Colombia	117	117
Congo	30	30
Côte d'Ivoire	15	15
Cuba	40	40
Czech Republic	70	59.9
El Salvador	92	70
EU	221	176
Fiji	40	40
Gabon	60	60
Guatemala	100	100
Guyana	100	100
Honduras	35	35
Hungary	86	68
India	150	150
Jamaica	100	100
Madagascar	30	30
Mauritius	122	122
Nicaragua	120	100
Paraguay	35	35
Philippines	100	100
Poland	120	96
St. Vincent and the Grenadines	170	130
South Africa	124	105
Swaziland	124	105
Thailand	104	99
Trinidad	100	100
Turkey	150	135
Zambia	125	125
Average in %	92	79

a. Figures are percentages unless otherwise indicated.
Source: UNCTAD (1997).

tiated a continuation of the agreement's preferences that ultimately resulted in the sugar protocol of the Lomé Convention. The protocol allows 16 countries in Africa, the Caribbean, and the Pacific region preferential entry into the protected EU market. Two countries, Fiji and Mauritius, hold roughly half the annual quota of approximately 1.3 million tons (figure 4.3).

Generally, regional agreements tend to propagate protectionist policies toward countries outside the agreement. In Poland, for example, protectionist policies were introduced in anticipation of a regional agreement. In the early 1990s Poland was in the process of privatizing its domestic sugar market while pursuing regional trade agreements with the EU. The legislative outcome was the September 1994 Sugar Industry Act, which established both the country's sugar marketing policy and its privatization policy. Under the act the Council of Ministers sets domestic production quotas for the domestic market (A-quota) and for subsidized exports (B-quota). Additional sugar (C-sugar) must be exported without subsidies. Levies on A- and B-quota sugar are intended to finance export subsidies. High tariff rates protect the domestic market, and a government agency purchases

Figure 4.3 Sugar Quotas for Preferential Imports from African, Caribbean, and Pacific Group Countries

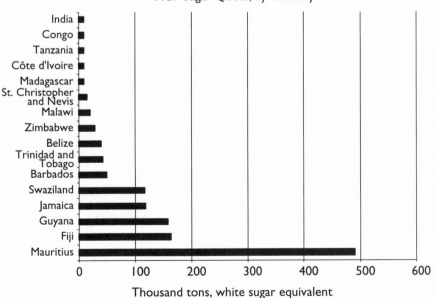

ACP Sugar Quota, by Country

Thousand tons, white sugar equivalent

Source: Harris and Tangermann (1993).

sugar in order to support minimum farm prices. In addition, some countries, such as Romania, have special access to the Polish market under the Central European Free Trade Agreement. Romania was granted an allowance of 5,000 tons of raw beet sugar at a reduced tariff in 1998.

The terms of trade in sweeteners between the United States and Mexico that are embodied in NAFTA also illustrate this point. Following a period of increasing government intervention, the Mexican government nationalized sugar mills during the 1970s. The experiment proved unsuccessful, and by 1990, when plans for NAFTA were first announced, Mexico had completed a substantial privatization of its sugar mills. Following privatization the government put in place fixed tariffs of 10 and 15 percent for raw and refined sugar, respectively. The result was a larger than anticipated flow of imports, and prices fell (figure 4.3).

In January 1991 the government intervened, setting a reference price defended by a variable tariff. The variable tariff remained in place as the terms of NAFTA were negotiated.[5] The terms of NAFTA called for a 15-year phased-in reduction in tariffs between the United States and Mexico that began on January 1, 1994. In addition, the governments of Mexico and the United States agreed to harmonize their tariff schedules for non-NAFTA countries by 1999. Shortly after signing the agreement, Mexico quickly moved its tariffs to levels close to those of the United States.

NAFTA also illustrates how new policy interventions can generate unexpected consequences and prompt irreversible policy-based investments. The agreement between Mexico and the United States affected tariffs for sugar and other sweeteners, most notably high-fructose corn syrup. The increased tariffs were a boon for the Mexican sugar industry, and new investments in sugar increased. But the protection also created opportunities to manufacture alternative sweeteners, since tariff rates for high-fructose corn sweeteners would fall faster than sugar tariffs (table 4.6). By 1996 imported sweeteners had begun to compete with domestic sugar as Mexican and U.S. firms announced new investments in Mexico. This development was in part attributable to the advantage NAFTA temporarily afforded corn sweeteners over sugar—an advantage that provided an opportunity for the industry to cover the high fixed costs associated with the sweetener industry (such as transportation systems and corn wet-milling plants). The industry was able to capture some of the benefits Mexican negotiators had expected to flow to smallholder cane producers and newly privatized Mexican sugar mills.

Dependence on the Trade Policies of Other Countries

Special access arrangements are an important component of the international sugar market. Two significant programs—those of the United States

Table 4.6 Selected Policy Variables for the Mexican-U.S. Agreement on Sugar Trade

Year	U.S. tariff rates for Mexican sugar exports — Within quota Raw	Within quota Refined	Above quota Raw	Above quota Refined	Duty-free quota Guaranteed	Duty-free quota Potential	Mexican tariff rates for high-fructose corn syrup (percent)	NAFTA year	Common U.S.-Mexican import duty for third-party countries (Cents per pound)
	Cents per pound				Raw equivalent tons				
1994	0	0	15.60	16.53	7,258	25,000	15.0	1	—
1995	0	0	15.20	16.11	7,258	25,000	13.5	2	—
1996	0	0	14.80	15.69	7,258	25,000	12.0	3	—
1997	0	0	14.40	15.26	7,258	25,000	10.5	4	—
1998	0	0	14.00	14.84	7,258	25,000	9.0	5	—
1999	0	0	13.60	14.42	7,258	25,000	7.5	6	—
2000	0	0	12.09	12.81	7,258	250,000	6.0	7	15.36 / 16.21
2001	0	0	10.58	11.21	7,258	250,000	4.5	8	15.36 / 16.21
2002	0	0	9.07	9.61	7,258	250,000	3.0	9	15.36 / 16.21
2003	0	0	7.56	8.01	7,258	250,000	1.5	10	15.36 / 16.21
2004	0	0	6.04	6.41	7,258	250,000	0.0	11	15.36 / 16.21
2005	0	0	4.53	4.81	7,258	250,000	0.0	12	15.36 / 16.21
2006	0	0	3.02	3.20	7,258	250,000	0.0	13	15.36 / 16.21
2007	0	0	1.51	1.60	7,258	250,000	0.0	14	15.36 / 16.21
2008	0	0	0.00	0.00	7,258	250,000	0.0	15	15.36 / 16.21

— Not applicable.

and the EU—are especially long-lived. As already mentioned, the Lomé Convention gives a number of countries in Africa, Asia, and the Caribbean with colonial ties to Europe quota-based preferential access to the protected EU sugar market. The United States also provides preferential access to developing countries, although it has long used tariffs on imported sugar as a source of revenue.[6] In addition, from 1934 until 1974 the United States employed import quotas and marketing allotments to manage domestic output and prices (Schmitz and Christian 1993.) At this time countries that had been granted tariff preferences were granted quotas along with domestic producers. During the volatile period from 1975 to 1981, when sugar prices reached record heights, the United States experimented with several programs, including some that obligated the government to purchase sugar at a minimum price. Tariffs were managed to prevent large government outlays. In 1982 quotas were reintroduced, and a modified tariff-quota scheme remained in place in 2000.[7] The U.S. Trade Representative rather than the U.S. Department of Agriculture manages the allotment of quotas to traditional U.S. trading partners (table 4.7).

Access to the protected U.S. and EU markets can be valuable. For example, Sturgis, Field, and Young (1990) estimate that U.S. sugar policies transferred as much as $120 million to the small economy of the Dominican Republic in 1984. Wong, Sturgis, and Borrell (1989) estimate that the Lomé Convention transferred more than $200 million to Mauritius in 1985. Participation in these programs can also reduce the risk of price volatility. Herrmann and Weiss (1995) for example, calculate that 17 to 42 percent of the welfare benefits associated with the EU program come from stabilization effects.

While the transfer and stabilization benefits are clearly significant, the effects of special access on development are subject to debate. For example, while reviewing the effects of the Lomé commodity protocols, the European Commission (1996) concluded:

> The impact of trade preferences has been disappointing by and large. Preferential arrangements, especially the protocols on specific products, have contributed significantly to the commercial success of some countries that managed to respond with appropriate diversification policies. But the bulk of ACP countries have lacked the economic policies and the domestic conditions needed for developing trade.

Similarly, the World Bank (1995) found that Fiji's preferential access to the EU and U.S. markets generated limited development impact.[8]

Table 4.7 U.S. Sugar Quota Allocations, 1996–97

Country	Allocation in tons	Country	Allocation in tons
Argentina	87,236	Nicaragua	42,604
Australia	168,387	Panama	58,833
Barbados	11,359	Papua New Guinea	7,258
Belize	22,198	Paraguay	7,322
Bolivia	16,229	Peru	83,179
Brazil	293,482	Philippines	273,881
Colombia	48,690	South Africa	46,199
Congo (Brazzaville)	7,258	St. Christopher-Nevis	7,258
Costa Rica	30,374	Swaziland	31,981
Côte d'Ivoire	7,258	Taiwan, China	24,396
Dominican Republic	357,060	Thailand	28,404
Ecuador	22,275	Trinidad-Tobago	14,020
El Salvador	52,747	Uruguay	7,691
Fiji	18,258	Zimbabwe	24,223
Gabon	7,258	Subtotal raw cane sugar	2,097,121
Guatemala	97,229		
Guyana	24,062	Mexico (NAFTA)	25,000
Haiti	7,258	Mexico (Sept. 1997	
Honduras	20,287	allocation)	—
India	16,229	Canada (Sept. 1997	
Jamaica	21,478	allocation)	—
Madagascar	7,252	Specialty sugars	1,656
Malawi	20,287	Other refined sugars	20,344
Mauritius	24,346	Subtotal refined sugars	47,000
Mexico	25,000		
Mozambique	26,375	Total	2,119,115

Source: USDA.

As discussed, under the EU and U.S. programs the lion's share of special-access quotas goes to a few countries. But even when the share of the total quota itself is relatively small, the effect on sugar industries in small countries can be profound. In some countries the sugar industry is highly dependent on special trade arrangements. In a handful of small countries, the agricultural sector and general economy also rely on sugar and special trading arrangements. According to data from the FAO, 10 countries depended on sugar exports for more than 10 percent of their export earnings between 1994 and 1996 (figure 4.4.) All had special trade arrangements during the period.

Figure 4.4 Sugar's Average Share of Total Merchandise Exports, Selected Countries, 1994–96

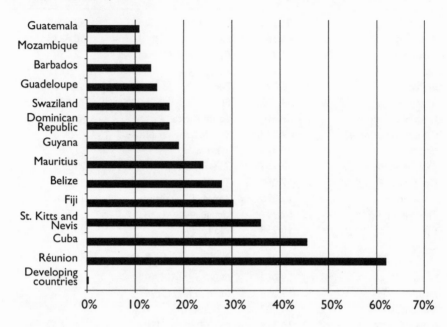

Source: FAO.

Special trade arrangements in sugar can be profitable while they are in place, but depending on foreign policy rather than world markets can be risky. Unlike market-related risks, policy changes tend to be abrupt and impossible to hedge. The turbulent history of the Cuban sugar industry illustrates this point.[9] The Cuban sugar industry grew fivefold between 1904 and 1925, reaching 5 million tons, or 23 percent of world production. Most of the sugar went to the protected U.S. market under a special trade arrangement. At the time U.S. companies were heavily invested in Cuba. Pollitt (1988) reports that by 1927, direct U.S. interests in Cuban sugar mills, railroads, and land exceeded $600 million, partly because U.S. banks had foreclosed on several large sugar mills in 1921. Pollitt also notes that U.S.-owned mills owned or leased 40 percent of Cuba's farmland in 1926–27 and accounted for an estimated 60 percent or more of output. By 1929 Cuban exports (some 77 percent of the island's sugar production) met half of U.S. sugar consumption. The livelihood of nearly two-thirds of the Cuban population depended directly or indirectly on sugar (Braga 1997).

In 1930, however, as the Depression hit the United States and domestic demand fell, the U.S. government moved to protect domestic producers and territorial production in Hawaii, the Philippines, and Puerto Rico. By 1932

Cuban sugar production had fallen to about 2.5 million tons and was commanding very low prices on the world market. Workers' incomes dropped significantly, and during the 1933 revolution farmers and workers seized many of the sugar mills. Following the revolution, the Cuban share of a much smaller U.S. market fell to 25 percent, and sugar production fell to slightly more than 2 million tons. The reduced export levels were institutionalized in the Jones-Costigan Act of 1934, which also increased the Philippines' quota of 1 million tons (this amount was later reduced to 800,000 tons). Between 1929 and 1933 some 38 mills were shut down. Because local communities were dependent on the mills for their livelihood, by 1937 the government had intervened to reopen 32 facilities.

Cuban sugar production recovered during World War II, reaching 6 million tons in 1947. About half of Cuba's sugar went to the protected U.S. market, while the rest entered the world market. But the Cuban Revolution of 1959 and the U.S. embargo of 1960 brought about a structural change in the Cuban economy and the sugar industry. During the next three decades, Cuba became dependent on Soviet-bloc countries not only as outlets for sugar but also (and more importantly) as trading partners for inputs, especially petroleum (Pollitt 1988, Pollitt and Hagelberg 1994). During the 1970s the implicit transfers grew (Early and Westfall 1996 and figure 4.5).[10] This relationship affected technology choices as well as decisions about output levels. When the Soviet bloc collapsed, the second Cuban sugar crisis occurred. From 1990 to 1992 production fell from 8.2 million tons to 7 million tons. As Pollitt and Hagelberg (1994) point out, the loss of premium sugar prices and Soviet credit facilities exacerbated falling export volumes, and Cuba's import capacity fell from 8.1 billion pesos in 1989 to 2.2 billion pesos in 1992. The 1993 crop fell to 4.2 million tons, costing the country over $450 million in lost export revenue (figure 4.6.)

Special trade arrangements often give rise to domestic controls that affect the way the benefits are distributed. The domestic arrangements in turn lead to entitlements. The Philippine market-sharing arrangement, the *quedan*, illustrates this point. Following the U.S. takeover of the Philippines in 1898, Philippine sugar interests were granted a series of preferences, partly at Cuba's expense. The Philippine government, following guidelines set out by the U. S. Department of Agriculture (USDA), surveyed the sugar industry and established a three-part quota that allocated specific amounts to the U.S. market, the domestic market, and reserves (Nagano 1988.) The three quotas were distributed among 47 mill districts, each of which contained hundreds of smallholders. Conflicts over cane pricing arose, especially during the 1930s. A sugar-sharing arrangement existed in most milling districts, but a series of surveys by the newly established National Sugar Board in the 1930s revealed large discrepancies in the percentage of sugar the mills took. The board instituted guidelines lim-

Figure 4.5 Prices Paid by the Soviet Union for Cuban Sugar

Soviet contract prices for sugar and implied subsidies

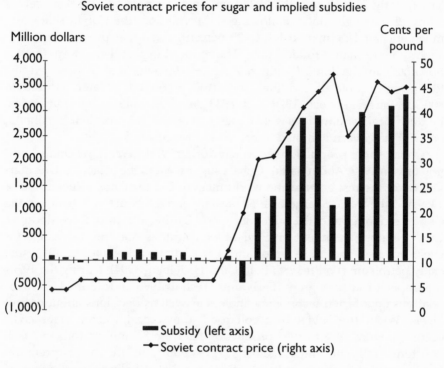

Subsidy (left axis)
Soviet contract price (right axis)

Source: Earley and Westfall (1996).

iting the millers' share to 30 to 54 percent in Luzon and 31 to 52 percent in Negros.

The system has grown in complexity, but it remains in place. The U.S. quota of 1.7 million tons comprised 12 percent of the 1998–99 *quedan* established by the Sugar Board's successor agency, the Sugar Regulatory Agency. Domestic markets are protected with a 65 percent tariff. Current policies result in market sharing among Philippine firms. This arrangement distorts marginal pricing, because production decisions are based on average revenues. It also stands in contrast to systems that base marginal production decisions on marginal profits, forcing marginal production onto world markets at going prices. The system also provides distorted incentives, as production levels also potentially affect access to protected U.S. markets. Consequently firms that do not fare well in domestic markets may survive because of profits from sales to the U.S. market. In addition fixed revenue sharing between producers and millers discourages millers from achieving better extraction rates.[11]

Figure 4.6 Sugar Production Swings in Cuba, 1960–96

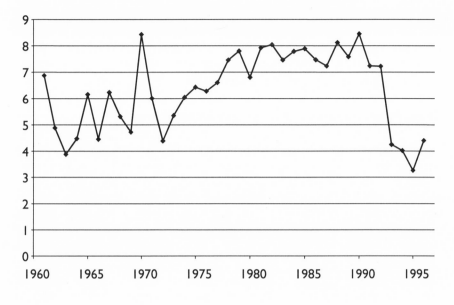

Source: FAO.

Mauritius provides an example of the way in which dependence on special access can generate legislative barriers to diversification. In that country special conditions for workers, special land market regulations, and other regulations specific to the sugar industry lock in resources to ensure that Mauritius produces enough sugar to meet its EU quota. As a result opportunities for productivity-enhancing diversification are limited and sugar production eats up virtually all the arable land—some 70 percent in 1998 (FAO 2000).

While special access to protected markets generates potential benefits, the allocation of those benefits depends on domestic policies. Domestic sugar industries do not always retain the benefits of special trading arrangements. Mlambo and Pangeti (1996) argue that in Zimbabwe the government, intent on political expedience, often set domestic prices below the cost of production during the transition to independence in 1979 (and subsequently throughout much of the 1980s). This policy transferred profits from special access to the EU and U.S. markets from the four private estates to domestic consumers.

In Fiji, the sugar industry, dependent on special access to the EU and U.S. markets, generates about 22 percent of the country's GDP, 40 percent of its agricultural GDP, and 40 percent of its export earnings. The program has brought marginal lands into sugar production, and some benefits are vested in potentially higher land prices. Still, much of the land had been farmed under 30-year leases negotiated around 1970. As the leases expire, the fight over how the benefits of these trade arrangements should be reflected in land rents has been bitter. The conflict is especially acrid because Indian-Fijians are 75 percent of Fiji's sugar farmers, and 73 percent of Indian-Fijians lease their lands (Reddy and Yanagida 1998).

Policies, Sugar Markets, and Sugar Production

Like the international sugar market, domestic markets are characterized by extensive interventions and a complicated political economy. As mentioned earlier, many of the interventions are based on special long-standing trade arrangements. Other issues important to domestic markets relate to the role of sugar as a basic food item, the physical characteristics of sugar production, and certain features of the industry's organization and of factor ownership.

Food Security

Because sugar is a basic food item, and because sugar prices are volatile, governments often intervene in sugar markets in order to maintain food security. But while it is often important as a basic food item, sugar is not a diet staple like rice, maize, and a handful of other crops. Governments nevertheless apply policies driven by the need to maintain food security to a handful of commodities that are perceived as essential, including sugar. Typically these policies, like those in China and India, are designed to protect the sugar industry.

Current policy in India dates back to the Defense of India Act of 1939, which aimed to limit speculation and hoarding during World War II, and to the tragic Bengal famine of 1942 that claimed 2 million to 3 million lives (World Bank 1996.) In 1955 the Essential Commodities Act established a wide range of policy instruments to control the storage, trade, and prices of food crops, including sugar. Over the years both the central and state governments imposed additional controls on the industry. In India sugar is produced by almost 5 million smallholders on plots that are generally less than one hectare. The country has more than 400 sugar mills, of which 60 percent are cooperatives, 15 percent public, and the remaining 25 percent private. Until the end of the 1990s, when the government began to grant licenses to private traders, the State Trading Corporation monopolized imports and exports. The government still sets import levels. The federal and state governments also subsidize farm inputs, especially water and fertilizer, and sometimes offer soft loans to mills. Mills are restricted in the amount of land they can own and may purchase cane only from administered zones.

The genesis of China's sugar policy is harder to trace, but the 1959–62 famine that killed 15–30 million people influenced the drive for self-sufficiency in all food items, including sugar (Riskin 1995.)[12] The country's domestic and trade policies are not consistent, however, and provide contradictory incentives. Trade with other countries—and sometimes trade among regions—is subject to regional and central government controls, and the government owns many sugar mills. Domestic sugar prices tend to be high—around 50 percent more than international prices in 1997 (FAO 1997).

Sugar Production

Sugar production has two cost components: field and processing. For most agricultural crops production, storage, and processing are independent activities, and markets exist for both processed and unprocessed commodities. But field and factory costs in the sugar industry (from cane to raw sugar) are interdependent. Despite this characteristic, fully integrated sugar companies are unusual outside of Sub-Saharan Africa.[13] In most countries, sugar producers and processors are separate economic entities that can achieve economic efficiency only through cooperative behavior.

Sugar cane is bulky and degrades soon after harvesting. The high cost of transporting it creates local monopolies and monopsonies. Conflicts between producers and processors are common and are often exacerbated by the need to share costs. For example, minimizing field costs often requires a planting and harvesting cycle that produces cane for processing during a relatively short period. But the increased sugar-processing capacities needed during this period raise mill owners' fixed costs. Spreading deliveries over an extended period minimizes processing costs. As a result scheduling and pricing conflicts often emerge between producers and processors and frequently spill over into political confrontations.

Land policies and ownership often influence sugar policies as well, for two reasons. First, policies on land ownership influence the organization of the industry, usually by limiting the scope for integrating production and processing. Second, since the value of land for sugar production and sugar producers' income levels depend on proximity to an efficient sugar mill, investment and production decisions tend to become matters of public debate in areas with many small or medium-sized cane growers. For this reason governments often intervene to take over failing sugar mills. Governments, on the whole, are rarely good at running sugar mills, and the mills are often resold to the private sector.[14]

The history of sugar production in Mexico illustrates these themes. Prior to the Mexican Revolution large landowners controlled and integrated cane cultivation and processing. The revolution resulted in a restructuring of the industry, especially in the state of Morelos, the heart of the country's sugar industry. But Morelos was also the center of the peasant-based Zapatista Movement (Crespo 1988). By 1921 many of the country's sugar mills had been destroyed and much of the irrigated sugar-growing land was transferred from the large plantations to peasant cooperatives. A new and successful structure emerged based on smallholder cane producers and private sugar mills with concentrated ownership.[15] The implicit mill cartelization was formalized in 1932 with the establishment of Azúcar, a miller-owned organization that was granted a marketing monopoly on sugar. The association set quotas and organized exports of subsidized sugar in order to maintain domestic prices above world levels. Financing was organized through a government-subsidized bank, Banco Azúcareros, SA.

Despite these changes, tensions between growers and millers remained high, and in 1938 the industry was reorganized. Government ministries were allocated voting rights in the cartel. Over time the government's role in the affairs of the sugar industry grew. Because local economies depended on the sugar mills, the mills were not allowed to fail. In many instances the government took over mills that were no long viable or that had been at the center of disputes with growers. By the mid-1980s the government owned 75 percent of the country's sugar mills, which by law could not own or lease land for cane production. Azúcar retained its marketing monopoly. The government intervened further by subsidizing cane growers, paying agricultural insurance premiums, and mandating special social security payments for sugar producers. Prices were regulated along the entire marketing stream. Producer prices were not directly linked to wholesale prices, and cane growers received a common payment regardless of the sugar content of their cane. Government-owned sugar mills were overstaffed and productivity levels declined. Despite its monopoly, Azúcar began running deficits that the Treasury was forced to absorb (Telléz 1995.)

REGULATING CANE PRICES AND SHARED REVENUES. In the examples above governments chose to solve the conflicts between cane producers and mill owners through forced vertical integration. Another approach involves mandating revenue-sharing rules. The value of cane delivered to a mill is determined by the sugar content of the cane and the ease with which the mill can extract the sugar. High-value cane has a low fiber content, a high sucrose content, and high juice purity—that is, low levels of soluble impurities—and is free of debris. Many factors along the production chain affect the quality of cane at the mill: natural endowments such as rainfall and soil quality; production methods, such as the variety of cane planted and the methods used to harvest it; and the promptness with which the cane is delivered.

Unfortunately, pricing systems that create the proper incentives require a degree of sophistication that is difficult to legislate and is likely to arise only from truly cooperative approaches. Poorly conceived approaches, while easier to administer, encourage misdirected efforts. For example, until recently growers in Colombia were paid according to the weight of the cane they delivered to the mill. The practice encouraged cane production but discouraged attention to quality. In Mauritius, the Philippines, and South Africa, sugar revenues are shared according to a fixed rate. Consequently a portion of the efficiency gains generated by new investments in sugar mills accrues to the cane growers. This practice effectively taxes improvements in milling efficiency. Table 4.8 provides a cross-section of various cane-pricing methods.[16]

MORE ON FACTOR MARKETS. As mentioned previously, the political economies of land and sugar are often intertwined. But land and sugar policies can be linked in other ways as well. In the Philippines only 10 percent of sugar cane farms are irrigated, although the returns to irrigation are substantial, increasing yields by 60 to 70 percent. Uncertainty over land reform, which limits incentives to improve land, is perhaps the primary reason so little land is irrigated. In a 1990 survey by the Management Association of the Philippines, 60 percent of respondents who together hold 72,000 hectares said that they had reduced or put off farming investments because of uncertainty over land reform (Borrell and others 1994).

Sugar cane production in St. Kitts and Nevis occupies almost half the islands' arable land. The sugar enters the United States and the EU under preferential trade arrangements. In 1975 the government intervened to nationalize the failing sugar industry, acquiring 52 privately owned estates and one sugar factory. As a result the government became the largest property owner in St. Kitts. In 1992 the government began leasing out land under 35-year agreements.

Water policies are often linked to sugar policies as well. Mlambo and Pangeti (1996) provide a step-by-step account of the efforts made by Zimbabwe's governments to provide water to the country's sugar-growing areas. In 1970 the government of Senegal signed a special agreement with the Compagnie Sucrière du Senegal that provided the firm with a free 99-year lease on land near Guiers Lake, with guaranteed free access to irrigation water (up to 20,000 cubic meters per hectare). The agreement also granted the company production and trade monopolies that were protected by quotas and tariffs. The arrangement remained in place for nearly 25 years, effectively immobilizing regional irrigation and land assets (World Bank 1995.) And in India, states and the national government provide farmers with access to subsidized water, power, fertilizer, and credit. Because producing sugar requires more of these inputs than most other crops in India, the policies favor sugar over other crops. And because rainfall and soil conditions differ across regions, the subsidies also favor some geographic areas over others (World Bank 1996.)

Table 4.8 Payments Systems for Cane

Country	Basis for sampling and testing — Individual growers	Average of growers	Cane analysis — Direct	Indirect	Extraneous matter	Relative payment scheme	Basis of payment[a]	Valuation of Cane[a]
Argentina		✓		✓	✓		TRS	Negotiated TRS
Australia				✓	✓	✓	CCS	Variable RS
Colombia (traditional)	✓[b]			✓			Weight of cane	Fixed RS
Colombia (new)	✓[c]						TRS	Fixed RS
Fiji	✓				✓		Weight of cane	Fixed RS[f]
India	✓		✓[e]			✓	Weight of cane	Fixed cane price[e]
Jamaica	✓[g]		✓[e]			✓	TRS	Variable RS
Mauritius	✓						TRS	Fixed RS
Mexico	✓[h]			✓	✓		TRS	Fixed RS
Philippines	✓		✓[i]				TRS	Fixed RS[l]
South Africa	✓					✓	Cane sucrose	Fixed RS[k]
Thailand	✓			✓	✓		Content	Fixed RS[m]
U.S. (Florida)	✓			✓	✓		CCS	Fixed RS
U.S. (Louisiana)	✓		✓[f]		✓		Cane sucrose	Fixed RS

Notes:

a. TRS = theoretically recoverable sugar; CCS = commercial cane sugar; RS = revenue share.
b. Individual samples of first-expressed juice, factory average fiber for particular cane variety.
c. Individual samples of first-expressed juice. This system is operating in several mills but not industrywide.
d. Fixed each year according to the industry average.
e. By core/press method.
f. Fixed in some states regardless of factory recovery, in others determined by factory recovery.
g. Cane testing for groups of growers when individual cane production is less than 500 metric tons per season.
h. Individual samples of first-expressed juice, factory average fiber.
i. Fixed according to the mill's total sugar output.
j. Sample taken after cane preparation and before milling.
k. From 1994–95 based on proceeds from two pools; from 1998–99 based on a single average sugar price for domestic and export sales.
l. Individual samples of first-expressed juice, factory average fiber.
m. Fixed at the industry level at 70:30 grower:miller. However, the cane price earned by individual growers takes account of individual CCS.

Sugar processing is capital intensive, requiring large fixed investments. Mills must acquire working capital to cover the period between the harvest, when mills buy cane, and the eventual sales of processed sugar. When governments direct credit to mills and farmers, sugar market reforms depend on the ability of mills, farmers, and financial institutions to forge new structures. During times of economic hardship, the new structures can be severely tested and sometimes fail. The Mexican experience again provides an effective example. During the privatization of the country's mills in 1990, many facilities were purchased by means of leveraged buyouts, with the mill serving as collateral. When the financial crises hit the Mexican market and interest rates rose dramatically, the highly indebted mills were unable to raise working capital. In September 1995 a debt-restructuring package worth 8.2 billion pesos was offered through Financiera Nacional Azúcarera (FINASA), a Mexican development bank—a move that meant FINASA's entire portfolio would be tied up in sugar-related assets.[17]

Sugar Market Reforms: Why and How

Policy interventions are pervasive in sugar markets, affecting global and domestic prices, incomes, and investment decisions. Although sugar markets were largely exempted from the trade reforms negotiated during the Uruguay Round of the GATT, in the 1990s a number of countries began the process of freeing domestic markets. As with other commodity markets, external events forced these changes in some countries (see chapter 1). Donors and multilateral lenders often encouraged reforms. In some cases reforms came about because of a change in the regime and were part of a broad agenda designed to reduce overall government intervention.

Governments that had collectively and individually intervened to manage commodity prices and price volatility began dismantling their interventionist systems and looking to private markets and market instruments to manage risk (Larson, Varangis, and Yabuki 1998.) Sweeping changes brought about by the breakup of the Soviet Union markedly altered the trade patterns of the former republics and their trading partners. Most countries, like Bulgaria, Poland, Hungary, Latvia, Russia, and Ukraine, took the first tentative steps toward creating private markets for sugar behind protective tariffs. Similarly in Indonesia the East Asian economic crisis triggered trade liberalization for several commodities, including sugar, although the government remains a significant owner of sugar mills and plantations.

Broad policy changes affecting the role of government, often the result of new electoral mandates, sparked domestic reforms in sugar industries in Brazil, Mexico, and Peru. Changes in international institutions' approaches to agriculture in development and the role of government in commodity markets also influenced market reform—indirectly through policy debate and directly through policy-based lending. Finally, the demise of commodity agreements in coffee and cocoa brought commodity market reforms to several countries (such as Brazil and Uganda), generating concurrent reform of the domestic sugar markets.[18] Often reforms were less sudden, motivated partly by a growing recognition of the failure of the public sector to perform and partly by the recommendations of donors and multilateral lenders. In Africa—for example in Chad, Côte d'Ivoire, and Kenya—the sugar industry is undergoing a slow process of privatization.

Many of the factors that motivated government intervention remain, however. In particular special trade arrangements still dominate exports from several countries, tensions between producers and processors are inherent in the organizational structure of many sugar industries, and conflicts remain over how to manage and price scarce water resources. And sugar reforms often take place amid reforms in factor and other markets. Thus, while the motivation to reform is often present, opposing forces can slow down the reform process.

Australia: Freeing Markets

Before Australia reformed its sugar policies, it maintained stringent production and marketing controls. These controls were first implemented in the 1930s to comply with the first International Sugar Agreement. Imports were restricted and regulations that established a two-tier pricing worked to the disadvantage of domestic consumers. In Queensland, where most of the country's sugar is grown, the Queensland Sugar Board set annual limits on the amount of sugar each mill could provide to the highest-priced "number 1 pool." Amounts that exceeded the quota were sold into the lower-priced export market. Farmers and processors discovered that they could profitably compete, even at international prices, and production expanded. Despite the implicit transfer from consumers to producers via the number 1 pool, marginal investment decisions were based on international prices. The industry, especially in Queensland, grew less dependent on domestic markets. Gains in milling efficiency flowed to millers, and farmers captured increases in field productivity because of well-structured cane-pricing rules.

Reforms began in 1989–90, when an import tariff replaced the import ban. The governments of Australia and Queensland reviewed the country's sugar policy in 1996. The review process itself was considered integral to the reforms because it established a broadly accepted factual basis for discussion. As a result of the review, the government eliminated that import tariff in July 1997 and converted the sugar board to the Queensland Sugar Corporation. The new corporation retains its monopoly on sugar marketing but sells to local refiners at export parity prices. In general the industry received the changes well. The reforms attracted new investments, and both production and milling capacity expanded. Adjustment difficulties occurred in the smaller New South Wales industry, which was more dependent on domestic markets. In response, the Australian government initiated a study examining ways the government can assist the industry during transition.

Brazil: Unwinding Cross-Subsidies

In the 1990s Brazilian policymakers began reforming the long-standing policies that had originated during the oil shocks of the 1970s (Borrell, Bianco, and Bale 1994). Brazil is one of the largest and most efficient sugar producers in the world, but for two decades up to two-thirds of its output was devoted to producing ethanol for the country's subsidized alternative fuel program, PROALCOOL. The government managed domestic supplies, allocating quotas to each of the more than 370 sugar mills and distilleries. The quotas were earmarked for the domestic sugar and ethanol markets, and above-quota production was eligible for export (and subject to export taxes). However, quotas were reallocated annually, and production above quota was frequently rewarded with a larger quota the following year. Domestic prices for sugar and ethanol were set to encourage the use of sugar for ethanol, and in most years the world price of sugar exceeded the domestic price. Further, regional producers faced differential tax rates on sugar and ethanol purchase prices. Beginning in 1995 steep export taxes replaced licensing as the primary instrument for managing the sugar trade, ushering in the first of many reforms.

Part of the reform process involved disentangling the interrelated controls on Brazil's sugar and ethanol markets. In 1996 the government took several important steps in this direction by reducing and then eliminating the export tax on sugar and deregulating the market for anhydrous alcohol (a sugar cane–based alcohol blended with domestic gasoline). In addition the government transferred the alcohol subsidy from fuel distributors to alcohol producers and moved toward establishing a uniform tax on sugar production.[19] The reforms aim in part to limit subsidies to a fixed quota per mill, so that additional alcohol production will be sold at market prices. The government also began looking at alternative ways to finance the program, including a "green tax" on gasoline.[20] In 1999 the deregulated sugar industry was still dependent on policies directing sugar toward domestic alcohol and fuel policies—a situation that developed partly because of the types of automobiles common in Brazil. The Brazilian automotive industry produces two types of cars: those that run on alcohol alone, and those that run on a blend of alcohol and gasoline. During the 1980s most new Brazilian cars were powered by alcohol (96 percent in 1986), but in the 1990s the number of alcohol-powered cars dropped markedly, and in 2000, 99 percent of new

Brazilian cars were running on blended fuel. Demand for alcohol declined. In response the government mandated purchases of cars powered by renewable energy sources and offered taxi drivers incentives to buy alcohol-powered cars. In addition the government used alcohol inventories to manage alcohol prices, affecting sugar mills' decision to produce alcohol or sugar from cane. In 1999 the government also temporarily boosted the required alcohol content for blended fuel from 20 to 24 percent in order to stimulate demand.

Thailand: Limiting the Distortions from Preferential Prices

Although costly to consumers, Thai sugar policies are designed so that marginal production decisions are based on world prices.[21] Under the Thai program imports are banned in order to raise domestic consumer prices. Three categories of sugar are produced: A quota (for domestic consumption), B quota (for export under long-term contracts), and C quota (for export at world prices). Around 60 percent of Thailand's sugar is produced as C-quota sugar. The A and B quotas are fixed each year, so the industry knows any additional production will command only world prices. Thus while the program transfers income from consumers to producers and millers, the transfers do not affect marginal production decisions.

Net revenue from the three types of sugar sales is split 70:30 between producers and millers, based on the average recoverable sugar content as determined by sampling. Averaging the sugar content discourages individuals from improving cane quality, but millers benefit by improving extraction rates and are penalized if those rates fall below 70 percent. In this way the system encourages millers to maintain their facilities. Thailand's approach can be useful for countries receiving preferential access to either EU or U.S. markets. The Thai system contrasts sharply with the approach taken in the Philippines, where preferential access to the U.S. market distorts marginal incentives.

Pricing Cane: Cooperative Strategies from Jamaica and Mexico

Well-conceived cane-pricing systems reward farmers for delivering high-quality cane to mills in an orderly fashion with no penalties for the mills' inefficiencies. Jamaica, which has many smallholder producers, developed a sophisticated set of incentives by continually improving its pricing system. The country had a tradition of paying cane growers that dated back to 1943. The system—based on individual measures of quality—had been modified over the years. Factory efficiency entered the payment formula in 1972, and in 1991 reforms put in place a revenue-sharing scheme based on relative performance. In the Jamaican system revenues are shared according to a 62:38

ratio when growers produce cane of average quality and millers achieve average efficiency. But growers receive higher prices for higher-quality cane, and millers earn more when efficiency improves, so the revenue shares differ from mill to mill. Sampling techniques and incentives to monitor cane are also more sophisticated (LMC 1997.) The system ensures that, at the margin, increased revenues from improvements in cane quality accrue to the grower, while millers capture any gains from milling efficiency.

Developments in Mexico show how improvements in incentives can be introduced even in a constrained environment. As part of a set of economy-wide reforms, the Mexican government began reforming the sugar industry. Two important legislative changes affected land ownership and cane pricing. In 1992 changes to the Mexican constitution allowed mills to enter into leasing arrangements with smallholders, although in practice sugar mills rarely lease large tracts. More significant in the short run, a presidential decree introduced a new payment system for sugar cane beginning with the 1991–92 season. The decree established a revenue-sharing system that divides the proceeds of sugar sales between cane growers and millers. Cane from many smallholders is assembled at the mill in "group" loads. Mill officials and growers' representatives monitor the cane deliveries. A committee of mill owners and growers establishes penalties that are applied based on debris content and delays in delivering the cut cane. Growers receive payments that are based not only on average quality levels but also on the mill's efficiency, providing a theoretical recovery rate for the mill. When the system was introduced, mills were assigned individual efficiency ratings, but by the 1994–95 season all mills had been assigned a common rating of about 82 percent. On average, mill efficiency in Mexico is closer to 80 percent. The system encourages mills to make efficiency gains, since any improvements accrue to the mills—and indeed several mills have exceeded the official rating. Once the sugar content has been established, an average price for standard sugar is used to value it, and this calculated value is split according to annual government directives. In 1996–97, the growers received 57 percent (LMC International 1997).

The Mexican example also shows how initial conditions and practical limits shape changes in pricing schemes. Because of the traditional government practice of setting pan-Mexican sugar prices, wholesale markets for domestic sugar are not well established, and setting an average price for standard sugar is difficult. Consequently the price is negotiated rather than established by market indicators. In addition, the system still prices sugar based on average cane purity and fiber content, penalizing growers who delay deliveries following cutting and growers who deliver debris. The system encourages some easy-to-measure improvements in quality but not a more sophisticated arrangement that would provide incentives for growers to deliver cane at off-peak times. However, the presidential decree allows

mills and growers to negotiate alternative systems that are mutually beneficial. At San Cristobal, the largest sugar mill in Mexico, growers agreed to
temporarily price their cane according to actual factory efficiency rates
when the mill's owners promised to invest $50 million dollars to improve
the plant's efficiency.

Privatizing Sugar Mills

Privatization is a common component of domestic sugar reforms. Most
countries have concluded that the state is ill suited to running sugar mills.
The process of privatization often reveals conflicting policy objectives, however. One goal of liberalization is to distribute the benefits of a more efficient
sugar industry to sugar consumers. But the need to generate revenues or
eliminate drains on the treasury may encourage governments to privatize
too quickly. Moreover, governments often face considerable pressure to
ensure that privatization does not result in mill closures. As a result governments often boost protection in order to improve the value of the mills
and speed privatization. Governments also face a number of other issues
during privatization, including how to cope with large accumulations of
debt and how to provide potential investors with the information they need
to make wise investment decisions.

USING TRADE PROTECTION. In practice most countries provide high levels of
protection to newly privatized sugar mills, at least temporarily. In providing
this protection governments implicitly tax future consumption to finance the
current government budget. Alternatively governments can fix low rates of
protection that are reflected in the value of the mills and in the prices bid during privatization. In some cases, however, state-owned mills deemed viable
in the long run are so poorly maintained that they fail to cover variable costs
at low rates of protection. For political and budgetary reasons, governments
are reluctant to subsidize the purchasing firms directly and instead choose to
tax future consumption in order to protect producers and workers

In Poland, for example, one purpose of the 1994 Sugar Industry Act was
to provide a stable and profitable environment for the sugar industry (albeit
at the expense of Polish consumers) during the privatization of the industry.[22]
High protection rates and even export subsidies were used to make the mills
more attractive to potential buyers. Despite these efforts the government still
owns most of the industry.[23] In Côte d'Ivoire the government was bound by
its GATT pledge to limit sugar tariffs to 33.3 percent. Yet it chose to provide
added protection while privatizing its industry by basing its 33.3 percent tariff on a reference price that included prices from protected EU and U.S. markets. In effect the system provided a tariff in excess of 100 percent for sugar
imported from world markets. The government of Burkina Faso took a

slightly different approach, lowering average rates of protection but establishing safeguard mechanisms based on a moving average of world prices to safeguard the newly privatized industry in case of sharp price declines.

WRITING OFF DEBT. Resolving debt issues is often a key component of the privatization process. The question of how to resolve large accumulations of debt can slow the privatization process, as it has for Muhoroni, a sugar parastatal in Kenya. Firms that would otherwise find the company attractive are unwilling to bid once they learn the ongoing cost of servicing the debt accumulated during the years of government management. In Brazil sugar mills borrowed heavily from the Sugar and Alcohol Institute Sugar Export Fund during the creation of Brazil's alcohol-fuel program. By 1996 the Bank of Brazil had been forced to renegotiate the debt, then valued at $4.5 billion.

Some governments are more willing than others to write off debt early in the privatization process. This approach provides a direct incentive for private investment and may leave newly privatized firms in a better position to raise working capital. And, as the earlier example from Mexico shows, failure to resolve debt during the privatization process may result in new interventions later.

Addressing the issue of accumulated debt was central to the Peruvian privatization process.[24] In 1969 the military government launched a sweeping agrarian reform program that began with the expropriation of the sugar plantations. Cooperatives were established and charged with running the mills, but in 1975 conflicts developed between the management of the cooperatives and sugar cane growers. As the financial integrity of the sugar mills crumbled, the government experimented with several different kinds of controls. In the early 1990s legislation freed cooperatives to dismantle or reorganize the existing structure, and four of the smallest sugar cooperatives chose to do so. By 1995 the eight largest sugar mills had amassed $538 million in debt to three government agencies and an undisclosed amount to other creditors, traders, and workers. In 1996 the newly elected government issued a legislative decree, the Extraordinary Program of Tax Regularization (PERTA), offering cooperatives three options for repaying their debt to government agencies:

- A cash payment of 40 percent of the debt (the other 60 percent would be forgiven);
- Capitalization of 30 percent of the debt, which would be converted to shares, with the balance forgiven; and
- Installments of 20 percent up front, with payments extended over six years following a two-year grace period (Chullen 1996).

At the government's urging, almost all cooperatives chose the second option.

THE ROLE OF INFORMATION IN PRIVATIZATION. During the initial stages of the privatization process in Peru, private capital was generally available. But it became clear early on that the poor management that often prompts privatization was also reflected in the firms' financial information management systems, making it difficult for all parties to value the firms. Moreover, the procedures governing private investment were unclear, for both making and responding to offers. As investors sought to line up majority stakes, one potential investor (the Kimberley Group) took to the street offering to purchase shares of the medium-size sugar company Paramonga from workers and to pay social benefits to retired workers. The ploy worked, and the firm bought about 55 percent of the workers' shares for approximately $20 million. But the process raised concerns about whether workers knew the value of their shares and were aware of alternative offers. Responding to these concerns, the National Supervisory Commission on Companies and Securities (CONASEV) intervened to suspend share trading at Paramonga.

Investors faced difficulties of their own as well. First, a lack of financial and business information, symptomatic of poor management practices, slowed decisionmaking. Investors interested in purchasing shares had trouble valuing firms because of poor record-keeping.[25] Cooperative members faced similar difficulties in evaluating offers. Early on CONASEV took an active role in getting information to the marketplace by requiring sugar companies to file audited financial reports. In addition the government established transition committees at each estate to facilitate the privatization process. The interventions slowed the privatization process, but by 1998 shares in all 12 of the sugar estates had been distributed. Two of the estates were fully privatized in 1997.

Reforms, Research, and Public Services

As we have seen, pricing systems create the incentives needed to improve the quality of cane. The improvements generally come from enhanced management and the application of existing technologies. The development, adaptation, and testing of new technologies are common goods that can benefit all members of the industry, a fact that has long been recognized. Most sugar-producing economies have an established history of research—for example Taiwan, China, which established the Sugar Cane Nursery and Trial Farm at Ta-mu-jiang (Hsinhwa) in 1900. Similarly the Arab Republic of Egypt's sugar research institute dates back to the 1930s.

In many countries where the government owns the sugar industry, the role of research becomes bundled with market activities. In some cases governments and industry participants fail to find a way to jointly fund research during the privatization process. Before privatization in Mexico a single organization managed the research agenda for the sugar industry.

With privatization research became much more dispersed. Some is conducted at the National Institute for Forestry, Agricultural, and Fishery Research (*El Instituto Nacional de Investigaciones Forestales, Agrícolas y Pecuarias*, or INI-FAP), some at universities such as the Universidad de Inversiones, and some at a research station in Chiapas. In addition almost every mill in the country conducts some research.

While the benefits of research are a common good, the government does not necessarily need to finance it. Since the industry benefits directly from new research, industry members are often willing to provide financing—for example, through a consumption or export levy—if they also have a voice in setting research priorities. The Mauritius Sugar Industry Research Institute is organized along these lines.[26] Following recommendations made by the Mauritius Economic Commission in 1947, the sugar industry decided to conduct its own research. It founded the Mauritius Sugar Industry Research Institute in 1953. The institute is financed by a cess on sugar production and is governed by a Board of Directors with 10 members: 7 representing millers, growers, and the Chamber of Agriculture, and 3 representing the government.

Nationalized sugar mills sometimes provide services to local communities. During privatization governments must be careful to ensure that appropriate institutions take on these tasks. Before privatization the sugar estates in Peru provided electricity, education, and health care and other social services to the community. And while the estates employed around 35,000 workers, up to 215,000 family members and retirees were also directly dependent on the services the estates provided. Although the process was slow and expensive, the government managed to transfer responsibilities to other organizations and agencies. For example, by 1996 Paramonga had transferred nine schools valued at $US 2.1 million to the Ministry of Education.

Lessons and Policy Recommendations

Unlike trade policies for coffee or cocoa, sugar policies are generally designed to subsidize producers at the expense of consumers. Often the benefits are dissipated through inefficient public ownership, captured by competing sweetener producers, or lost to rents on land. Yet the accumulated effects of such policies also give rise to well-defined groups that depend on continued interventions. Often these groups include entire communities that rely on existing policies and the survival of local mills. Since reform usually means structural changes, including at least some mill closings, the political and socials costs of reform are high. For this reason governments have been reluctant to pursue reforms in sugar markets as readily as reforms in other commodity markets (such as coffee and cocoa) even though the economic benefits of such reforms are significant, especially relative to costs.

In general the benefits of domestic reforms accrue primarily to consumers and the economy at large through productivity increases that result when resources flow to optimal uses. Recent experience suggests that sugar reforms are more likely when governments include them in a package of overall market reforms designed to spur lagging economies (as occurred, for instance, in Brazil, Mexico, and Peru). Moreover, governments will pursue true trade liberalization when the costs of reform are relatively low for the industry and the benefits more apparent, as was the case in Australia and Brazil.

Because sugar policies generally tax consumers to subsidize producers, the policies do not directly affect the government budget. In fact import taxes often raise revenue. As a result budgetary crises do not necessarily trigger reforms of sugar policy. However, public ownership of sugar mills also places the burden of new investment in the plants on the public ledger, and public funds are generally limited and their availability is unpredictable. As machinery depreciates and the efficiency of such mills declines, a crisis emerges. Soon the need to raise capital spurs privatization. This experience has been repeated in much of Africa and Latin America, including Chad, Kenya, Mexico, and Peru.

Trade regimes and preferential trade agreements give rise to their own distortions, as they did in Fiji, Mauritius, the Philippines, and St. Kitts, and reliance on the policies of other countries can be risky. When governments join or prepare to join regional trade agreements, new distortions are often introduced, as happened in Mexico and Poland. In contrast the potential gains from multilateral trade liberalization are significant and accrue primarily to developing countries.

Because the consequences of reform differ from country to country, and because of differences in initial conditions, no single blueprint exists for sugar market reforms. But research overwhelmingly suggests that developing countries would benefit not only from multilateral reform but also from unilateral reform. Realizing the potential gains from reform requires establishing a framework that puts in place the proper incentives for both domestic industries and international trade. Finding the political support for sugar reform requires lowering the cost of the transition for those countries and for groups most likely to bear a disproportionate share of those costs, especially the loss of income and wealth. Lessons from earlier experiences suggest that a successful reform strategy has several components:

- For multilateral reforms of sugar markets to succeed, developing countries need to push large sugar-producing and -consuming countries to change their domestic sugar regimes. During the Uruguay

Round negotiations, neither the EU nor the United States was prepared to make significant changes to its domestic regime. In the end the round had a limited effect on the global market.

- The handful of countries that depend on special access to protected sugar markets requires assistance during the reform process. When these countries lose protected markets, the governments will not have the resources to soften the impact on the industry, as Cuba's experience illustrates.
- Even when subsidies exist—either to protect consumers or because of preferential trade agreements—countries must take unilateral action to limit the distortionary effects, as Thailand's experience shows.
- Sugar market reforms may entail reforms in other markets as well. The link between Brazil's sugar and energy policies is one example.
- Clear analysis that identifies and quantifies the direct and indirect economic and welfare impacts of policy changes can provide a consistent and objective framework for negotiating change. Australia's experience supports this notion.
- Mills slated for privatization are often burdened with debt or require large initial capital improvements. Governments provide added trade protection in order to improve the profitability of domestic sugar firms, hoping to entice private investors and speed privatization. This approach taxes consumers and may support competing industries such as corn sweeteners. Peru's experience shows that debt relief is a less distortionary alternative.
- Information about asset values must be available during privatization. Investors need accurate and timely information in order to make wise investment choices. As we saw, the Peruvian government addressed this issue by putting in place uniform reporting rules that provide information to both buyers and sellers during privatization.
- Services provided by large estates before privatization must be transferred to another provider. Sometimes large government-owned estates provide workers common goods such as education and health care. Peru's experience shows that careful planning can minimize disruptions in public services. In Mauritius the government also plays an organizing role in privately financed research.
- Governments must play a constructive role in resolving conflicts between producers and mill owners. The physical characteristics of sugar production can lead to conflicts that often prompt poorly devised government interventions. To avoid such problems, governments can follow Jamaica's example in setting cane-pricing rules, which create the proper economic incentives.

Some Final Thoughts

Public interventions are commonplace in domestic and international markets for sugar. Many of them are long-lived and rooted in historic trade arrangements, fears of shortages, and conflicting interests between growers and sugar mills. Arrangements rooted in colonial eras still shape policies and trade in the United States, the EU, and many developing countries. Responses to key events are frequently added to old policies, or they may precipitate new ones. Throughout the 20th century events encouraged interventions, and the prevailing economic thinking on the role of agriculture in development was used to justify them. Once the policies were in place, households and investments became dependent both on them and on the institutions that support them. These policies and institutions remain in place even as their usefulness fades. Most countries that have experimented with public ownership of sugar-producing estates and mills have found this approach untenable. At the same time successful experience with liberalization in other commodity markets has encouraged several countries to rethink their existing sugar policies. As a result most countries have initiated some measure of sugar market reform.

In addition events related to NAFTA, the Cotonou Agreement, and the expansion of the EU may significantly change the EU and U.S. sugar regimes. Such changes would have important ramifications for many countries. Countries dependent on the sugar policies of other countries can learn from Cuba's turbulent history and begin the difficult process of becoming independent.

No single country experience can teach us all we need to know about successful sugar market reform. But successful solutions for common problems associated with sugar market reform—such as how to determine cane quality, encourage and finance research, and share revenue from joint production fairly—can be found by drawing selectively on country experiences. Finally, the experiences of many countries show that governments intervene in markets for many reasons. In some cases the circumstances that motivated past policies have changed, even when the legacy of those interventions remain. In other instances the underlying problems that have motivated interventions in the past still remain, even when policymakers realize that current approaches have failed. Successful market reform goes beyond eliminating failed policies to finding lasting solutions.

Notes

1. Brazil is an exception.

2. For example, this method is not designed to measure the effects of exchange rates policies. Krueger, Schiff, and Valdés (1992). Among the critics of this method are Strokov and Meyers (1996).

3. For example, see Lord and Barry (1990) for a report on the concentration of benefits in the U.S. fructose corn syrup market and Webb, Lopez, and Penn (1990) on the subsidy component of sugar producer revenue in developed countries.

4. Sugar was an extreme example of the way countries commonly managed the tariffication of the agricultural sectors during the Uruguay Round (Hathaway and Ingco 1996).

5. The NAFTA sweetener agreement, which covered sugar and high-fructose corn syrup, proved especially contentious. One particular point of disagreement was a side-letter that amended the language of the signed version.

6. Preferential treatment was initially a policy instrument designed to protect U.S. interests, especially in Cuba.

7. Domestic marketing allotments were reintroduced briefly in 1990.

8. Prasad (1998) challenges this view. He also notes that challenges to special access arrangements are likely to succeed and calls for an orderly transition to free markets.

9. Pollitt (1988) provides an interesting account of this "first" sugar crises.

10. Because the ruble was not convertible, measures of implied subsidies are open to challenge. See Earley and Westfall (1996), Pollitt and Hagelberg (1994), and Perez-Lopez (1988) for further discussion.

11. See Borrell and others (1994) for a discussion of the costs of Philippine policies.

12. Ironically, the food shortages resulting from the failed Great Leap Forward also pushed the government toward a heavy reliance on internal market mechanisms.

13. Fully integrated sugar industries frequently originated as colonial plantations and in many instances were nationalized at the end of the colonial era. Often the nationalized sugar companies retained monopolies or other special privileges. In Indonesia, for instance, the Dutch plantations were converted into government-owned "people's plantations." In Chad a colonial company was transformed into a joint venture involving the government, the private sector, and a French multinational.

14. Although small and medium-sized producers complicate the political economy of the sugar industry, family-owned farming systems are among the world's most efficient sugar producers. Family ownership creates strong incentives toward long-run stewardship and reduces the costs of monitoring performance. In terms of efficiency, smallholder farms in Thailand compare favorably with large and medium-sized sugar farms in Australia, France, and the United States.

15. By 1934 the top six *ingenios* processed about 56 percent of the country's sugar (Crespo 1988).

16. See LMC (1997) for a more complete discussion of the details, benefits, and drawbacks of the various cane-pricing methods.

17. In some instances smallholder debt can burden local or even national banking systems as well. Reddy and Yanagida (1998) point out that Fijian banks depend heavily on sugar.

18. Earlier agreements on sugar were unsuccessful as well. See Gilbert (1985, 1987, 1996) for a brief history of commodity agreements.

19. Prior to October 1997 the government taxed producers in high-cost production areas at lower rates.

20. Brazil's reforms to its sugar-ethanol market began at a time when markets in "green energy"—usually wind or hydro-based—were developing in Australia, Canada, and the United States. Further, the Clean Development Mechanism established under the Kyoto Protocol should have facilitated this process. See Jacoby, Prinn, and Schmalensee (1998).

21. Borrell et al. (1994) provide a useful contrast between the incentives established by the Thai and Philippine sugar policies.

22. The sugar industry was privatized as part of the economywide privatization begun in 1989.

23. Of the 76 sugar refineries in Poland, 13 are completely privatized, and all but 2 have issued shares. Foreign companies have significant investments in 10 of the mills and controlling interest in at least 4.

24. The government of Uganda took a similar approach when privatizing its cotton industry. See chapter 5.

25. Inadequate record-keeping is a common problem when sugar mills and estates are being privatized. For example, in Kenya the government was unable to establish clear title for several of the sugar parastatals.

26. Visit http://www.cgiar.org/isnar/hosted/msiri/msiri.htm to learn more about the Mauritius Sugar Industry Research Institute.

References

Borrell, Brent, and Ronald Duncan. 1992. "A Survey of the Costs of World Sugar Policies." *World Bank Research Observer* 7(2):171–94.

Borrell, Brent, José R. Bianco, and Malcolm D. Bale. 1994. *Brazil's Sugarcane Sector: A Case of Lost Opportunity*. Policy Research Working Paper 1363. Washington, D.C.: World Bank.

Borrell, Brent, Derek Quirke, and David Vincent. 1991. *Sugar: Winning in a Corrupt World Market*. Canberra: Centre for International Economics.

Borrell, Brent, Derek Quirke, Beulah de la Pena, and Lourdes Noveno. 1994. *Philippine Sugar: An Industry Finding Its Feet*. Canberra: Centre for International Economics.

Braga, Michael. 1997. "To Relieve the Misery: Sugar Mill Workers and the 1933 Cuban Revolution." In Jonathan Brown, ed., *Workers' Control in Latin America, 1930–79*. Chapel Hill: University of North Carolina Press.

Chalmin, Philippe. 1988. "Important Trends in Sugar Diplomacy before 1914." In Bill Albert and Adrian Graves, eds., *The World Sugar Economy in War and Depression, 1914–40*. London: Routledge.

Chullen, Jorge. 1996. "Solving the Cooperatives' Puzzle: The Peruvian Sugar Industry in Transition." *F.O. Licht's International Sugar and Sweetener Report* 128(29): 661–65.

Coleman, Jonathan, and Donald Larson. 1993. "Tariff-based Stabilization of Commodity Prices in Venezuela." In Stijn Claessens and Ronald Duncan, eds., *Managing Commodity Price Risk in Developing Countries.* Baltimore: Johns Hopkins University Press.

Crespo, Horacio. 1988. "The Cartelization of the Mexican Sugar Industry, 1924–40." In Bill Albert and Adrian Graves, eds., *The World Sugar Economy in War and Depression, 1914-40.* London: Routledge.

Drèze, Jean. 1995. "Famine Prevention in India." In Jean Drèze, Amartya Sen, and Athar Hussain, eds., *The Political Economy of Hunger: Selected Essays.* Oxford: Oxford University Press.

Earley, Thomas, and Donald Westfall. 1996. *International Dynamics of National Sugar Policies.* Rome: Food and Agriculture Organization.

European Commission. 1996. "Green Paper on Relations between the European Union and the ACP Countries on the Eve of the 21st Century: Challenges and Options for a New Partnership." Brussels: European Commission.

FAO (Food and Agriculture Organization of the United Nations). 1997. FAOSTAT (FAO Statistical Database: www.fao.org). Rome.

_____. 2000. FAOSTAT (FAO Statistical Database: www.fao.org). Rome.

Gardner, B. L. 1993. "Political Economy of Agricultural Pricing Policy." *World Economy* 16(September):611–19.

Grissa, Abdessatar. 1976. *Structure of the International Sugar Market and Its Impact on Developing Countries.* Paris: Organisation for Economic Co-operation and Development.

Gilbert, Christopher L. 1985. "Futures Trading and the Welfare Evaluation of Commodity Price Stabilization." *Economic Journal* 95(September):637–61.

_____. 1987. "International Commodity Agreements: Design and Performance." *World Development* 15(May):591–616.

_____. 1996. "International Commodity Agreements: An Obituary Notice." *World Development* 24(January):1–19.

Hathaway, Dale, and Merlinda Ingco. 1996. "Agricultural Liberalization and the Uruguay Round." In Will Martin and L. Alan Winters, eds., *The Uruguay Round and the Developing Countries.* Cambridge: Cambridge University Press, pages 30–58.

Harris, S., and S. Tangermann 1993. "A Review of the EC Sugar Regime." In Stephen Marks and Keith Maskus, eds., *The Economics and Politics of World Sugar Policies.* Ann Arbor: University of Michigan Press.

Harris, S., A. Swinbank, A. and G. Wilkinson. 1983. *The Food and Farm Policies of the European Community.* New York: Wiley.

Herrmann, Roland, and Dietmar Weiss. 1995. "A Welfare Analysis of the EC-ACP Sugar Protocol." *Journal of Development Studies* 31(6):918–41.

Jabara, Cathy, and Alberto Valdés. 1993. "World Sugar Policies and Developing Countries." In Stephen Marks and Keith Maskus, eds., *The Economics and Politics of World Sugar Policies.* Ann Arbor: University of Michigan Press.

Jacoby, Henry, Ronald Prinn, and Richard Schmalensee. 1998. "Kyoto's Unfinished Business." *Foreign Affairs* 77(4): 54–64.

Koester, U., and P. Schmitz. 1982. "EC Sugar Market Policy and Developing Countries." *European Review of Agricultural Economics* 9(2):183–204.

Krueger, A. O., M. Schiff, and A. Valdés, eds. 1992. *The Political Economy of Agricultural Pricing Policy.* Baltimore: Johns Hopkins University Press.Larson, Donald, Panos Varangis, and Nanae Yabuki. 1998. "Commodity Risk Management and Development." World Bank Working Paper 1963, Washington, D.C.: World Bank.

Larson, Donald, Panos Varangis, and Nanae Yabuki. 1998. "Commodity Risk Management and Development." World Bank Working Paper 1963, Washington, D.C.: World Bank.

LMC International. 1997. *An Evaluation of Cane Payment Systems in Selected Sugar Industries Worldwide.* Mimeo. Oxford, United Kingdom.

Lopez, Rigoberto. 1989. "Political Economy of U.S. Sugar Policies." *American Journal of Agricultural Economics* 71(1):20–31.

Lord, R., and R. Barry. 1990. *The World Sugar Market: Government Intervention and Multilateral Policy Reform.* Washington, D.C.: Economic Research Service.

Matthews, A. 1985. *The Common Agricultural Policy and the Less Developed Countries.* Dublin: Gill and Macmillan.

Mlambo, A. S., and E. S. Pangeti. 1996. *The Political Economy of the Sugar Industry in Zimbabwe, 1920–90.* Harare: University of Zimbabwe Publications.

Messina, William A., Jr., and James Seale, Jr. 1993. "U.S. Sugar Policy and the Caribbean Basin Economic Recovery Act: Conflicts between Domestic and Foreign Policy Objectives." *Review of Agricultural Economics* 15(1):167–80.

Nagano, Yoshiko. 1988. "The Oligopolistic Structure of the Philippine Sugar Industry during the Great Depression." In Bill Albert and Adrian Graves, eds., *The World Sugar Economy in War and Depression, 1914–40.* London: Routledge.

OECD (Organisation for Economic Co-operation and Development). 1997. *Agricultural Policies in OECD Countries: Measurement of Support and Background Information.* Paris.

Perez-Lopez, Jorge. 1988. "Cuban-Soviet Sugar Trade: Price and Subsidy Issues." *Bulletin of Latin American Research* 7(1):1–13.

Pollitt, Brian. 1988. "The Cuban Sugar Economy in the 1930s." In Bill Albert and Adrian Graves, eds., *The World Sugar Economy in War and Depression, 1914–40.* London: Routledge.

Pollitt, Brian, and G. B. Hagelberg. 1994. "The Cuban Sugar Economy in the Soviet Era and After." *Cambridge Journal of Economics* 18(December):547–69.

Prasad, S. 1998. "Fiji and the Sugar Protocol: A Case for Trade-based Development Cooperation." *Development Policy Review* 16(March):39–60.

Reddy, Mahendra, and John Yanagida. 1998. "Fiji's Sugar Industry at the Crossroads." *Pacific Economic Bulletin* 13(1):72–87.

Roberts, I., T. Graeme, and S. Murphy, "EEC Sugar Policies and World Market Prices." *Quarterly Review of the Rural Economy* 3(4):309–19.

Schmitz, Andrew, and Douglas Christian. 1993. "The Economics and Politics of U.S. Sugar Policy." In Stephen Marks and Keith Maskus, eds., *The Economics and Politics of World Sugar Policies*. Ann Arbor: University of Michigan Press.

Sturgis, Robert, Heather Field, and Linda Young. 1990. "1990 and U.S. Sugar Policy Reform." ABARE (Australian Bureau of Agricultural and Resource Economics) Discussion Paper 90.4. Canberra: Australian Government Publishing Service.

Strokov, Sergei, and William H. Meyers. 1996. "Producer Subsidy Equivalents and Evaluation of Support to Russian Agricultural Producers." Center for Agricultural and Rural Development Working Paper 168, Iowa State University, Ames, Iowa.

Téllez, Luis. 1995. "Privatization of the Sugar Market in Mexico." In Dina Umali-Deininger and Charles Maguire, eds., *Agriculture in Liberalizing Economies: Changing Roles for Governments*. Washington, D.C.: World Bank.

Valdés, Alberto. 1987. "Agriculture in the Uruguay Round: Interests of Developing Countries." *World Bank Economic Review* 1 (September):571–93.

Valdés, Alberto, and J. Zietz. 1980. *Agricultural Protection in OECD Countries : Its Cost to Less-Developed Countries*. Washington, D.C.: International Food Policy Research Institute.

UNCTAD (Inited Nations Conference on Trade and Development). 1997. "Prospects for the World Sugar Economy in the Light of the Uruguay Round Agreements." Paper presented at the Asia Pacific Sugar Conference, sponsored jointly by the government of Fiji and the Food and Agriculture Organization of the United Nations, Geneva, October 1997.

Webb, A., M. Lopez, and R. Penn. 1990. *Estimates of Producer and Consumer Subsidy Equivalents: Government Intervention in Agriculture, 1982–87*. Washington, D.C.: Economic Research Service.

Wong, Gordon, Robert Sturgiss, and Brent Borrell. 1989. "The Economic Consequences of International Sugar Trade Reform." ABARE Discussion Paper. Canberra: Australian Government Printing Service.

World Bank. 1995. *Report and Recommendation of the President of the International Development Association to the Executive Directors on a Proposed Credit of SDR 29 Million (US$45 Million Equivalent) to the Republic of Senegal for an Agricultural Sector Adjustment Credit*. Report P-6610-SE. Washington, D.C.

_____. 1996. "India: Achieving Economic Gains in the Indian Sugar Cane Sector: The Place of Uttar Pradesh and Maharashtra." Report 15678-IN. Washington, D.C.

Zietz, J., and A. Valdés. 1986. "Potential benefits to LDCs of trade liberalization in beef and sugar by industrialized countries. *Weltwirtschaftliches Archiv* 122 (1): 93–112.

Zhiren, Jia, and Jiao Nianmin. 1997. "Developments in the Industrial Use of Sugar in China from 1970–96 and Its Future Prospects." Paper presented at the Asia Pacific Sugar Conference, sponsored jointly by the government of Fiji and the Food and Agriculture Organization of the United Nations, Geneva, October 1997.

5

Policy Reform Experience in Cotton Markets

John Baffes

DEVELOPING COUNTRIES account for three-fourths of world cotton production.[1] Cotton is the main source of cash for many low-income farmers and the chief source of foreign exchange for a number of developing countries. In 1993–94 cotton accounted for more than 40 percent of total merchandise export earnings in Mali and Uzbekistan and for 30 percent in Benin, Chad, and Sudan. Cotton's contribution to the overall economy of several countries is substantial—in some cases close to 10 percent (table 5.1).

For decades the cotton market has been subject to marketing and trade interventions. Townsend and Guitchounts (1994) estimate that in the early 1990s more than 90 percent of cotton was produced in countries with some type of government intervention in the cotton sector.[2] They also estimate that if free-market policies prevailed in the cotton sector worldwide, cotton production would increase and prices would decline. A more recent study shows that government assistance to the cotton industry in 1997–98 topped $2 billion in China, $754 million in the United States ($156 million of it for export assistance), $320 million in Greece, $290 million in the Arab Republic of Egypt, and $205 million in Turkey (ICAC 1999a).

In the late 1990s, however, state involvement began to decline and in some cases changed markedly. Until the early 1990s, for instance, government enterprises handled all cotton marketing and trade throughout East Africa. By the early 1990s Tanzania, Uganda, and Zimbabwe had begun liberalizing marketing and trade regimes for cotton, albeit to differing degrees. These changes shifted many responsibilities, such as providing input financ-

Table 5.1 Cotton's Importance to Developing and Transition Economies, 1993–94

Country	Cotton's contribution		Per capita Income (current $US)
	Merchandise exports (percent of total)	Overall economy (percent of total GDP)[a]	
Mali	42.91	6.45	243
Uzbekistan	42.46	8.32	928
Chad	31.90	5.60	170
Sudan	26.34	—	—
Benin	26.16	8.33	349
Togo	22.87	5.65	295
Tajikistan	19.74	8.08	455
Tanzania	17.78	2.52	113
Turkmenistan	15.26	10.81	1,161

— not available.
[a] Ratio of the value of cotton (at world prices) to GDP. The world price was taken to be the December average of the A Index minus $.10/lb (an allowance for converting the price from c.i.f. [cost, insurance, and freight] Northern Europe to f.o.b. [free on board]).
Source: International Monetary Fund, *International Financial Statistics*, and author's calculations.

ing and responding to price volatility, from the state to private entities. Major challenges accompany this transition, both for the governments involved and for the individuals whose livelihood depends on cotton.

This chapter focuses on the cotton policy reforms initiated by several countries during the 1990s. It looks at three East African countries— Tanzania, Uganda, and Zimbabwe—and at several West African countries. The East African countries have largely completed their reforms. In West Africa the reforms have been limited and sporadic, but new reform efforts appear more promising. The chapter also examines cotton reforms in four countries outside Sub-Saharan Africa: Egypt, Mexico, Pakistan, and the United States. Egypt and Pakistan both taxed cotton in order to subsidize textiles. They introduced some reforms in the 1990s (Pakistan to a greater degree), but interventions into the cotton industry remain an issue. The situation in Mexico and the United States differs from that in Egypt and Pakistan in one important respect. Mexico and the United States subsidized rather than taxed cotton, and the reforms (which are part of larger efforts to reform the entire agricultural sector) attempt to compensate producers for loss of income from the direct support programs.

We chose this mix of countries for a number of reasons. Because the reforms in the East African countries are largely complete, they offer useful lessons for other countries, such as China and Uzbekistan, where state enterprises still play a key role in the cotton sector. The West African countries also present a contrast to East Africa. They have state enterprises much like those that prevailed in East Africa, but while cotton production has stagnated in East Africa (and collapsed in Uganda) yields and production in the western region have grown. Further, the situation in Egypt and Pakistan highlights the importance of delinking the cotton and textile industries—as well as the government's unwillingness to do so. Finally, Mexico and the United States took a unique approach to reform that has addressed the issue of subsidies.

The World Cotton Market

Most countries produce cotton, but the Northern Hemisphere accounts for about 90 percent of global production. World cotton production in 1997–98 was around 20 million tons. China and the United States account for about 20 percent of world production apiece, followed by India and Pakistan (15 percent) and Uzbekistan (8 percent) (table 5.2). Other significant cotton producers are Argentina, Australia, Brazil, Greece, the Syrian Arab Republic, Turkey, and West Africa. About 30 percent of cotton production is traded internationally, with the United States, Uzbekistan, and West Africa accounting for more than half of world exports. Other major exporters are Argentina, Australia, and Greece. Four major producers (China, India, Pakistan, and Turkey) do not export cotton and occasionally even import substantial quantities to supply their textile industries.

Imports of cotton are more uniformly distributed than exports. In 1997 the eight largest importers—Brazil, Indonesia, Italy, the Republic of Korea, Mexico, Taiwan (China), Thailand, and Turkey—accounted for half of cotton imports. Imports, then, are less concentrated than exports, which are dominated by the two countries that account for 40 percent of exported cotton.

The Policy Environment

Cotton-producing countries commonly use one or more of several interventions to impact cotton marketing and trade. These interventions include taxes, subsidies, and controls such as import duties and quotas and generally involve state enterprises. They result in four main types of output-oriented distortions:

- **Taxation** through a state marketing enterprise that imposes fixed cotton prices. This type of intervention is common in Central Asia, where the state handles both domestic marketing and international trade. In Uzbekistan, for example, cotton is taxed both explicitly and implicitly through a multiple exchange rate regime, with cotton growers receiving only a fraction of the world price. Egypt and Syria also have extensive controls on both production and prices. In West Africa domestic

Table 5.2 World Cotton Production, Exports, and Yield Profiles, 1997–98

Producer	Production		Exports[a]		
	000 tons	Percent of total world	000 tons	Percent of total world	Yield kgs/ha
North America	**4,304**	**21.50**	**1,708**	**28.67**	**771**
Mexico*	209	1.04	75	1.26	1,042
United States	4,092	20.44	1,633	27.41	762
South America	**842**	**4.21**	**299**	**5.02**	**389**
Argentina	295	1.47	220	3.69	347
Brazil*	370	1.85	0	0.00	420
West Africa	**970**	**4.85**	**838**	**14.07**	**424**
Benin	151	0.75	134	2.26	397
Côte d'Ivoire	145	0.73	122	2.05	601
Mali	216	1.08	193	3.24	434
North Africa	**432**	**2.16**	**154**	**2.59**	**797**
Egypt	342	1.71	72	1.21	948
Sudan	88	0.44	82	1.37	497
Rest of Africa	**386**	**1.93**	**191**	**3.21**	**225**
Zimbabwe	105	0.53	83	1.39	334
European Union	**464**	**2.32**	**286**	**4.80**	**930**
Greece	348	1.74	200	3.36	890
Spain*	116	0.58	60	1.01	1,078
Central Asia	**1,551**	**7.75**	**1,349**	**22.65**	**618**
Tajikistan	106	0.53	107	1.80	488
Turkmenistan	180	0.90	58	0.97	375
Uzbekistan	1,139	5.69	1,050	17.63	768
China*	**4,602**	**22.99**	**6**	**0.10**	**1,066**
South Asia	**4,335**	**21.66**	**187**	**3.14**	**356**
India	2,686	13.42	82	1.38	304
Pakistan	1,556	7.77	74	1.24	526
Australia	**689**	**3.44**	**575**	**9.65**	**1,611**
Middle East	**1,392**	**6.95**	**307**	**5.15**	**1,092**
Iran	132	0.66	10	0.17	548
Syria	355	1.77	230	3.86	1,479
Turkey*	833	4.16	23	0.39	1,153
WORLD	**20,015**	**100.00**	**5,957**	**100.00**	**592**

[a] Exports include intraregional trade.
* Net importers.
Source: ICAC, *Cotton: Review of the World Situation,* August 1998.

enterprises and a French state enterprise control the marketing and trade of cotton output and inputs.

- **Taxation** in the form of border interventions intended to tax cotton producers and support domestic textile industries. India, Pakistan, and Turkey have interventions of this nature.
- **Support** aimed at increasing producers' income. Cotton producers in Greece and Spain receive heavy support under the Common Agricultural Policy of the European Union (EU), sometimes as much as twice the world price. U.S. cotton producers also receive a moderate level of support. (During the 1990s government support accounted for an average of one-fourth of the market price of U.S. cotton.) This type of support can be pursued through price interventions (as in the United States and the EU) and through state enterprises or buyers of last resort.
- **Support** through border interventions. In China such support takes the form of high import tariffs.

In addition to output-oriented distortions, distortions are also widespread in credit, fertilizer, irrigation, and other input markets.

The Multifibre Arrangement (MFA) created under the auspices of the General Agreement on Tariffs and Trade (GATT) also affects the world cotton market. The MFA allows industrial countries to restrict textile imports from developing countries, effectively protecting textile industries in industrial countries and distorting the location of textile-processing activities. Martin (1996) estimates that the MFA imposes an implicit tax of about 20 percent on cotton products relative to synthetic fiber products. The MFA agreement is being phased out, and all import quotas are to be eliminated by 2005. The phase-out is expected to encourage the relocation of processing facilities to developing countries and to boost the demand for cotton.

To some extent interventions in the cotton markets of developing countries are driven by import-substitution policies intended to transfer resources from cotton to textiles. This link to the protection of the textile industry has been an obstacle to reforms. Cotton sector reform requires either eliminating textile protections or replacing them with a direct subsidy. The textile industry opposes removing protections, and policymakers are reluctant to finance new subsidies with taxes. Thus in textile-producing countries cotton reform initiatives depend on whether (and how) the cotton industry is linked to the textile industry and on the government's willingness to remove or replace textile protections.

The way cotton is produced also affects the nature of distortions and consequently the pace of reforms. During the ginning process around 30 to 35 percent of seed cotton (the farm product) becomes cotton lint—what we refer to as cotton. The rest becomes cotton oil or cotton meal.[3] In some circumstances ginning operations are natural monopsonies because weak transportation networks or high initial investment allow one ginnery (often a state enterprise) to become a monopsonist. In several cases the monopsonistic structure of the ginning industry has led to contract farming, with the ginners financing cotton producers and then buying the cotton at a prearranged price.

Two additional factors affect the cotton market. The first is the price of synthetic fibers, which currently account for more than half of world fiber consumption. The second is Chinese policy, since China holds almost half of the world stock of cotton (4.4 million tons of the total world stock of 9.4 million tons of cotton in 1996–97).[4]

The World Price of Cotton

The most widely quoted price for cotton is an index calculated as the average of offer quotations by cotton trading agents in northern Europe. It is constructed daily by Cotlook Limited, a private information dissemination company based in Liverpool (the most important cotton trading center in Europe since the 18th century), and published weekly in the *Cotton Outlook*. The cotton price index for Middling 1³⁄₃₂' cotton (often referred to as the Cotlook A Index) is an average of the 5 least expensive of 14 styles of cotton traded in northern Europe (table 5.3). The Cotlook B Index, which represents a coarser quality of cotton, is the simple average of the three least expensive of eight styles.[5]

Price Discovery and Hedging

The New York Cotton Exchange (NYCE) is the dominant cotton exchange. Established in 1870, it has been trading cotton futures almost uninterruptedly since then. The NYCE offers futures and option contracts of up to two years, using Memphis No. 2 cotton as the cash price equivalent for quality specification and delivery purposes. Numerous commodity exchanges have traded cotton futures contracts at various times.[6] But the lack of a non-U.S. hedging instrument has long complicated the process of trading cotton futures.

Because the NYCE futures contract has limited use as a hedging instrument outside the United States, in 1992 the NYCE launched the World Cotton Contract with the A index as the cash price equivalent.[7] The contract never took off, for a number of reasons. First, no equivalent spot market existed with well-defined quality specifications and physical delivery locations. Second, many feared that the settlement price (the A index) could be manipulated. And third, trading took place exclusively in U.S. dollars, so the contract did not meet the needs of the many hedgers outside the United States who want to use other currencies.

Table 5.3 Composition of the Cotlook A and B Indexes
(U.S. cents per pound)

Origin	October 17, 1996	January 2, 1997	July 31, 1997
United States (Memphis Territory)	83.00	84.00	85.25*
United States (California/Arizona)	83.00	84.00	87.50N
Mexico	79.75	NQ	NQ
Paraguay	NQ	NQ	NQ
Turkey	NQ	NQ	NQ
Syria	NQ	79.50*	79.50*
Greece	74.00*	79.00*	NQ
Central Asia	71.00*	75.50*	79.50*
Pakistan	76.00*	NQ	NQ
India	NQ	NQ	NQ
China	NQ	NQ	NQ
Tanzania	78.00*	NQ	NQ
Africa CFAF	75.00*	79.00*	80.00*
Australia	80.50	84.00*	87.00*
COTLOOK A INDEX	74.80	79.40	82.25
United States (Orleans/Texas)	79.50	80.00	81.50
Brazil	NQ	NQ	NQ
Argentina	NQ	78.50	NQ
Turkey	74.50*	78.50*	NQ
Central Asia	69.00*	72.50*	77.00
Pakistan	72.50*	NQ	NQ
India	NQ	76.00*	NQ
China	NQ	NQ	NQ
COTLOOK B INDEX	72.00	75.65	—

N = Not offered in volume or used in the composition of the A index.
NQ = Not traded on that day.
* = The A and B index components from which the simple average is taken.
— Fewer than three cotton varieties actively traded that day.
Source: Cotton Outlook.

The East African Experience

The three East African countries examined here—Uganda, Tanzania, and Zimbabwe—share a number of similarities. All three used state enterprises to intervene in the cotton market, effectively taxing cotton. During the late 1980s and late 1990s these state enterprises went bankrupt, and the performance of the cotton sector declined (Tanzania and Zimbabwe) or collapsed (Uganda). And all three countries had active textile industries that were being subsidized at the expense of cotton. In the end the cotton sector's performance was so poor that reform was the only feasible option (table 5.4).

Commodity Market Reforms

Table 5.4 Cotton Production and Area Planted in East Africa, 1990–98

	Uganda		Zimbabwe		Tanzania	
	Production (000 tons)	Area (000 ha)	Production (000 tons)	Area (000 ha)	Production (000 tons)	Area (000 ha)
1990–91	8	89	72	273	51	320
1991–92	7	134	88	235	106	450
1992–93	9	174	75	246	48	430
1993–94	5	71	60	230	43	344
1994–95	6	74	38	194	94	172
1995–96	10	120	104	246	84	344
1996–97	20	95	101	313	66	283
1997–98	7	38	105	315	45	350
1998–99	25	250	130	320	55	350

Note: Shading indicates year of reform.
Source: ICAC, *Cotton: Review of the World Situation*, various issues.

The Situation before Reform

UGANDA. Prior to the 1970s, Uganda ranked third among African countries in cotton production, behind Egypt and Sudan. Cotton was introduced to Uganda in 1903, and production grew rapidly until the mid-1930s, when coffee began to compete as an alternative cash crop. Cotton production continued to increase steadily, however, peaking at 900,000 hectares in 1970 with a record output of 87,000 tons of cotton.

Most activities in the cotton industry were administered under monopolistic arrangements. The Ministry of Agriculture was responsible for cotton research and seed multiplication. Responsibility for cotton seed for planting and oil milling fell to the Lint Marketing Board (a state enterprise), which also undertook lint marketing (both domestically and for export) and regulated the industry. Cooperatives—each with its own network of producers and ginning operation—were responsible for primary marketing and processing.

The political instability, poor governance, and inappropriate macroeconomic policies of the 1970s and 1980s had a devastating effect on the Ugandan economy and hit the cotton sector especially hard. Cotton production collapsed, plunging to a record low of 2,000 tons in 1987. Seed multiplication activities were disrupted, as were research and extension. Cooperatives failed to pay farmers cash for their cotton, and inefficient ginning marketing and operations generated high overhead costs.

TANZANIA. Cotton was introduced in Tanzania in the early 20th century, but production began to expand significantly only after 1945. Cotton soon became Tanzania's most important cash crop in terms of employment and the second most important in terms of export earnings. Cotton is a smallholder crop in Tanzania that is grown on farms of 0.5 to 10 hectares (the average is 1–2 hectares). Only around 10 percent of farmers use irrigation or fertilizer.

The cooperative movement emerged in the early 1950s, when relations between ginnery owners (most of them foreign) and cotton farmers started to deteriorate. Several hundred farmer associations were formed, and the groups began successfully handling crop purchasing. They soon formed cooperative unions and became involved in building ginneries, training staff, and taking over ginneries and cotton oil mills from foreign owners. They also promoted the mechanization of cotton farming.

Shortly after independence the government, seeking to increase its control over cooperatives, established a unified cooperative service and gave the cooperatives a marketing monopoly. The cooperatives were formally abolished in 1976 and aspects of marketing turned over to the Tanzanian Cotton Authority. The government set the prices paid to farmers, establishing uniform prices for an entire season across the country.

The cooperatives were reinstated in 1984. Under the new structure the unions and village-level farmer associations acted as agents for the renamed Tanzanian Cotton Marketing Board (TCMB). The associations stored and sold cotton to certain cooperative unions for a fixed price, and the unions processed the seed cotton for a fixed margin. The TCMB managed sales to domestic and international buyers. Despite the changes most of the cooperatives managed to stay alive only with government subsidies and donor support.

ZIMBABWE. Commercial production of cotton in Zimbabwe started in the early 1920s. A comprehensive cotton research program and research station were set up in 1925. By using advanced technologies such as insect control and developing improved seed varieties, the country became one of Africa's most important cotton producers. Initially cotton marketing was the responsibility of a committee under the Grain Marketing Board. The Cotton Marketing Board (CMB) was established in 1969 to handle cotton marketing.

Until 1994 the CMB controlled most aspects of cotton production, from the sale of planting seed to the purchase of cotton from farmers. Ginning and the marketing of cotton and cotton seed also fell under its purview. The CMB had eight ginneries and was the sole buyer of cotton (the country's single private ginnery had to buy cotton from the CMB on contract). The CMB also regulated the industry. It announced producer prices well in advance, so the state absorbed all the price risk.

The CMB grew into an inefficient organization plagued by poor governance and high operating costs. The board's weak management and subsidized cotton sales—often at half the international price—to the domestic textile industry resulted in serious financial difficulties. Cotton production fell by almost half during the 1980s, producers were not paid on time, and when they were they often did not receive full payments. By the late 1980s it had become clear that the CMB would have to be restructured or the cotton industry would collapse. A severe drought in 1991–92 contributed to the sector's woes, causing a further 60 percent decline in production.

The Reforms

During the late 1980s and early 1990s the state enterprises of the three African cotton producers went bankrupt. The performance of the cotton sector declined (Tanzania and Zimbabwe) or collapsed (Uganda). And all three countries had active textile industries that were being subsidized at the expense of cotton. In the end the cotton sector's performance was so poor that reform was the only feasible option (table 5.4).

UGANDA. In 1992, with World Bank assistance, Uganda embarked on a major reform program that included the liberalization of the cotton industry (World Bank 1994). The government redefined its role in the cotton industry, taking on some new responsibilities (especially during the transitional phase) and shedding others. Ginning and the marketing of cotton and cotton inputs were liberalized, and research, seed multiplication, extension services, and credit delivery mechanisms were strengthened. To increase the efficiency of the ginning industry, gins were transferred to creditworthy operators.

At the time of the reforms the cooperatives were crippled by bad debt. Potential ginning capacity was much greater than actual capacity, and rundown ginneries needed infusions of new capital. Management knew little about how to restructure their facilities, however. To address the problems, the government established the Business Advisory Service, a temporary agency that worked with cooperatives to draw up new business plans. In return for restructuring their businesses, the ginneries would receive limited debt relief. Temporary lines of credit were established through the Bank of Uganda's Development Finance Department to provide working capital for the restructured firms. Some cooperatives were able to sell assets and finance smaller, more efficient business. Others entered into joint ventures with foreign partners. Some businesses were simply liquidated. One international cotton company established a new ginning operation.

Government participation in the cotton sector now takes place almost entirely through the Cotton Development Organization (CDO), although the CDO also collaborates with other institutions (table 5.5).[8] The CDO is intended to represent the cotton industry as a whole and to monitor the pro-

Table 5.5 Public Institutions Involved in Uganda's Cotton Industry

Implementing agency	Responsibilities	Coordinating ministry
Cotton Development Organization (CDO)	Regulatory framework, monitoring, and technical services, including seed management	Ministry of Trade and Industry
Ministry of Agriculture Extension Services	Integrated extension services	Ministry of Agriculture
National Agricultural Research Organization (NARO)	Support to national agricultural research	Ministry of Agriculture
Development Finance Department (DFD), Bank of Uganda	Seasonal and medium-term credit	Ministry of Finance
Agricultural Policy Committee (APC)	Policy framework, including the restructuring of the cotton ginning industry and supervision of the Business Advisory Services (BAS)	An interministerial committee coordinated by the Ministry of Planning

Source: Sabune (1996).

duction and marketing of cotton. A 12-member board of directors that includes public and private sector representatives governs the organization.[9] Among other things the board approves expenditures, senior staff appointments, procurement procedures, and business plans. An auditor-general reviews the CDO's accounts and by law must report the findings to the legislature.

To carry out its mandate, the CDO can charge for its services, borrow, manage property, and levy a cess (local tax). The initiating statute also places explicit limits on the CDO's authority, however. The cess cannot be more than 2 percent, although the Ministry of Agriculture, which is responsible for the CDO, can vary or rescind the cess by statutory instrument. The types of penalties the CDO can levy for noncompliance are limited. Further, it is obliged to give all new entrants a registration permit, even if they have not previously been engaged in the cotton industry. (Businesses can renew their registrations automatically by paying the prescribed fees.)

Several cotton-related activities have been shifted to the private sector, including transportation, ginning operations, input provision, and exports. A total of 24 ginneries were operating in 1997, many below full capacity. Three of the ginneries were leased, 13 were operated by unions, 2 were run by joint ventures, and 6 were under private ownership. Some of the ginners were also cotton exporters. By the 1997–98 season cotton production had rebounded from its low of 2,000 tons in the late 1980s to 25,000 tons—a significant achievement. Producer prices fluctuated between 55 percent and 65 percent of world prices because of the continuing inefficiencies in the industry (transportation and ginning performance, for instance).

TANZANIA. Cotton reform in Tanzania began in 1989–90, when the government launched the Agricultural Adjustment Program. This program transferred ownership of seed cotton to the regional unions, with the TCMB providing fee-based marketing services for final sales and input purchases. Price controls on cotton were gradually relaxed. In 1991–92 the government announced only indicative prices. Cooperatives were free to determine their own producer prices for the next season, although the unions chose to offer uniform prices throughout the country. The biggest step came in 1993–94, when the government formally eliminated the cooperatives' monopoly and allowed competition in cotton marketing and processing.

In 1994–95 eight private ginneries were constructed, opening up another marketing channel. By the 1995–96 season the private sector response to reforms had become stronger, and by 1996–97 private businesses were purchasing more than half of all cotton. Private traders and ginneries were able to capture a considerable share of the market because they offered higher prices than cooperative unions. Some private ginneries were also involved in contract farming, providing inputs (seeds and occasionally fertilizer) to producers who agreed to supply cotton in return. The ginneries and producers usually established a minimum price at planting time, but this price could be adjusted if the market price was higher during the harvest.

Under the TCMB about two-thirds of the country's cotton was exported. The rest was used to supply the domestic textile industry. When the government stopped supporting the textile industry, it was unable to withstand international competition, and the textile mills went out of business.

ZIMBABWE. Zimbabwe appointed private sector representatives to the CMB in 1992, leaving just one government representative. The CMB's mandate at the time was to develop a privatization plan for all aspects of cotton trade and marketing. Various regulatory controls (such as seed quality regulations and cotton grading) were transferred from the CMB to the Ministry of Agriculture. In 1993 the government announced that the cotton market would be open to new entrants, bringing the CMB's monopoly to an end. In 1994 all subsidies to the textile industry were discontinued.

In July 1994 the CMB began having difficulty paying for cotton, and a number of commercial growers started to buy their seed cotton and have it ginned at the only private gin. In September 1994 the CMB's monopoly was formally terminated, and it became the Cotton Company of Zimbabwe (CCZ), with the government holding all shares. The government assumed all of the CCZ's debts, allowing the agency to start out with a clean balance sheet, and discontinued all subsidies to the textile industry.

Private companies have moved into ginning and marketing in the country. As of 1994 the CCZ still owned 80 percent of the ginning capacity in Zimbabwe and operated a network of buying centers and collection points throughout the major cotton-growing areas. The Commercial Cotton Growers Association, a cooperative owned by growers who farm 25 hectares or more, joined with an international cotton company to form a new firm, Cotpro, that provides competition for the CCZ.

In 1995 the CCZ leased two of its gins to Cargill, a U.S.-based agribusiness. Cargill started buying seed cotton, putting itself in direct competition with the CCZ and Cotpro. In 1996 it bought the two gins it had been leasing from the CCZ. In October 1997 the CCZ was privatized. The government holds 25 percent of the shares, small-scale farmers 20 percent, institutional investors and the general public 15 percent each, large-scale farmers and the National Investment Trust 10 percent each, and employees 5 percent.

Although only a few seasons have passed since cotton was fully liberalized, the cotton industry has improved in several ways. First, cotton production is up substantially, from 85,000 tons in 1997–98 to 130,000 tons in 1998–99. Some 30 percent of the 1997–98 cotton harvest was marketed entirely by private entities (Cargill accounted for 22.5 percent and Cotpro for 7.5 percent). Private companies now transport most cotton. Competition has pushed the price farmers receive to close to 80 percent of international prices, and producers are being paid faster.

Some problems remain, however. Primary among them is one we have already seen: the lack of a non-U.S. hedging instrument. While large companies such as Cargill can manage risk through a diversity of operations, one-commodity local companies such as Cotpro need some kind of hedging instrument. Lack of research is the second most important problem. Cotton research remains underfunded, although the Cotton Research Institute has developed some new cotton varieties. Finally the CCZ still holds a legal monopoly on the supply of planting seed, and the government sets maximum prices for seed, effectively shutting other seed suppliers out of the market.

The West African Experience

The modern cotton industry in West African countries was pioneered by the French state-owned Company for Textile Fiber Development (*Compagnie Française de Développement des Fibres Textiles*, or CFDT).[10] As countries gained independence they established their own national cotton companies. The CFDT retained a minority shareholding position (usually holding around one-third of shares) in these companies and entered into technical agreements with them. It also retained an ownership interest in companies engaged in processing cotton by-products. The national cotton companies have a legal monopsony in seed cotton, and most have a monopoly in ginning, marketing, and providing inputs to farmers. They announce a base buying price for seed cotton before planting starts, sometimes supplementing this price with a second payment. Any supplement is based on the company's financial results for the season and is paid on production the following season. Village producer associations handle intermediate input credit and seed payments, and input credits are deducted from payments for cotton. Nearly all cotton is exported, and a large share of exports is marketed by the CFDT's affiliate, the Cotton Company (*Compagnie Cotonière*, or COPACO).

Aided by productive research in Africa and France, cotton growing expanded rapidly in West Africa, increasing more than fourfold between 1974 and 1996. In 1996–97 the region produced 877,000 tons, or 5 percent of world production (table 5.6). It is the third-largest cotton exporter after the United States and Uzbekistan, accounting for almost 15 percent of world exports. Farmers use chemical inputs and seed varieties adapted to local conditions to produce high yields and consistently top-quality cotton. High repayment rates for input credits and well-organized producer associations bolster the industry.

The system has a number of weaknesses, however. The prices West African producers receive tend to be very low. From 1983 until 1995 farmers received 37 percent more in Zimbabwe and 60 percent more in India for similar types of cotton (table 5.7). Since the 1994 devaluation of the CFA franc, prices in Zimbabwe and India have been 80 percent to 100 percent higher than prices in West Africa. The services the cotton companies provide (extension, rural road maintenance, and transportation to move seed cotton to gins) account for some but not all of these price differences. Governments usually absorb much of the difference between domestic and world prices in the form of various taxes. The absence of competition in domestic markets results in operating inefficiencies in state companies and creates opportunities for rent seeking and corruption.

The annual determination of cotton prices reflects the relative bargaining power of a number of groups—producers, governments, managers of the state-owned cotton companies, the CFDT, and in some cases private ginning firms. The uniformity of cotton input and output prices across entire countries subsidizes producers close to ginning centers and taxes those farther away. Planned delivery schedules to ginning plants severely limit farmers' opportunities to profit through inventory management. And the system does not respond flexibly to changes in world market conditions. For example, in the late 1980s and early 1990s low world prices and an overvalued currency

Table 5.6 Cotton Production and Area Planted in Selected West African Countries, 1990–98

	Benin		Burkina Faso		Chad	
	Production (000 tons)	Area (000 ha)	Production (000 tons)	Area (000 ha)	Production (000 tons)	Area (000 ha)
1990–91	59	123	77	166	60	207
1991–92	75	144	69	186	68	283
1992–93	69	139	69	177	47	199
1993–94	103	235	51	150	37	158
1994–95	98	230	63	184	61	203
1995–96	141	282	64	160	62	208
1996–97	143	383	90	200	86	285
1997–98	151	380	138	280	110	400
1998–99	150	399	140	297	91	420
	Côte d'Ivoire		Mali		Togo	
1990–91	116	199	115	205	41	80
1991–92	87	190	114	215	42	78
1992–93	106	224	135	246	42	80
1993–94	116	219	101	201	35	65
1994–95	93	242	128	270	52	93
1995–96	96	204	169	336	31	96
1996–97	114	211	190	420	47	108
1997–98	147	244	216	498	73	137
1998–99	160	248	215	498	72	144

Source: ICAC, *Cotton: Review of the World Situation*, various issues.

Table 5.7 Grower Prices in Selected Developing Countries, 1989–90–1994–95 (percentage of c.i.f.)

	1989–90	1990–91	1991–92	1992–93	1993–94	1994–95
Benin	0.39	0.35	0.41	0.51	0.33	0.33
Burkina Faso	0.39	0.35	0.41	0.46	0.25	0.25
Chad	0.37	0.33	0.39	0.48	0.26	0.27
Côte d'Ivoire	0.45	0.35	0.41	0.46	0.30	0.35
India	0.78	0.68	0.90	1.17	0.90	0.77
Togo	0.39	0.35	0.41	0.48	0.31	0.32
Mali	0.35	0.31	0.37	0.46	0.26	0.30
Zimbabwe	0.37	0.53	0.90	0.70	0.86	0.85

Note: c.i.f. = cost, insurance, and freight.
Source: Varangis, Larson, and Thigpen (1995); Pursell (1998).

led to the de facto bankruptcy of a number of state cotton companies. The companies had to be drastically restructured, supported by injections of money from national governments and international aid organizations.

Sporadic Reform Initiatives

A few West African countries, including Benin and Côte d'Ivoire, have introduced reforms to deal with the system's shortcomings, but the reforms have been sporadic and very limited.[11] Benin reorganized its national cotton company, the National Refining Society (*Société Nationale de Raffinage*, or SONARA), between 1989 and 1991. Private companies on contract to SONARA began supplying inputs and providing transportation for both inputs and cotton. Three private gins began operating in 1995–96. SONARA owns eight gins (35 percent of the private gins), and the CFDT is part owner of one private gin. Each gin has a quota of 25,000 tons of seed cotton, which SONARA supplies at the official price plus transportation costs. Farmers do not enjoy the benefits of even limited competition, since the private ginneries pay the same price as SONARA. Any benefits of this pricing system go to the ginning operations. The government has addressed this problem by replacing the single, season-long price announced prior to planting with a two-tier system. Under this system producers receive a supplement once the cotton is sold if the world price climbs above a certain level.

In Côte d'Ivoire the state-owned Company for Textile Development (*Compagnie Ivoirienne de Développement des Textiles*, CIDT) controlled the industry until 1996. It sold inputs to farmers on credit, provided extension and other services, purchased seed cotton and ginned it, and established prices. Output had stagnated in the late 1980s but rose again after the devaluation of the CFA franc in January 1994, reaching almost 250,000 tons in 1997–98. To improve incentives for farmers and the private sector in general, the government undertook privatization of its 10 ginneries; by 1998 six had been privatized. Finally, following a two-year transitional period, the CIDT will no longer provide services to producers, instead contracting with private ginneries. Two private groups, including a producer group, are planning to build new ginneries, potentially raising the total ginning capacity to more than 400,000 tons by 2001.

Concerted Reform Efforts

The early sporadic reforms occurred in only two countries. In 1998 the governments of West African cotton-producing countries and other stakeholders, including the national cotton companies, the CFDT, input suppliers, and the World Bank, discussed a more concerted effort to reform the entire cotton industry. These discussions resulted in two proposals: retaining the cotton companies but reforming and regulating them, and introducing free entry and competition (ICAC 1999b).

The first approach involves a number of steps:

- Setting prices at levels appropriate to a competitive environment;
- Giving producers equity in the national cotton companies and more influence over key decisions, especially price setting;
- Subcontracting with private firms for activities such as providing inputs and transportation; and
- Eliminating subsidies on sales of cotton lint and cottonseed to domestic textile firms and oil mills.

The advantage of this option is that it reduces the risk of damaging the current system—which has many desirable aspects—with more far-reaching reforms. Maintaining the system's ability to recover research and extension costs and its high repayment rates on input loans is especially important. The option has two weaknesses, however. First, domestic prices are unlikely to move with world prices (a supposed goal of the reform process), because large shares of national income are at stake. The price-setting mechanism remains inherently political because a number of interest groups are involved in the negotiations. Second, the proposal is incompatible with initiatives to establish free trade among countries in the region under the two regional arrangements.[12] New trade arrangements would require reforming the cotton industry again.

Another approach, which involves free entry and competition, is more along the lines of the reforms in Uganda and Zimbabwe. It calls for:

- Opening the sector to competitive entry at all levels and linking domestic prices to international levels (prices would vary according to transportation costs and the season);
- Maintaining and strengthening research, extension, and phytosanitary activities, in which the government's role is essential;
- Strengthening farmer groups and facilitating their participation in voluntary contract farming arrangements;
- Freeing the cotton industry from sector-specific taxation and subjecting it to economywide taxes only; and
- Increasing the efficiency of regional ginneries by harmonizing reforms of cotton trade across West African cotton zones.

In some countries free entry may be all that is needed to generate a competitive system. In most countries, however, the national cotton monopoly needs to be privatized and restructured into a number of successor companies. Such a move would signal the government's commitment to open markets and ensure that producers in every region have access to competitive markets for their seed cotton.

Other Reform Initiatives

This section moves outside Africa to briefly examine the reform process in Egypt, Mexico, Pakistan, and the United States. Two of the countries (Egypt and Pakistan) taxed the cotton industry prior to reforms, while two (Mexico and the United States) subsidized it.

Egypt

Egypt is typical of countries where partial reform efforts fail because of the government's unwillingness to separate interventions in the cotton and textile industries. Before 1961, when the government nationalized the cotton industry, production, ginning, and marketing were all private sector activities.[13] After 1961 the Egyptian Cotton Organization took over all activities, setting farm prices at the beginning of the season and determining export prices and quantities. The government went even further, deciding which varieties were to be planted and where. Producers received less than the world price so that the government could provide the textile industry with subsidized cotton.

In 1993 the government initiated a series of reforms designed to reform the cotton industry. But the new marketing and trade regime, under which farmers sold cotton for export at free-market prices, lasted just one season. In November 1994 the government intervened to protect textiles by halting further exports. The system of fixed prices was reinstated for the 1995–96 season.

Pakistan

Before 1971 growers produced and traded cotton under liberal marketing and trade policies. About 70 percent of cotton production was traded through the Karachi Cotton Exchange, which was established in 1955 by the Karachi Cotton Association (Farooqui, Keaton, and Miller, 1958). In 1971, however, the government introduced a new price program that made the Cotton Export Corporation (CEC), a public agency, the bulk purchaser of cotton. The program was fully implemented in 1976 and provided cotton producers with guaranteed prices, levied export duties to protect textiles, fixed ginning charges, and ultimately dictated how much cotton was to be exported (Huque 1987).

Reforms introduced in 1987 allowed private competition with the CEC in cotton exports, and in 1988 private agents were allowed to procure cotton directly from open markets. The implicit protection provided to the textile industry was converted into an explicit export tax. The result is that marketing and trade are in private hands, but the cotton industry is taxed to benefit textile production.

Mexico

Until 1994 Mexico subsidized its cotton industry. Cotton producers received not only output subsidies but also subsidies for inputs, especially for credit and irrigation. When the North American Free Trade Agreement (NAFTA) negotiations were initiated in the early 1990s, the Mexican government began reducing its support to the cotton sector. As a result cotton production declined from 251,000 tons in 1991–92 to 43,000 tons in 1992–92. A spate of diseases exacerbated the situation.

In 1994 the Mexican government replaced guaranteed prices with direct income support payments for nine commodities, including cotton. The payments will remain in place for 15 years (fixed in real terms for 10 years and declining for the next 5), or until 2009. Initially producers had total flexibility in using their land (including abandoning it), but changes introduced in 1996 required that the land remain in agricultural use. Both the area planted and production volumes increased following the reforms, but the increase reflected mainly higher domestic demand following the NAFTA-induced relocation of a number of textile operations to Mexico (table 5.8).

United States

Between 1950 and the early 1970s, the U. S. government maintained large cotton stocks. For example in 1966 the Commodity Credit Corporation (CCC) accounted for 73 percent of cotton stock carryover (Emery 1975).[14] In the 1980s the United States introduced supports for cotton (and grain) producers through so-called deficiency payments.

In 1996 the deficiency payments were replaced by a direct income support program intended to make production decisions independent of market prices. The program, the FAIR Act, will be in effect until 2002 (Mexico has a similar program). During that period producers of seven commodities (of which cotton is one) will receive fixed payments (Baffes and Meerman 1998). In addition to direct payments through the FAIR Act, U.S. cotton producers receive support through additional programs and the loan rate.

Assessing the Reforms and Lessons

The liberalization of cotton followed a similar pattern in most East African countries, although the reform strategies differed. Unlike coffee prices, cotton prices did not collapse.[15] Despite the relatively strong prices, Uganda's state cotton company went bankrupt, in large part because of political instability and poor management. For this reason Uganda's liberalization efforts

Table 5.8 Cotton Production, Area Planted, and Net Exports in Egypt, Mexico, Pakistan, and the United States, 1990–98

	United States			Mexico		
	Production (000 tons)	Area (000 ha)	Net Exports (000 tons)	Production (000 tons)	Area (000 ha)	Net Exports (000 tons)
1990–91	3,376	4,748	1,696	175	231	7
1991–92	3,853	5,245	1,444	179	251	7
1992–93	3,531	4,510	1,132	30	43	(147)
1993–94	3,513	5,175	1,493	24	33	(168)
1994–95	4,281	5,391	2,043	99	156	(85)
1995–96	3,897	6,478	1,583	212	318	(49)
1996–97	4,362	5,467	1,237	235	243	(107)
1997–98	4,304	5,584	1,299	209	201	(260)
1998–99	3,270	4,454	785	219	237	(288)
	Pakistan			Egypt		
1990–91	1,638	2,662	272	296	417	(33)
1991–92	2,180	2,836	444	291	358	(47)
1992–93	1,539	2,836	251	357	353	(19)
1993–94	1,367	2,805	(7)	416	371	117
1994–95	1,478	2,653	(119)	255	303	26
1995–96	1,801	2,997	285	242	298	(1)
1996–97	1,594	3,148	(35)	346	387	36
1997–98	1,556	2,959	54	342	361	72
1998–99	1,500	3,026	11	232	339	100

Note: Numbers in parentheses indicate imports.
Source: ICAC, *Cotton: Review of the World Situation*, various issues.

had few opponents, because there were no potential losers. Zimbabwe followed a similar pattern. The state cotton company was effectively bankrupt (producers were not receiving payments in full or on time), although the event that actually triggered liberalization was probably the 1991–92 drought. In Tanzania the virtual bankruptcy of the state company led to the initiation of reforms.

In West Africa, however, cotton production and yields increased throughout the 1980s and 1990s (table 5.6). Thus the proximate cause of the liberalization efforts of 1998 was low producer prices. But state companies continue to handle the marketing of inputs for cotton, preventing other subsectors from expanding. Reforms in West Africa are still at the discussion stage, and focus on one of two approaches: reforming the cotton monopsonies or allowing free entry and competition.

The three countries discussed in detail here used different approaches to reform. Uganda focused mainly on privatizing marketing and trade, leaving only regulatory functions and quality control to the Cotton Development Organization. Zimbabwe began by changing the management of the CMB, turning it into a private corporation, and introducing private sector competition. The final step toward full liberalization and privatization was the sale of shares of the CMB to private individuals.

In Uganda three years passed before there was a supply response to the reforms. Production in the 1998–99 season recovered to 25,000 tons, and grower prices rose to 50–60 percent of world prices—still low, but higher than before the reforms. A number of new small entrants (mostly traders and exporters) are operating in the sector. Cotton production in Zimbabwe is also up, with farmers receiving between 80 and 90 percent of world prices. New private traders, exporters, and ginners have given new dynamism to the rural sector.

The picture is less encouraging in Tanzania. Production doubled in 1994–95 (the year following the reforms), rising from 43,000 to 94,000 tons. But it dropped back to prereform levels in 1997–98. Cargill could not get enough cotton and was forced to close its two ginneries. In their study of the Tanzanian cotton market, Kahkonen and Leathers (1997) blame the lack of competition, high transport costs, inefficient ginning operations and low prices (well below expected levels) for the collapse in production. Finally, Egypt and Pakistan have not completed their reforms because the governments are unwilling to delink cotton and textiles, and the cotton industries in Mexico and the United States still receive government assistance.

We can draw a number of lessons from the experiences with reform discussed in this chapter.

These lessons cover a number of issues in the cotton industry:

- Reforms in the cotton sector must address the need to restructure ginning operations because of the monopsonistic nature of the market at the ginning stage.
- Even when markets are fully liberalized, the government must continue to play an active role, especially in regulation, research and extension, dissemination activities, and occasionally in credit provision.
- Insuring against price risk remains a concern. Differences in quality among cotton types prevent NYCE cotton futures from being used as a hedging device outside the United States, although the NYCE is the only exchange with sufficient liquidity to create such an instrument. Small producers cannot be expected to hedge at the NYCE or any other

exchange, but a futures contract could be used as a price discovery mechanism. A contract for a type of cotton similar to, say, West African cotton could be used to set prices for contract farming arrangements or to negotiate forward contracts.

- The link with the textile industry is often an obstacle to reform, although it need not be. Reforms in the cotton industry can proceed independently of reforms in textiles (as happened in East Africa but not in Egypt and Pakistan). But the government must be willing to support textiles with funds from the central budget instead of with taxes on cotton. Ultimately the textile industry must also be reformed.

- Smallholder credit is a problem and may present an obstacle to reform. Growers need seeds, fertilizers, and chemicals in order to produce cotton. Prior to reform state cotton companies provided small farmers with these inputs in exchange for cotton. This arrangement effectively eliminated any potential moral hazard problem, since the state company was the only buyer.

Notes

1. The United States, the European Union (EU), and Australia account for the rest.

2. Cotton-producing countries with little or no government intervention in marketing and trade include Argentina, Australia, El Salvador, Guatemala, Israel, Nicaragua, Nigeria, Paraguay, Peru, and Venezuela.

3. The most valuable by-product of seed cotton is cotton oil. In 1998 some 3.97 million tons of cotton oil were produced, and 6 percent of this amount was traded internationally. Cotton oil averaged $718 per ton in 1998.

4. Varderrama (1993) estimates that a decline of about 53,000 tons in China's net trade adds $.01 to the Cotlook A Index.

5. Offering prices are ¢/lb., c.i.f. northern Europe, cash against documents on arrival of vessel, including profit and agent's commission. The quotations represent forward (nearby) delivery, normally up to two months. *Cotton Outlook* staff compile the quotations by interviewing cotton traders in northern Europe and factoring in other relevant market developments. The offering prices are published, together with the day's indexes, around 2:30 p.m. UK time. Quotations include cotton growths not offered in volume, but these quotations are not included in the indexes. The quotations reflect the competitive level of offering prices, so a buyer would normally expect a slightly lower price. Two sets of indexes run concurrently when old and new crops are available, one with nearby and one with forward quotes (the dual

index system). Forward indexes have been introduced as early as February and, in the case of the B Index, as late as July.

6. These exchanges include the Alexandria Cotton Exchange, the Bombay Cotton Exchange, the Bremen Cotton Exchange, the Chicago Board of Trade, the Le Havre Cotton Exchange, the Hong Kong Commodity Exchange, the Karachi Cotton Exchange, the Liverpool Cotton Exchange, the London Commodity Exchange, the Osaka Sampin Exchange, the São Paulo Commodity Exchange, and the Shanghai Cotton Exchange.

7. The absence of a non-U.S. hedging instrument for cotton has long been recognized. *Cotton Outlook* (December 12, 1997, p. 3) reported: "The lack of an international trading instrument other than the No. 2 [NYCE] contract—one which consistently reflects broad world cotton market developments but is capable of being used as 'hedge'—continues to be a shortcoming of the current pricing system."

8. Other institutions involved in the cotton industry are the National Agricultural Research Organization, Ministry of Agriculture Extension Services, Development Finance Department of the Bank of Uganda, and Agricultural Policy Committee.

9. The board of the CDO comprises the chairman, who is appointed by the Minister of Agriculture; representatives of the ministries of agriculture, trade and industry, and finance and of the National Agriculture Research Organization; six private sector representatives (two cotton growers, one oil miller, one ginner, one exporter, and one representative of the textile industry); and the managing director, who is appointed by the board.

10. Cotton in West Africa is produced mostly in eight countries: Benin, Burkina Faso, Cameroon, the Central African Republic, Chad, Côte d'Ivoire, Mali, and Togo. The West African countries have formed a monetary union arrangement with France. Their domestic currency (the CFA franc) is linked to the French franc at a rate of 100:1 (prior to the 1994 devaluation, the rate was 50:1). On January 1, 1999, the CFA franc was linked to the euro through the French franc.

11. Some private sector activity in ginning operations has also taken place in Togo.

12. The West African Monetary Union (*Union Economique et Monétaire Ouest-Africaine*, or UEMOA) and the Economic and Monetary Community of Central Africa (*Communauté Economique et Monétaire de l'Afrique Centrale*, or CEMAC).

13. Egypt went through a cycle of liberalization in the mid-1800s (Hafez 1946). Cotton in Egypt was first commercially grown in the 1820s. The government handled most aspects of production, marketing, and trade in an effort to promote the textile industry. In 1849 the cotton sector was fully liberalized, and in 1861 Egypt established the world's first Cotton Futures Exchange in Alexandria. The Egyptian cotton industry came under state control in 1961, and the exchange was officially suspended.

14. One casualty of this policy may have been the New Orleans Cotton Exchange. Established in 1871 (almost the same time as the New York Cotton Exchange), the New Orleans Exchange terminated operations in 1964.

15. In the last 10 years, the A Index has fluctuated around an average of 70¢/lb, reaching a low of 55¢/lb in October 1993 and a high of 116¢/lb in May 1995.

References

Baffes, John, and Jacob Meerman. 1998. "From Prices to Incomes: Agricultural Subsidization without Protection?" *World Bank Research Observer* 13 (2):191–211.

Cotton Outlook. Various issues. Liverpool: Cotlook Limited.

Emery, Walter L. 1975. "Understanding the Cotton Futures Market." In H. Jiler, ed., *Forecasting Commodity Prices: How the Experts Analyze the Markets*. New York: Commodity Research Bureau, Inc.

Farooqui, Hameed M., Clyde R. Keaton, and Guy W. Miller. 1958. *Agricultural Marketing in Pakistan*. Karachi: Amin Book Company.

Hafez, Abdel-Rahman, M. 1946. *The Alexandria Cotton Market*. Cairo: Fuad University Press.

Huque, Heshamul. 1987. *Cotton Production in Pakistan: A Story of Success*. Karachi: Pakistan Central Cotton Committee.

ICAC (International Cotton Advisory Committee). 1999a. *Government Measures Affecting the Cotton Sector*. Washington, D.C.

_____. 1999b. *Statements of the 57th Plenary Meeting*. Washington, D.C.

Kahkonen, Satu, and Howard Leathers. 1997. "Is There Life After Liberalization? Marketing of Maize and Cotton in Zambia and Zimbabwe." Preliminary draft prepared for the U.S. Agency for International Development. Institutional Reform and the Informal Sector (IRIS) Center, University of Maryland.

Martin, Will. 1996 "The Abolition of the Multi-Fibre Arrangement and its Implications for Fiber Markets." Paper presented at the conference "The WTO and the Uruguay Round Agreement: Implications for South Asian Agriculture," Kathmandu, April 22–24.

Pursell, Garry. 1998. "Cotton Policies in Francophone Africa." Development Research Group. Washington, D.C.: World Bank. Mimeo.

Sabune, Jolly. 1996. "Experiences of Uganda with Privatization of its Cotton Industry." Paper presented at the 55th Plenary Meeting of the International Cotton Advisory Committee, Tashkent, Uzbekistan.

Townsend, Terry. 1996. "Marketing Cotton in Africa." Paper presented at the Workshop on Development in Africa, Abidjan, Côte d'Ivoire, June 30–July 4.

Townsend, Terry, and Andrei Guitchounts. 1994, "A Survey of Cotton Income and Price Support Programs." *Proceedings of the Beltwide Cotton Conferences*, Washington, DC.

Varangis, Panos, Donald Larson, and Elton Thigpen. 1995, "What Does Experience in Other Cotton-Producing Countries Suggest for Policy Reforms in Francophone Africa?" International Economics Department. Washington D.C.: World Bank. Mimeo.

Varderrama, Carlos. 1993. "Modeling International Cotton Prices." *Proceedings of the Beltwide Cotton Conferences*. National Cotton Council of America, Memphis, Tenn.

World Bank. 1994. "Uganda: Cotton Sub-Sector Development Project." Staff Appraisal Report No. UG-PE-2977. Washington D.C.

6

Cereal Market Liberalization in Africa

Jonathan Coulter and Colin Poulton

IN THE 1980s AND 1990s many countries in Sub-Saharan Africa began reforming their cereal marketing systems, reducing state intervention in order to encourage private trading. Most governments initiated the reforms in response to pressure from international financial institutions and generally as part of wide-ranging structural adjustment programs. The reforms were necessary in light of the unsustainable burden interventionist policies had imposed on government finances and macroeconomic stability. Despite this fact the reforms were politically contentious, and governments often implemented them reluctantly. This chapter reviews experience with cereal marketing liberalization in Sub-Saharan Africa prior to 2000 and suggests ways to improve the performance of the liberalized systems.[1]

Sub-Saharan Africa is a relatively minor producer of cereals, accounting for only 4.2 percent of world production (table 6.1). Only South Africa exports significant quantities of grain to countries outside the continent, but the volume is very small compared to the volumes exported by countries such as the United States and Argentina. Yet cereal market reform in Sub-Saharan Africa merits special study. In most African countries cereals are staple foods, and effective marketing systems are vital to food security. Cereal production also provides a livelihood for large numbers of small farmers. Moreover, with the notable exception of South Africa, Sub-Saharan Africa is relatively underdeveloped in terms of both physical infrastructure and institutional environment, so that market reform is a particularly challenging task.[2]

**Table 6.1 Cereal Crop Production in Sub-Saharan Africa
(millions of tons)**

	1990	1991	1992	1993	1994	1995	1996	1997	1998	1999
Maize	23.2	22.7	19.8	25.0	25.4	25.4	27.9	25.4	25.3	26.6
Sorghum	11.1	15.1	16.1	14.8	16.6	16.1	19.6	18.1	19.5	19.0
Millet	10.7	10.5	10.9	10.7	12.1	11.7	12.4	12.2	13.5	12.8
Rice (paddy)	9.2	9.9	9.9	10.3	9.5	10.4	10.6	11.5	11.5	11.7
Wheat	2.0	2.2	2.1	2.0	2.0	2.2	2.6	2.6	2.7	2.1
Total	56.2	60.4	58.8	62.8	65.6	65.8	73.1	69.8	72.5	72.2

Source: Food and Agriculture Organization.

The findings in this chapter are based largely on four short case studies of reform experiences in Ghana, Mali, Tanzania, and Zimbabwe. Mali, Tanzania, and Zimbabwe entered the 1980s with marketing boards that held a statutory monopoly on procuring and distributing grain. Prices were pan-territorial (regardless of transport costs), and a series of margins related consumer and producer prices, with an allowance for the costs and charges of the intermediate organizations.

Despite these similarities the experiences of the three countries differed in several important ways:

- Mali suffered periodic food crises induced by drought and had only one important export crop (cotton). Yet Mali's financial situation was relatively strong, since membership in the CFA franc zone enforced financial discipline. Mali experienced only one period of major inflation immediately after the devaluation of the CFA franc at the end of 1993.
- Tanzania experienced a radical socialist transformation in the 1960s and 1970s, resulting in a nationalized banking system that was used extensively to bail out financially strapped parastatals and government-controlled cooperatives. Tanzania's weak public finances stood in stark contrast to public finances in Mali.
- Zimbabwe gained its independence only in the 1980s and unlike the other two countries had to cope with a dualistic agricultural economy inherited from its colonial days.

In Ghana, Mali, and Tanzania economic policies before liberalization resulted in an overvalued currency and low prices for agricultural producers. But in Ghana most trade had always been in private hands, making the economy a particularly useful case study. Traders were stigmatized as speculators, however, and in 1981–82 a campaign against those considered guilty of hoarding resulted in the seizure of substantial quantities of grain and other goods. As in the other countries preliberalization credit policies were biased against private agricultural trade and toward the parastatal sector.

Grain Markets in Africa

Root crops and plantains predominate in much of West Africa. But in most of Sub-Saharan Africa the coarse grains—mainly maize, sorghum, and millet—are the main staple foods. Sorghum and millet still predominate in regions bordering the Sahel, the semidesert southern fringe of the Sahara, but elsewhere maize has become the main crop, particularly for trade. Except in areas of low rainfall, maize produces higher yields than millet and sorghum, in part because of new high-yielding varieties, and in most of southern and eastern Africa consumers prefer it.

Rice is an important crop in certain areas, particularly West Africa, but much of the rice supply is imported from countries in the Far East where production costs are low. Wheat is important in urban areas, but while production is high in southern Africa, most wheat is imported.

As Jones (1998) argues, grains and other staple foods are essential to economic development, political stability, and the welfare of the poor. Urbanization, industrialization, and agricultural specialization cannot occur without an efficient food-marketing system to replace household food production. Low-income households may spend 30–50 percent of their food

Table 6.2. Cereal Imports and Exports in Sub-Saharan Africa (millions of tons)

	1990	1991	1992	1993	1994	1995	1996	1997	1998
Imports									
Maize	1.0	1.1	4.2	2.6	2.3	1.6	1.3	2.1	2.0
Sorghum	0.1	0.4	0.5	0.3	0.5	0.3	0.2	0.2	0.2
Rice	2.6	3.1	3.2	3.1	3.2	3.2	3.1	3.6	4.0
Wheat*	4.9	5.6	5.7	5.5	6.0	5.1	5.2	6.4	8.9
Total imports	8.6	10.2	13.6	11.5	12.0	10.2	9.8	12.3	15.1
Exports	1.4	0.7	0.3	1.4	1.8	1.2	0.7	0.7	0.8
Net trade balance	7.2	9.5	13.3	10.1	10.2	9.0	9.1	11.6	14.3

* including the wheat equivalent of imported flour.
Note: Trade in commodities amounting to less than 50,000 tons is not reported. A large proportion of cross-border trade among African countries is not recorded.
Source: Food and Agriculture Organization.

budget just on food grains, so that price increases hit the poor hardest (Newbery 1989). In addition a large number of consumers who depend on purchased grains belong to farming households. Even in grain-producing areas with surpluses, most households usually do not produce enough grain to meet their needs. A few farmers are responsible for the surplus; the rest must buy additional grain at market prices.

Key Characteristics of Grain Markets

The low value-to-weight ratio of grains makes them costly to transport, leads to wide price swings between times of surplus and deficit, and makes organizing outgrower schemes (contract farming) to enhance production difficult. Together with climatic disadvantages, the low capitalization of smallholder agriculture, and ecological factors, the low value-to-weight ratio forces peripheral areas of Africa to import both food and feed grains and makes the continent a net importer of grain compared with the rest of the world. At the same time urbanization and changing tastes are increasing the continent's dependency on imported food.

Low elasticities of supply and demand also contribute to price volatility. To accommodate these inherent realities of grain markets in Africa, prices need to vary by location and season, and neighboring countries need to use trade as a tool to guarantee food security. But this practice is often in opposition to political imperatives for national self-sufficiency and panterritorial and panseasonal pricing. The contradiction between logistical and other realities on the one hand, and political imperatives on the other, makes the grain market reform particularly problematic and encourages renewed government intervention (sometimes known as second-generation controls), which itself discourages private investment in grain marketing.

The implication of these characteristics is that in order to prosper under liberalized marketing systems, smallholder farmers in many areas of Africa need to diversify. These farmers need to move away from the production of food crops that generate surpluses, particularly maize, which governments have often promoted in preference to all other crops.

Logistical Disadvantages in Cereal Markets

The physical and economic characteristics of cereals distinguish these commodities from other durable agricultural products. The most important characteristic, particularly for coarse grains, is the low value-to-weight ratio. A typical price for American No. 2 yellow maize is around $110 f.o.b. (free on board) Gulf ports, while white maize of the kind consumed in Africa sells typically sells at a premium of US$10–15 per ton.[3] Despite this premium, the value of white maize is low in relation to transport costs within Africa, leading to large differences between import and export parity prices. The transportation problem in Africa is acute, as the necessary infrastructure is poorly developed in most areas. Transportation costs are highest for landlocked countries like Zambia. According to the Zambian Food Reserve Agency, the costs per ton of importing South African white maize to Lusaka and the southern Congolese border in January 1999 were as follows:

White maize f.o.t. (free on truck), Gauteng zone, South Africa $94
Delivered to Lusaka, Zambia $190
Delivered to Congolese border $225

These figures show that the costs of transporting the maize to Lusaka and the Congolese border are as much or more than the FOT cost of the grain itself.

Estimates of the cost of importing maize from the United States show a cost of more than $93 per ton, depending on the port (table 6.3). Congestion at a port may mean that the cheapest route is not available.

The total shipping costs are virtually the same as the f.o.b. Gulf price.

High shipping costs affect Africa's ability to export. Most of the productive maize-producing areas are located in the interior plateaus of the continent, including the northern area of South Africa (formerly the Transvaal), the Southern Highlands of Tanzania, and Western Kenya. However, in supplying international markets, Africa is on a very weak competitive footing compared with other major grain producers such as the United States, which have low-cost rail- and water-based transportation systems. South Africa frequently exports maize but is seriously handicapped with regard to transportation. Despite efficient rail and port handling systems, the cost of

Table 6.3. The Cost of Shipping Maize from the United States to Lusaka, Zambia, 1995 (dollars per ton)

F.o.b. U.S. Gulf to Lusaka, via:	Ocean freight and insurance	Port charges, bags, and bagging costs	Inland freight and insurance	Total, including losses and contingencies (5 percent of costs from CIF[a])
Dar es Salaam	44.5	25.0	75.9	150.4
Maputo	27.0	22.0	70.5	124.1
Beira	27.0	22.0	41.0	93.1

a. CIF = costs, insurance, and freight.
Source: Zambian Food Reserve Agency.

shipping grain from the major grain-producing areas of Transvaal to f.o.b. Durban is around $30 per ton, or close to three times the cost of shipping by barge from Chicago to New Orleans.

For similar reasons, inland locations of Africa sometimes experience difficulty competing in coastal markets with imports from other continents, particularly when liberalization has reduced trade barriers. In two of the three ports cited in table 6.3, the cost of inland freight is higher than the cost of importing grain from the United States. The situation is particularly marked in West Africa, where coastal states import large quantities of rice from the Far East.

High transport costs provide some theoretical justification for government support to mitigate price fluctuations in landlocked countries. The problem is particularly serious if a whole region (such as southern Africa) has an aggregate surplus or deficit. In the absence of any form of intervention by the governments involved or of a fully developed futures market (except in South Africa), in years of surplus prices could fall to near zero export parity levels, while in years of surplus they could rise to high import parity levels (over $250 per ton in places like Lusaka). In the case of southern Tanzania, a maize-producing area around 1,000 km from the sea, prices would be totally unremunerative in times of regional surplus in the absence of some form of public price stabilization (Coulter 1994).[4] Pinkney (1993) argues that massive price variability in southern Africa would have adverse consequences for both producers and consumers.[5]

Other Handicaps in Grain Production

These logistical disadvantages have important implications for Africa's liberalized grain markets and together with a number of other factors make Africa a net importer of food and feed grains. The related factors include:

- Climatic disadvantages, including unreliable rainfall patterns over much of southern Africa;
- Low capitalization of smallholder agriculture;
- Ecological factors such as the vulnerability of tropical soils to intensive mechanized cropping (a notable constraint on intensification in West Africa); and
- Growing demand for imported cereals, mainly wheat and rice, due to urbanization, a desire for convenience in food preparation, and changing tastes.[6]

The absence of inputs and technical support also constrains grain production. Structural adjustment has squeezed the budgets of extension departments and left behind leaner and more cautious banking sectors with little interest in smallholder farmers, since lending to this group is likely to involve high transaction costs and repayment problems. But private agribusinesses have successfully used outgrower schemes to develop small-holder production of a range of crops, including cotton, tobacco, and vegetables for export. The agribusinesses supply inputs and technical support, but the farmers must market their crop through the companies. Unfortunately these schemes rarely work with cereal crops, as in the absence of an effective procurement monopoly farmers can easily sell the grain to other buyers who do not deduct the cost of inputs and technical support.[7] The lack of legal remedies and farmers' experience with government and donor-funded schemes (in which credit is often not repaid) encourage this practice.[8] The agribusinesses cannot afford the high costs of monitoring deliveries and repayment and therefore refrain from funding grain production.

Given the failure of seasonal credit markets for smallholder agricultural production, smallholder farmers must pay cash or else barter for their inputs. The financial circumstances of most smallholders make this situation an important obstacle to the adoption of modern technology that can increase yields (in instances where such technology remains profitable after a devaluation, the removal of input subsidies, or both).

Food grains crops have another disadvantage: the short-run price elasticities of both demand and supply for these grains in aggregate tend to be low. Fluctuations in production or demand are likely to translate into large price swings. One way of moderating such swings is through trade, but as we have seen poor logistics and the high cost of transport hinder commerce, and politicians tend to accord a low priority to the development of cross-border trade.

The Policy Conundrum

Liberalization policies easily fall afoul of major political priorities in newly independent states, where political leaders want to ensure that their countries can feed themselves without depending on supplies from elsewhere and that all farmers (even those far from markets) can sell food grains at a profit. Consequently politicians are sometimes unwilling to admit either that producer prices should vary by location and by season or that their countries should depend on trade as a means of guaranteeing food security.[9] Investing in transportation and infrastructure and promoting regional trade would greatly mitigate Africa's logistical disadvantages in commodity trading, but too often governments try to address the outcome rather than the cause by subsidizing domestic trade through parastatal marketing arrangements.

This problem poses a real conundrum for grain markets in Africa. State-controlled systems have by and large proved financially unsustainable for grain marketing, more so than for cash crops. Marketing revenues for cash crops are higher, while pricing issues are less location-specific, involve fewer interest groups, and thus are somewhat less politically charged. At the same time the extreme political sensitivity of grain crops means that liberalization is rarely fully realized. Liberalizing governments tend to move from state control to second-generation controls that involve considerable ad hoc intervention of a kind that renders private decisionmaking difficult.

Implications for Smallholder Farmers

In order to prosper under liberalized marketing systems, the best strategy for African smallholder farmers is often to diversify. In areas with a strong comparative advantage, they can sensibly continue producing marketable grain surpluses. In other areas they can benefit from assistance in identifying alternative cash crops with higher value-to-weight ratios and lower input requirements or other locally viable activities. Considerable efforts in this direction are already being made—for example with the extension of cotton production in Mozambique, Zambia, and Zimbabwe, efforts to encourage cassava and sweet potato plantings in Malawi and elsewhere, and the production of soybeans in northern Ghana. Similarly the production of pulses such as grams and pigeon peas (for export to India) in Kenya and Malawi and the development of export horticulture in Zimbabwe offer alternatives to surplus-generating crops.[10]

What Prompted Market Reforms?

Coarse grains have assumed major importance in African postindependence politics. In eastern and southern Africa, governments made an implicit social contract with the African majority to redress the neglect of smallholder agriculture during the colonial period (Jayne and others 1999). In doing so the new governments made use of the controlled marketing systems colonial governments began developing in the 1930s, believing that expanding these systems could spread the benefits accruing to settler farmers to millions of indigenous smallholders (Jenkins 1997). Public resources were devoted to raising yields through the provision of technical assistance, high-yielding varieties, and fertilizers. Given their need to unite diverse ethnic groups, the governments of newly independent countries could not contemplate varying producer prices according to transport costs, as such a move might be politically divisive. For this reason panterritorial pricing became sacrosanct. The social contract also incorporated the understanding that governments were responsible for ensuring cheap food for the urban population, and in some countries, particularly in West Africa, this policy took precedence over the interests of farmers.

This approach succeeded to varying degrees in raising smallholder incomes and promoting consumer welfare. In many cases the existence of an assured market provided a vital incentive for producers to adopt new technology, so much so that Jayne and Jones (1997) speak of a "smallholder green revolution" in eastern and southern Africa. But the approach was costly to implement and invariably resulted in an unsustainable drain on public finances. In the 1970s and 1980s in Tanzania, the parastatal National Milling Corporation and cooperative unions accumulated losses or doubtful debts (which ultimately had to be assumed by government) in excess of $600 million, mainly because of grain trading (Coulter and Golob 1991). In the early 1990s the deficits of Zimbabwe's Grain Marketing Board were 5 percent of GDP (Jenkins 1997). And by the late 1980s Zambia's subsidies to the maize sector had reached 17 percent of the government budget (Howard and Mungoma 1997). Costs were high owing to input subsidies, low repayment rates on loans, and the need to subsidize the transportation of grain from remote areas.[11]

This situation, coupled with analogous problems in other sectors, resulted in budgetary deficits and macroeconomic instability, and from the early 1980s gave international financial institutions major leverage over domestic agricultural policies in Africa. These institutions believed that governments were using extractive or low pricing policies that adversely affected production.[12] In many countries official monopolies could not be maintained and illegal private trade was flourishing. The practical effect of controlled single-channel systems was to subsidize supplies to a relatively privileged urban group at the expense of producers. In view of this situation, one by one African governments signed on to structural adjustment programs that required wide-ranging reforms and reduced the state's ability to intervene in grain markets.

While the cost of maintaining single-channel systems was a matter of considerable concern to local finance ministries, by and large governments implemented reforms reluctantly and, as noted earlier, only under pressure from international financial institutions. Even so policy reversals were frequent, state interventions continued, and official directives were inconsistent. These problems can be attributed to:

- *Widespread mistrust of markets among policymakers and government officials, particularly in countries like Mozambique and Tanzania, where governments had previously embraced socialist ideas.* Moreover in many countries (particularly in eastern and southern Africa), few people had ever experienced the working of private grain markets.
- *Governments' commitment to the local populace under the implicit social contracts, which involved (among other things) input subsidies and assured markets for grain at panterritorial prices.*
- *Normal political processes that require politicians to respond to local interests and pressures, often with little consideration for the long-term conse-*

quences.[13] These processes are a factor in all governments—socialist, free market, or other—and pose the most intractable problem for would-be reformers. The recent increase in farm support in the United States confirms this observation.[14] The likelihood of opportunistic intervention is particularly great with staple crops in poor countries because the population is highly dependent on staples, both as producers and consumers.

The Impact of Liberalization

Liberalization appears to have been largely successful with regard to the level of consumer prices, the producer's share of consumer prices, the quality and variety of products offered to consumers, and the impact on public finances (in the last case when liberalization measures have been carried through). There has been no overall impact on the level of grain production, and the impact has been negative in eastern and southern Africa. Limited available information suggests that liberalization may have decreased overall price stability. The effect on beliefs and attitudes has been mixed.

How is the relative success of liberalization measured? Production levels and farmgate prices are the key indicators of the success of reforms. The assumption is that society benefits if both are higher, a notion that often does not hold true for food crops. For example, if liberalization raises producer prices, the net benefits may be negative because high prices can have an adverse impact on consumers, including the majority of farming households that are typically short of food. Likewise if liberalization causes production to fall and imports to rise, the overall impact is not necessarily adverse, since the allocation of resources within the economy may have improved. Farmers may be producing more high-value cash crops because in the absence of pan-territorial pricing grain production no longer makes sense.

We argue, then, that the efficiency of grain market liberalization can be measured most effectively using the following yardsticks:

- The level of production, but only in as much as it is a proxy for the nutritional status of populations;
- The average level of consumer prices (low prices are preferable);
- Economic efficiency in terms of the producer's share of consumer prices;
- The stability of prices over time, as stable prices enable farmers that produce surpluses to foresee revenues and make use of purchased inputs and allow consumers to budget for food expenditures;
- The quality and variety of products offered to consumers; and
- Public finances—that is, the need to continue government subsidies.

Grain Production

Official figures indicate that per capita grain production in Africa as a whole has remained static for the last 20 years. However, the impact of liberalization varied across countries, and the findings presented below suggest that these figures hide important regional differences. To a greater extent than in West Africa, countries in eastern and southern Africa seem to have used their marketing boards to promote the production of high-yielding varieties. These are the countries where production was most affected by the (partial) withdrawal of state services. Liberalization also affected the four countries under discussion differently. Per capita production rose significantly in Ghana, the country where changes were least pronounced, climbed slightly in Mali, and declined in Zimbabwe.[15] Per capita production has declined in Tanzania since 1989 (figure 6.1).

Jayne and Jones (1997) present evidence that per capita production generally fell after liberalization efforts began in southern and eastern Africa. Of six countries surveyed—Kenya, Malawi, South Africa, Tanzania, Zambia, and Zimbabwe—only Tanzania enjoyed an increase in production in 1990–95 over 1980–89. All six countries saw per capita production reduced

Figure 6.1. Per Capita Cereals Production in Case Study Countries and in Africa as a Whole, 1980–98

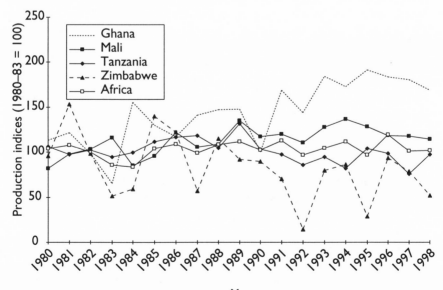

Source: FAOSTAT.

in amounts ranging from 18 to 39 percent. Jayne and Jones attribute the overall decline to the effects of policy reform. The state-led smallholder green revolutions observed in Kenya and Tanzania in the 1970s and in Zambia and Zimbabwe in the 1980s had become fiscally unsustainable, and private marketing systems had not been able to stimulate more intensive production. As a result the region continued to move toward a structural food deficit (Jayne and Jones 1997).

Our own observations suggest that this diagnosis is at least partially correct. Caution is needed in interpreting these production figures, however, since the period between 1990 and 1995 includes the most serious drought year (1992) ever recorded in southern Africa and a second drought in 1995. Some of the decline may also be attributable to the incomplete liberalization efforts and the contradictory approaches that were adopted. Most significantly a fall in per capita production is not altogether surprising in view of the physical and economic characteristics of grain.

Consumer Prices

Available research findings indicate overwhelmingly that consumers have gained from liberalization and that there has been a major increase in market efficiency. Jayne and others (1996) examine trends in real food prices in six Sub-Saharan countries (Ethiopia, Ghana, Kenya, Mali, Zimbabwe, and Zambia) and find that grain and meal prices declined in Mali (after 1982), Kenya (after 1988), and Ethiopia (after 1990). In Kenya, Mali, Zambia, and Zimbabwe, the negative impact on low-income consumers was wholly or partly offset by other reforms providing access to food products that had previously been unavailable because of regulation. A number of factors contributed to a decline in real consumer food prices:

- The removal of trade barriers, a reform that improved the transmission of declining real world prices into domestic economies (Ghana and Mali);
- Increased food aid flows during the reform period (Ethiopia and Mali); and
- Increased competition in food marketing and processing, accompanied by lower costs—developments that reduced marketing margins (Kenya, Mali, Zambia, and Zimbabwe).

In Kenya, Zambia, and Zimbabwe demand for unrefined maize meal was widely viewed as negligible, but by 1994 unrefined maize accounted for 40–60 percent of total urban meal demand. The availability of this type of maize, which sold for 60–75 percent of the price of roller meal, helped offset the adverse effect of eliminating consumer subsidies on roller meal (Jayne and others 1995). Many beneficiaries were small farm households that are typically net buyers of grain. The developmental significance of this shift cannot be overstated. If households can buy grain more cheaply, they do not need to devote as many resources to becoming self-sufficient and can diversify into cash crops with a relatively high value. A later survey of rural consumers in Kenya showed that 60 percent felt that maize had become more available to consumers since liberalization, while 31 percent felt it was less available (Jayne and others 1999). Finally Badiane and others (1997) draw evidence from the countries discussed here to determine that average real prices for maize declined during liberalization.

Producer Prices

The removal of panterritorial prices has invariably favored farmers close to major urban markets compared with those in remote locations, but otherwise the effects of reforms on producer prices have varied from country to country. Preliberalization policies taxed smallholder production in much of West Africa, for example, and not surprisingly real producer prices rose with liberalization. Jayne and others (1998) report that in Ethiopia average real prices for maize and white teff (the country's primary cereal crop) rose after liberalization in areas with a cereal surplus but fell in most regions with deficits. The researchers attribute the lower price spreads (at least in part) to the efficiency of liberalized marketing systems. However, distinguishing the impact of liberalization from the effects of peace—which came to the country around the same time—is difficult.

In contrast Jayne and Jones (1997) argue that preliberalization policies supported producer prices in much of southern and eastern Africa. Producers located far from markets benefited from the transportation subsidies inherent in panterritorial pricing. Even when an overvalued currency implied an indirect tax on producers, the effect was offset by subsidies on purchased inputs and other investments in the public marketing system. The beneficial impact of liberalization on real producer prices is thus restricted to the most accessible areas, but even there it has often been offset by larger increases in the prices of purchased inputs.

Price Stability

Seasonal price variability is necessary to the efficient functioning of a liberalized marketing system, as it provides producers with incentives to store crops. But the variability in spot wholesale markets is often far in excess of what should be required to cover carrying (capital and storage) costs.[16] Data for Uganda for 1995–97 and Zambia for 1994–95 to 1997–98 show average real price increases of 80 percent or more over six monthly periods. However, it is difficult to make definitive statements about price stability, both because comprehensive data is lacking and because in many African countries official grain monopolies often operated stable price regimes that hid dramatic price variations in unofficial parallel markets.

Seasonal price variability has been high since liberalization, mainly because the private sector has been slow to step in when governments have reduced their role in storing grains. This failure can be attributed to:

- Uncertainty regarding public policies on international trade—for instance, whether they will be applied consistently—so that speculative storage is perceived as hazardous;
- Uncertainty over the disposal of remaining public stocks and food aid, which governments may feel they need to ensure food security or stabilize prices, so that the overhang inhibits private storage decisions;
- Weak systems of crop forecasting that make it difficult to determine whether a surplus or deficit situation exists;
- An absence of information on private stockholding (except in South Africa, where such information is required by law);
- Weak financial frameworks and banking sectors;
- A shortage of creditworthy customers dealing in grain and of sound collateral for lending, because real estate outside of urban areas is not accepted as collateral and warehouse receipt systems that allow banks to lend against the security of stock-in-trade (inventory credit) are in their infancy; and
- Farmers' reluctance to store crops in the volumes required to ensure intraseasonal price stability, either because the farmers need ready cash or, in wetter climates, because they fear storage losses from insects, rodents, or molds.[17]

These factors are particularly evident in Ghana and Tanzania and are echoed in Zambia. In Mali the situation is more satisfactory because farmers often store millet and sorghum without threshing for several years (both grains can be stored for such periods). In Zimbabwe government storage remains high, crowding out storage by farmers, traders, and millers.

Some price-stabilizing measures are difficult to implement in African countries. In an economy with many small traders and farmers, determining the level of the stocks that are being held is almost impossible. Probably the most important steps governments can take to bring relative stability to the market are creating a transparent trade regime and maintaining a low level of public stocks in order to minimize the overhang effect.[18] If traders are really free to import and export grain and have the necessary access to foreign exchange, a country can import a degree of price stability from the international market. In the case of yellow maize, a notable spike in 1996 to around $190 per ton was the single aberration from the relatively stable price (f.o.b. U.S.-Gulf port) of $100 to $130 per ton. A transparent trade regime may permit the financing of domestic trade transactions in hard currency, a measure that eases domestic funding constraints. Allowing stock-in-trade to be used as collateral through a credible system of warehouse receipts can facilitate these processes.

Grain Markets

Jayne and Jones (1997) found evidence that some features of the reformed market systems promote growth and serve to reduce dualism—for instance by improving smallholders' access to urban markets and eliminating barriers to movement. But these incentives have not been sufficient to offset the effects of cutbacks in government transfers, which were an integral part of the formerly controlled systems.

Tanzania exemplifies one effect of liberalization: the emergence of large numbers of informal traders. While this development is a welcome one, atomistic competition has some disadvantages. Even if they approach the ideal of perfect competition in terms of static efficiency, small informal traders have significant dynamic disadvantages. Their small scale and limited resources and education hinder their capacity to innovate. Further they are generally unable to enter into long-term contractual arrangements, largely because they do not have the capital and cannot access bank finance, and they store for very short periods. The larger players are able to take advantage of the new policy environment, engaging in interseasonal storage, acquiring specific assets such as grain dryers and stores, developing long-term contractual relationships with industrial users, and introducing new forms of packaging. Markets work most efficiently when small and large traders coexist.

In order to overcome the shortage of market information, capital availability, and a sound legal framework for contract enforcement, informal traders tend to deal through networks.[19] However, this situation has the effect of making markets imperfectly competitive (Barrett 1997). Badiane (1998) also notes that a trader's social network and reliance on retaining profits can constrain business expansion.

Despite these observations we have encountered considerable evidence of progressive market behavior stemming from liberalization. Entrepreneurs seek to enhance their competitive position in the marketplace in a variety of ways—for example by tailoring the terms of sales to customers' requirements, increasing the range and quality of products offered, and improving packaging. In state-controlled systems the kind of competitive pressure that stimulates such improvements is often lacking.

Public Finances

When liberalization is carried through to its conclusion, as it was in Mali and Tanzania, it results in major financial savings for the government. In Zimbabwe, however, the government did not carry through with liberalization but instead sought to maintain high levels of public procurement with inflexible panterritorial pricing structures. The immediate impact was to increase the cost to the government budget. Similarly a high level of budgetary losses characterized the initial stages of liberalization in Tanzania (until 1990).

Mozambique also found that liberalization saved on public support to the parastatal sector. Until the early 1990s the parastatal AGRICOM managed grain marketing with financial assistance from the Swedish Government. AGRICOM was liquidated in 1993 and replaced by another parastatal, the Instituto de Cereais. This agency has survived by forming an unusual association with a private trading company and dollarizing borrowing—which, up to 1999, it unfailingly reimbursed.

Zambia's reform program eliminated maize subsidies. But the government still subsidizes imported fertilizers and sometimes grains as well. There have been various official credit programs to support emergent farmers and traders, but invariably the level of default has been high. Indeed much of the default can be viewed as a form of tacit subsidy. The overall impact of liberalization on public finances has never been reckoned. However, a review of the liberalization of maize marketing calculates that direct food subsidies (which averaged ZK 15–20 billion per year in current terms in the five years prior to 1993) were replaced by indirect subsidies that could amount to ZK 43 billion for the marketing years 1993–94 and 1994–95 (MAFF 1995). These figures underscore the high costs associated with incomplete liberalization processes, inflation notwithstanding.

Obstacles to Reform

Misgivings about reform and a lack of genuine commitment on the part of government decisionmakers are among the major obstacles to reform, as we have seen. Other factors that hinder reform are weaknesses in the wider policy environment and the financial framework, the poor performance of restructured marketing boards, the reluctance to free up cross-border trade, and uncoordinated donor support.

Lack of Wholehearted Government Commitment

Lack of commitment is the greatest obstacle to reform. Among the countries under discussion, Zimbabwe is the clearest example of an economy that lacks the leadership to successfully pursue reforms. Ghana and Tanzania also have commitment problems, as evidenced in the imposition of discretionary controls over international trade, the use of food reserves to preserve panterritorial pricing (in Tanzania), and a reluctance to restructure or eliminate dysfunctional marketing boards. Likewise Zambia's liberalization process has been rendered incomplete by the government's decision to use the Food Reserve Agency in unintended ways, including for importing commercial grains and fertilizer. The government's proclivity for ad hoc intervention and its lack of clarity in promulgating and applying rules has dampened investor confidence and diminished the dynamism of the liberalized marketing system. In addition the government of Zimbabwe has given companies operating large roller mills preferential access to cheap maize supplies, implicitly discriminating against small hammer mills. In 1997 the government of Ghana created a similar situation by suddenly giving some importers duty-free access to the market.

Jayne and others (1999) describe a second generation of controls that involve distribution programs run by governments or nongovernmental organizations (NGOs). These programs, which subsidize inputs and output prices for smallholders, undermine private trading incentives. They in fact create their own vicious circle: since the subsidies make it impossible to recover real costs, the private sector is reluctant to engage in activities that involve subsidies. Sometimes it is simply the fear of government intervention that discourages private players. The lack of private sector response in turn creates a vacuum that can be used to rationalize an even greater government role.

Lack of commitment may reflect ideological opposition, pressure from vested interests, or bureaucratic failure. The Kenyan experience provides the strongest example of the power of vested interests. In the late 1980s and early 1990s, the European Union (EU) tried to help the Kenyan government liberalize its cereal markets against a background of rent-seeking in controls over the movement of grain and nepotism in the running of the marketing board (NCPB). The exercise proved frustrating to the consultants and officials involved, and the overall benefits were questionable.[20] During the 1990s, however, Kenya made considerable progress in liberalization, particularly in slimming down the NCPB. Jones (1998) suggests that this success was largely the result of a shift in the interest of politically influential groups, which had been extracting rents from marketing controls but turned to evading import duties on imported maize.

Unlike the other countries under discussion, Mali has a system for addressing and resolving problems of commitment. This system makes use of the coordinating role of the Program for Restructuring the Cereals Market (PRMC) in building consensus among donors and government decisionmakers, with the conditionality attached to international financial institutions' support as a last resort. Although certain urban groups that were adversely affected by the devaluation of the CFA franc at the end of 1993 pressed for a reversal of the liberalization process, the government has maintained the proliberalization policies.

Mali's success can be attributed both to its consensus-building mechanism and to the efforts of far-sighted individuals on both the government and donor sides. Donor organizations showed considerable self-discipline when they joined the government in forming the PRMC, because they combined their financial contributions and agreed that decisions on disbursement would be made by consensus. This arrangement limited the potential for striking bilateral deals (such as dumping food aid) that could undermine the sense of unity and send contradictory signals to the host government. As underlined in Coulter (1994), lack of donor coordination can introduce contradictions into the liberalization process[21].

The most outstanding example of effective grain market liberalization in Africa so far is South Africa, and its success owes much to the commitment of the government. South Africa abolished its single-channel marketing system and its Maize Board after 1995 without adverse effects on food security and without precipitating a stampede out of maize production. Key to this success was the government's lack of interest in preserving the old system, which had been constructed primarily to protect white farmers. The government did not try to create food security reserves or buffer stocks and otherwise minimized opportunities for the discretionary exercise of power. Laws and rules affecting trade are now drawn up in consultation with industry groups and are applied fairly.

Table 6.4 provides a snapshot of the remaining constraints to effective liberalization in 13 African countries. Mali, Senegal, and South Africa are the only countries where policies can be described as unambiguously proliberalization and where there are no second-generation controls.[22] Other countries vary in the coherence of their approaches. When faced with marketing problems, for instance, governments are generally quick to tackle symptoms such as localized shortages or complaints about low prices. But they are much slower to address causes such as poor logistics, high transaction costs, or simply the wrong mix of crops for local circumstances.

Most of the discussion so far has focused on central government policymakers' commitment (or lack of it) to liberalization. Yet commitment is also important at the local level, where village, district, and regional administrations can hinder marketing activity by imposing and enforcing high taxes or levies and bureaucratic licensing requirements. In some countries the liberalization of marketing is reported to have eased the burden of such controls on traders. However, controls remain significant at the local level, even in countries where national policy has changed.[23] Local controls may be imposed because of hostility to liberalization at the grass-roots level, for rent-seeking purposes, or to raise revenue for local administrations. The rev-

Table 6.4. Progress of Liberalization in Nine African Countries

Country	Year	Major changes	Areas of incomplete liberalization
Benin*	1990	Parastatal downsized to minimal food security function	Continuing regulation of fertilizer importation, distribution, and pricing (leading to parallel market)
			Local movement restrictions remain and periodic trade bans
Ethiopia	1990	Liberalization of internal trade	Pervasive presence of kella charges on grain movements
			Government control of imports and exports
			Food aid depressing domestic price levels
			Important role for "party-statals"
Ghana	1990**	End of minimum producer prices	Parastatal overstaffed and unreformed
	1993	Government starts encouraging private storage and exports	Discretionary provision of import permits and duty exemptions
			Ad hoc government intervention in trade lending and fertilizer imports
			Weak crop forecasting and market information system
Kenya	1988	Limited unlicensed maize trade allowed	
	1992	Liberalization process practically halted	
	1996	Major downsizing of parastatal (NCPB)	Discretionary provision of import permits and duty exemptions
Malawi	1987	End of trading and milling monopoly	Heavy parastatal involvement in trade and storage crowding out private sector
	1987	Strategic grain reserve established	Panterritorial pricing
			Government control of exports

(Table continues on the following page.)

Table 6.4. (continued)

Country	Year	Major changes	Areas of incomplete liberalization
Mali	1981	Liberalization of coarse grain trade, 1981	No major policy contradictions
	1987	Drastic downsizing of parastatal (OPAM) to manage national security stock and complementary functions. Range of "accompanying measures" to develop domestic trade	
	1987	Liberalization of rice marketing	
Madagascar*	1986	Expanded marketing role for private sector	Some restrictions on grain movement, import/export, and trade entry remain
	1991	All input and output prices liberalized	
	1995	Rice import tariff reduced	
Mozambique	1993	Closure of parastatal AGRICOM	Role of new parastatal founded in 1993 remains unclear
	1996	End of minimum pricing regime	Licensing restrictions on cross-border trade with Malawi, the main market for northern surpluses
South Africa		Liberalization of internal and external trade	None
	1997	Closure of Maize Board	
	1996	SAFEX lists maize contracts	
Senegal*	1994	Parastatal (SAED) relinquished control over paddy marketing	No major policy contradictions (but no private suppliers of seasonal credit had emerged by 1997)
	1995	All rice marketing margins liberalized, import monopoly (CPSP) dismantled, and SAED privatized	

Country	Year		
Tanzania	1984	Gradual liberalization of trading, from 1984	Ad hoc regulation of export trade, including bans
	1990	End of parastatal trading role for NMC	Ad hoc district-level controls on grain movement
	1990	Strategic grain reserve started	
	1991	Recognition of co-ops as private institutions	
Zambia	1992	End of public trading monopoly	Continued de facto subsidization of agricultural inputs
	1995	Creation of Food Reserve Agency with limited and well-defined functions	Government uses FRA to import grains and fertilizer, crowding out public sector
Zimbabwe	1992	Gradual liberalization of trading	Parastatal import and export monopoly
			Heavy parastatal trade and storage crowds out private sector
			Continued panterritorial and seasonal pricing
			Subsidies to consumers of roller meal since 1998

Notes:
* See Badiane and others, (1997.)
** No formal marketing monopoly ever existed in Ghana.

enue problem could become increasingly serious as ongoing decentralization programs give local administrations added authority and financial
responsibilities.

Weak Policy Environments and Financial Frameworks

Badiane (1998) refers to the general problem of partial liberalization that
occurs when distorting policies and regulations in sectors directly related to
agricultural marketing—such as rural transportation and finance—are left
outside the reform process. An incomplete reform process jeopardizes the
efficient takeover of services by private traders. The same situation develops
when countries choose to exclude some output or input markets or certain
segments of distribution chains from the reform process.

Weak public finances and a poor institutional framework in the financial
sector generally affect agricultural reforms. Most African countries are
undergoing some sort of financial sector reform, but interest rates of upward
of 20 percent annually are still common. Rates are also variable and at times
very high in real terms. In Zambia in 1993–94 annual rates rose to over 100
percent, causing widespread insolvency among commercial farmers. Few
African countries have escaped high and variable interest rates, although
those in francophone Africa have been able to enforce tight monetary discipline through common regulatory systems. As we have seen, this discipline
may be one of the reasons Mali's reforms have gone further and enjoyed
more consistent support from decisionmakers than those of the other countries under discussion. With the exception of the one-time CFA franc devaluation, public sector morale has not been constantly undermined by inflation, and interest rates have been consistently low by African standards.

African banking sectors tend to be weak, to have limited branch networks, and to operate with high margins (spreads). In Ghana buoyant
markets for treasury bills often diminish banks' willingness to adopt innovate lending practices. The worst problems have occurred in countries like
Mozambique and Tanzania, where the emergent private sector initially
found itself handicapped by largely inoperative and insolvent government-owned banks. The liberalization of agricultural markets tends to
take place alongside reforms of financial institutions. But the initial impact
of greater commercial awareness on bank staff is often to make them more
wary of lending to the agricultural sector, while the new policy framework
usually proscribes government attempts to direct credit towards agricultural activities.

Apart from the need for day-to-day working capital, grain traders and
processors need considerable amounts of credit to cover seasonal storage
requirements and to invest in fixed assets. Available credit usually falls far
short of what is needed to meet these needs, for several reasons: inadequate

financial services, a limited number of creditworthy customers, and a lack of eligible collateral. International banks, which are gradually increasing their involvement in Africa, can offer some relief, but their presence creates a form of financial dualism that favors a few traders and millers with links to international commodity brokers and the option of borrowing in dollars. Those borrowing in local currencies avoid exchange risks, but the cost of credit is often high and unpredictable. Most indigenous traders have little or no access to bank credit and must use equity or informal borrowing to finance working capital (at a high implicit or explicit cost). This financial dualism is reinforced by the difficulty many traders encounter in obtaining foreign exchange.

The Poor Performance of Restructured Marketing Boards

Liberalization programs invariably streamlined marketing boards, limiting their functions to supporting a predominantly private marketing system. In South Africa the marketing board was eliminated altogether. Some countries (including Ethiopia, Kenya, Malawi, and Zimbabwe) seek to maintain their marketing boards as major commercial players that compete directly with the emergent private sector and usually have a role as buyer of last resort, manager of price stabilization reserves (otherwise known as stocks), or both. In other countries, such as Mali, Tanzania, and Zambia, marketing boards have been converted into limited food reserves for use only in emergencies. In Ghana the board was encouraged to diversify its services and expand into new areas, including third-party storage and importing, and left to survive as best it could. However, it was not restructured, became insolvent, and has practically ceased operating.

Jones and Jayne (1997) note that the policy of turning marketing boards into buyers and sellers of last resort has not emerged as a successful model. Politicians are generally unwilling to delegate real autonomy to the management of marketing boards, exposing the boards to large trading deficits. A contradiction also exists between the boards' efficiency objectives, which imply a withdrawal from unprofitable activities, and the objectives of the role of buyer and seller of last resort, which implies a withdrawal from profitable activities to make room for the private sector. The failure to adequately separate the boards' social functions and commercial activities often results in increased market uncertainty. In this situation the boards often take steps to improve their financial trading accounts in ways that exacerbate uncertainty rather than reduce it. At the same time price stabilization schemes impede private storage and marketing activities in two ways. First, they dampen spatial and seasonal price variations. Second, the schemes are often implemented unevenly in deference to short-term political considerations rather than a consistent long-term policy.

Fewer problems of this kind develop when parastatals are downsized into food reserves. However, as we have seen, the Tanzanian Strategic Grain Reserve went beyond its reserve function and for many years operated as a price support agency in remote producing areas. The Zambian Food Reserve Agency has likewise been required to carry out functions that exceed its original mandate. Strong political factors and a lack of confidence in the private sector have motivated these decisions. In contrast Mali's food reserve has kept within its original mandate, but this may be because the donors were involved (through the PRMC) in financing and decisionmaking.

Problems with Cross-Border Trade

In many areas, particularly West Africa, most agricultural trade among neighboring countries is informal. By one estimate 10 times more millet and sorghum was traded in Mali through informal channels than through official channels in 1988–89, despite an official export campaign. Similar findings were noted in the Ghana (see annex 6.4). Work by Ackello-Ogutu and Echessah (1997) indicates that unrecorded trade flows for all products between Kenya and Uganda accounted for 60 percent of the value of official registered trade. The study also highlights the importance of sound domestic road infrastructure in encouraging small-scale cross-border trade.

Despite many promises progress in liberalizing official cross-border trade in agricultural commodities has been limited, particularly in southern and eastern Africa. Politicians fear that opening borders to trade will result in food shortages as vital domestic supplies leave the country and that the authorities will be blamed. This situation inhibits both long-term production planning and more formal marketing endeavors that are based on security of access to markets in neighboring countries. In Tanzania, for example, an export ban prevented the southern highlands area from capitalizing on its location and becoming a maize supplier within the subregion.

Mozambique provides another example of this phenomenon. The country has very poor roads and little other transportation to link the north and south of the country, which stretches 2,500 km. The north usually produces a surplus of maize, while the capital (Maputo) is constantly in deficit, but under normal circumstances it is simply uneconomical to move maize from the north to Maputo. Imports from nearby South Africa have ameliorated the problem somewhat, as have exports of surplus maize from the north, either to Malawi by rail and road or to the world market by sea, depending on prices. In 1997 exports to Malawi rose to about 100,000 tons, bringing major economic benefits to the northern economy. Yet official policies on exports remain ambivalent. The concept of self-sufficiency continues to predominate in public debates, and the Council of Ministers considered imposing a 50 percent export duty on maize. At the same time local officials sometimes hinder trade by attempting to keep grain from leaving their districts, prevent Malawian traders from entering the country, or both (Jayne and others 1999).

Given the reluctance of most governments to liberalize cross-border trade, informal grain movements provide a vital safety valve. However, the history of the rice trade in West Africa shows that the effect of such movements is not always benign. Given the lack of uniform protection in neighboring countries, these movements often serve as means of importing rice from the Far East into countries with low tariff protection and then shipping the rice as contraband to countries with higher protection. This activity increases the continent's dependence on supplies from outside Africa and at times facilitates rent-seeking activities by politicians, merchants, and officials (Coste and others 1991). Given that Asia has a head start in rice production, arguments for infant-industry protection and antidumping measures have some legitimacy. But in the absence of common trade policies or customs unions among neighboring countries, governments often have difficulty applying such policies in a coherent manner.

The Lessons of Liberalization

Efforts to liberalize Africa's cereal markets have met with varying degrees of success. But liberalization is now a fact of life throughout the continent. Our analysis of the strengths and weaknesses of liberalization efforts leads us to the following conclusions:

- *The liberalization of cereal marketing in Sub-Saharan Africa was necessary and inevitable in view of the costs imposed by the state-dominated systems and the financially unsustainable expectations they created among beneficiaries.* The primary problem has been accommodating variable pricing structures that reflect differential transport and transaction costs and the seasonal characteristics of grain markets. This problem would not exist if politicians were willing to delegate decisionmaking to professional managers, but powerful political imperatives (such as Zimbabwe's social contract) prevent this reassignment of responsibility.
- *Liberalization accelerated the demise of state-led smallholder green revolutions in certain countries of southern and eastern Africa.* Given the high level of public subsidies and marketing board losses these programs engendered, the gains appear by and large to have been a temporary and unsustainable phenomenon.
- *Most countries have been unable to reach a consensus on liberalization that would ensure consistent implementation of reforms.*

Liberalization has progressed so far that going back to state monopolies is unlikely to be either financially feasible or politically acceptable. Thus the main lessons we need to learn concern what can be done to improve the operation of existing systems. Above all we believe that African countries need to develop a guiding policy framework in line with current realities and that this framework should form the basis of political commitments between the government and the populace at large (a new social contract). Governments must be able to deliver on these commitments in the long term. The key elements of the new framework would be:

- *A clear legal basis for market liberalization.* When governments decide to backtrack on reforms, they frequently use laws from the era of state control. This practice will be more difficult if such laws are abrogated and new ones introduced that are in line with the new policy framework.
- *Reduced costs for producing and distributing grain.* Given Africa's competitive disadvantages on the international stage, strong efforts are needed to minimize transportation, transaction, and financing costs. Transportation is usually the most important component of marketing costs, and much can be achieved by improving road networks and maintaining them. Based on comparisons with Asian countries, Hine, Ebden, and Swan (1997) find that the cost of transport services in Africa can be reduced. For instance some tariff rates in Tanzania are two to five times higher than in Pakistan and Indonesia. A variety of approaches exist that can potentially reduce transaction and financing costs. These include establishing associations of farmers to contract with banks and agribusinesses, improving market information services, developing arbitration systems to provide low-cost dispute resolution services, organizing weekly fairs or markets, and creating warehouse receipt systems and commodity exchanges. Most of these approaches are currently being tested through pilot initiatives to determine which are most appropriate and how they should be introduced.
- *Authorized cross-border trade and a consistent international trade regime that provides any needed protection through tariffs.* These reforms will allow countries to equalize supply and demand and provide markets for populations in border areas. Often such measures are difficult for politicians to accept, but they are vital to the efficient marketing of bulky grain crops.
- *Minimal public stocks.* Stocks should be minimized with due regard for genuine food security requirements that cannot be met by other means. In addition strict rules regarding disposal should be in place.
- *Diversification based on market opportunity and comparative advantage.* Instead of seeking to develop smallholder agriculture by supporting a single target food crop like maize, governments should adopt a more

decentralized approach, encouraging farmers to specialize according to comparative advantages in geographical location and operational scope. Most farmers grow food crops mainly for subsistence, and productivity depends heavily on the workings of the entire farming system (including cash crops and livestock).

Decentralized initiatives involve considerable up-front costs in terms of infrastructure, training, and support services. Some services will be provided by the private sector, but considerable government, donor, and NGO involvement is also needed. In southern Africa the NGO community has been leading the way with this kind of project involvement. Finding the right balance of private initiatives, self-help programs, and public provision is a challenge in its own right, and ever-present political pressures for quick fixes need to be scrupulously avoided.

One way to accomplish these goals is on a regional basis—that is, by groups of countries, such as those of the Southern African Development Commission (SADC) or the Economic Commission of West African States (ECOWAS)—establishing a single authority to regulate the grain trade within common borders. This method will generate far greater benefits than unilateral actions, since neighboring countries can make cross-border trade an explicit part of their food security strategies and establish a strong set of institutions (including commodity exchanges and market information systems) to support the process.

Because of the nature of the political process, however, there is no assurance that such an approach will materialize. An alternative approach requires reformers to lower their expectations about what they can really achieve. One possible scenario involves gradually modernizing local trading systems, with local companies forging alliances with international grain traders and individual politicians—but within a distinctly nontransparent policy framework that continues to generate high levels of intraseasonal price variability and other market failures.

Some countries must still make decisions about the strategy and phasing of liberalization. These countries can learn several important lessons from the experience of countries where reforms are more advanced:

- *Allow public procurement prices to vary on both a seasonal and geographical basis, eliminate controls, and radically alter legal texts.* The experiences of Kenya and Zimbabwe raise questions about the wisdom of partial liberalization and reforms that are phased in over a long period. In such situations governments may put off making critical decisions.
- *Make maximum use of market mechanisms to stabilize prices, notably by developing private storage, regional trade, and risk management tools for prices.* Forward contracting is the most viable risk management tool in

most African countries. There is some scope for hedging on the South African Futures Exchange (white and yellow maize contracts) and the Chicago Board of Trade (yellow maize, wheat, soybeans, and other commodities), but high basis risks limit the use of these contracts.

- *Use research to inform the reform process.* Those designing support programs should study other countries that provide successful models of reform, notably Mali. Moreover, an ongoing research process should inform decisions on liberalization. Here again Mali provides a valuable model. The PRMC and its members have funded valuable research on pricing policy (Staatz, Dione, and Dembele 1989), ways to increase the use of small grains (Boughton and Reardon 1997), and rice policy (Baris and others 1996).

As we noted earlier the experience of landlocked countries such as Zambia and Zimbabwe provides some theoretical justification for using marketing boards to stabilize prices.[24] However maintaining reasonable costs and preventing distortions will require governments to delegate the management of the boards to apolitical technocrats, much as European governments have recently done in managing their money supply. Stabilization activity will need to be gradually scaled back as logistical constraints to trade are removed and private mechanisms of risk management developed. None of the cases known to the authors suggests that African governments will implement such an approach. But we have noted cases in which governments have established institutions with very limited postliberalization mandates and then expanded these mandates into systems of second-generation control. We therefore conclude that under the present circumstances the combination of liberalization and limited interventionism is unlikely to produce the desired results.

Notes

1. Because of space constraints we focus our attention on marketing reforms for maize, the most extensively produced and consumed cereal in Sub-Saharan Africa. We also discuss other cereals (such as rice, sorghum, and millet) when they are important to overall national cereal production, consumption, or both. The findings are based primarily on Coulter (1994).

2. In South Africa production of maize for the market is concentrated in the Transvaal, an area dominated by commercial farmers and well served by both road and communications infrastructure. As argued later in the chapter, the politics of maize in South Africa also exhibits important differences from those of cereals in most Sub-Saharan African countries.

3. On a world scale white maize is produced and traded in much smaller volumes than yellow maize, which is used on a massive scale in the production of

compound animal feed. The market is relatively thin and prices more volatile. In recent years the premium over yellow maize has varied between -$2 to $50 per tonne.

4. Prices will not fall to export parity levels if the crop is stored for sale in the next season. Storage is unlikely, however, since a good harvest in the following year may maintain prices at depressed levels. The lack of hedging mechanisms, the weaknesses of the financial sector, and uncertainties in the policy environment reduce the value of storing crops still further.

5. According to Pinkney's model, a free regional market involving Malawi, Zambia, and Zimbabwe would experience a 44 percent price deviation from the target in 1 of every 3 years and a 72 percent deviation in 1 of every 10 years. The coefficient of variation would be 44 percent. Pinkney's analysis takes no account of forward contracting or the possible development of a futures market. These instruments would reduce the variability of producer prices, at least for large producers. Pinkney also does not take into account the possibility that when prices are high consumers will switch from refined meal to lower-priced whole meal.

6. To these disadvantages we can add the protectionism of northern countries and the competitive advantages decades of such protectionism have created—the anticipated effects of the recent Uruguay Round agreement to raise world prices for commodities such as yellow maize notwithstanding.

7. Procurement monopolies were effective in a few countries prior to liberalization, though more often there was large scale evasion through parallel markets.

8. In a liberalized marketing system, attempts to supply inputs on credit are likely to generate a culture of default, if past experience with failed government programs and even credit programs run by nongovernmental organizations is to be believed (Poulton, Dorward, and Kydd 1998). In addition genuine repayment problems occur when crops fail or prices plummet. Parastatal lenders and official cooperatives operating within single-channel marketing systems usually face serious problems of this kind but are able to be more acute when there are many buyers.

9. This concern is manifest with maize, but in the case of wheat and rice many governments are resigned to increasing their dependence on imports.

10. Not all smallholders will be direct beneficiaries of diversification, at least in the short run. In this regard research by Michigan State University has established that cotton industries in Mozambique and Zimbabwe are tending to screen out risky farmers with little land (Tom Jayne, personal communication, 1999).

11. In many cases the inefficiency of parastatal enterprises also contributed to the cost burden.

12. See for example World Bank (1981) and Bates (1981).

13. As the British politician R.A.B. Butler said, "A week is a long time in politics."

14. A recent OECD report notes that developed country support to agriculture has reached levels not seen since the mid 1980s. Figures quoted show that the reversal has been particularly acute in the United States.

15. Contrary to the figures quoted here, data quoted by Egg (1999) show that cereal production in Mali grew by 4.7 percent annually between 1980 and 1997, a rate that far exceeds population growth (2 percent).

16. Ghana and Tanzania exemplify this scenario. They are discussed in annexes 6.4 and 6.1, respectively.

17. Nevertheless it is usually farmers who store the bulk of marketable surpluses. Sometimes the only way they can obtain a worthwhile price is by storing grain until it becomes scarce and prices rise.

18. The successful handling of food distribution after the 1992 drought in southern Africa suggests that countries do not need large reserves in order to maintain food security, providing they have good early warning systems and can rely on international support.

19. See for example Bryceson (1993) and Seppala (1998) on Tanzania.

20. See Bates (1989) for an account of the background situation, as well as the short account by Coulter (1994, pp. 10–11).

21. A classic example of poor donor coordination was the funding of about 1,000 village stores in Tanzania, at a time when the country was liberalizing its maize market. The stores were built for cooperative societies which were part of the old order and were largely bypassed by emerging marketing intermediaries (Coulter 1994).

22. Senegal depended heavily on rice even before liberalization and simply could not afford the controlled system after the devaluation of the CFA franc.

23. See Mehta (1989) for a discussion of how liberalization in Mali eased the burden of such controls. For the more common discussion of the ongoing burden of localized controls, see Abdulwahid (1995) on Chad; Anyango (1996) on East Africa; Golob, Stringfellow, and Asante (1996) on northern Ghana; Ikiara (1998) on Kenya; and Santorum and Tibaijuka (1992) on Tanzania.

24. Such a case cannot easily be made for coarse grains in Mali, even though this country is, like Zimbabwe and Zambia, landlocked. Research has shown that high producer prices benefited only a small percentage of producers and that the short-term producer response was likely to be weak (see annex 6.2 and Staatz, Dione, and Dembele 1989). The largely incidental nature of surpluses in a mainly subsistence-based production and the absence of purchased inputs may explain the poor responsiveness of prices.

Annex 6.1
Tanzania: Still Awaiting a Supply Response

How Liberalization Was Implemented

Maize is Tanzania's staple food crop, while rice and small grains (millet and sorghum) play a subsidiary role. The liberalization that began in 1985, under pressure from the World Bank, gave official recognition to trends that were already well established. The National Milling Corporation (NMC), a marketing organization that is supposedly a monopoly, had long struggled to supply enough maize meal to the capital, Dar es Salaam. This was not helped by the fact that its system of panterritorial producer pricing had encouraged a concentration of production in four regions of the Southern Highlands—Iringa, Mbeya, Ruvuma and Rukwa—which were between 600 and 1,300 kilometers from Dar es Salaam. As politically deter-mined producer prices for maize grain, and consumer prices for maize meal, gave the NMC a smaller and smaller margin on its operations, its debt mounted, its purchases declined, and Dar es Salaam became more and more dependent on "illegal" parallel market supplies provided by private traders dealing in domestically produced grain. The cost to government ascended to hundreds of millions of dollars. the NMC and associated regional cooperatives accumulated debts that were regularly refinanced by the Bank of Tanzania, this in turn contributing to an inflationary spiral (Coulter and Golob 1992).

Structural adjustment policies caused bank lending to become tighter, and the state-controlled institutions lacked sufficient funds to exercise their position as monopoly buyer. Progressively, the private trade was allowed to extend its radius of action. In 1990, the NMC ceased to have any responsi-bility for buying and selling grain and was to restrict itself to milling, while a 150,000-ton Strategic Grain Reserve (SGR) was created under the Ministry of Agriculture to deal with food emergencies. Between 1990–91 and 1996-97, the quantities of maize procured by the SGR varied between 23,000 and 85,000 tons.

The liberalization of Tanzania's grain market is a result of the high cost and unsustainable nature of the state-controlled system, and pressure from international financial institutions (IFIs). For most of the time, the process has not been comprehensively "owned" by government itself, and not sur-prisingly the overall strategy has often lacked clarity and coherence. For long the SGR functioned more as a price support agency than as a food security reserve, purchasing overwhelmingly from the Southern Highlands, at panterritorially fixed procurement prices, and storing so as to cushion the negative impact of the liberalization policies on the four regions. This continued up to the 1996-97 marketing season, when the reserve started procuring larger quantities close to Dar es Salaam.

Another policy inconsistency concerned donor-funded "village storage" programs. About one thousand 300-ton stores were built around the country during the 1980s and early 1990s, notionally in support of the new, liberalized marketing system, while in fact they were designed for an ailing system of cooperative grain procurement. The stores were largely bypassed by farmers and private traders. Farmers generally distrusted collective storage and preferred to hold their maize on the farm in traditional cribs, and release it on to the market as and when they needed to sell. Notwithstanding the fact that some stores served other valuable purposes, for example, as dance halls and public registry offices.

The government's general commitment to liberal economic policies has strengthened under the leadership of President Benjamin Mkapa, who came to office at the end of 1995. Macroeconomic management has improved, leading to a fall in inflation and consequently lower interest rates.[1] An ambitious program of privatization should, at last, dispose of the major assets of the NMC, chiefly mills and storage facilities.[2] However, commitment to liberalization takes time to filter down through the government system. At district level, there remains a tendency to impose restrictive levies and licensing requirements on trading activities—a problem that could be exacerbated by the ongoing program of bureaucratic decentralization. At the end of 1997, government was still regulating the export trade in an ad hoc manner. A system of quotas and licences had been created to restrict exports on the grounds of conserving national stocks—some traders alleged that quotas and licences could be bought and sold corruptly (Norvell 1998).

Impact on Market Structure and Conduct

The private marketing system that emerged in the early 1990s was rudimentary and hampered by shortages of trade finance and limited specialization in the functions of intermediaries. High interregional price fluctuations for maize reflected limited integration of the country's different markets (Gordon 1988, Scarborough 1989). The banking system awaited reform, and there was virtually no credit for private traders. Wholesale merchants in Dar es Salaam held minimal transactional stocks of maize, and virtually all storage of commercial maize surpluses (excluding stocks held by the SGR) was carried out by the farmers themselves, with varying success, depending on the availability of insecticides and the impact of an exotic storage pest, the larger grain borer.

With the gradual demise of the NMC, consumers in major urban centers had to switch from buying maize meal to maize grain, and this led to the installation of a large number of hammer mills, in both urban and rural areas, where consumers would take their grain to be milled on a "custom" basis.

During the 1990s, traders involved in the assembly end of the marketing chain have remained relatively unsophisticated. Recent research by both Risopoulos and others (1998; Appendix 2) and Seppala (1998) suggests that they engage in the maize trade because it requires little capital—for example, trucks can be hired and shared among several traders who travel together. However, they do not appear to see this activity as a long-term venture, but seek to progress to more profitable lines of activity. Problems in obtaining capital, resulting from the extremely weak financial sector, coupled with the relatively low margins in maize trading, may account for much of this weakness.

By contrast, some larger grain traders and millers have emerged at the urban wholesale trading level. Commercial storage activity is now more common and tends to be conducted by large, general agricultural commodity traders (often Asian-owned) seeking to exploit opportunities in cross-border markets and food aid tenders, as well as in the domestic market. Increasingly these companies trade or work in partnership with major international grain traders, such as Glencore, Cargill, and Louis Dreyfus. Notwithstanding greater storage activity, interseasonal price spreads have been very large (table A6.1).

The explanation for why there has not been more intraseasonal storage, given these price spreads, may be found in the following factors:

- *Unpredictability of price movements.* Whilst spreads are large in some consumption centers, according to data from the Marketing Development Bureau (MDB), it is difficult to predict when prices will peak, because of the unpredictability of the *vuli* ("minor") rains in northern Tanzania, where two maize harvests per year are possible. In

Table A6.1 Average Monthly Maize Wholesale Price in Dar es Salaam, 1993–94 to 1995–96, Highs and Lows (T Shs)

Year	Low	Month	High	Month	Percentage of increase
1993–94	4,750	July	9,000	Jan–Feb	90
1994–95	5,250	Aug–Sept	14,500	January	176
1995–96	7,000	July	18,800	April	169

Source: MDB (1997).

1997–98, good *vuli* rains are reported to have caused losses to larger farmers in Dodoma who stored in anticipation of high prices in Dar es Salaam in early 1998. An alternative explanation, however, is the arrival of food "aid" in response to the perceived problems caused by El Niño, suggesting that certain government interventions may still discourage private storage activity.

- *Lack of capital.* Although respected international financial institutions have begun to establish themselves in Dar es Salaam and, more recently, Mwanza, they have little outreach to the agricultural sector. Of the two (ex-)parastatal banks with extensive branch networks outside Dar, one has only been looking for lending opportunities for the past two seasons, whilst the other is still too saddled with bad debts to take on new lending commitments. Collateral remains a major obstacle for lending to private entrepreneurs, in the agricultural sector and elsewhere, and in view of this the grain trade may be ripe for the development of warehouse receipt financing.

The early 1990s have witnessed the rise of a few large-scale private millers, producing a higher quality branded meal than that still produced by NMC. A survey by Mdadila and Associates (1995) found that four private roller mills (three in Dar es Salaam and one in Dodoma) were operating at, or close to, their combined, installed capacity of 75,000 tons of maize meal per year. Nevertheless, they complained of fierce competition from the rising number of small-scale hammer mills operating in the capital. Despite large intraseasonal price rises, these larger millers were buying sporadically throughout the year, because of a lack of storage space and working capital.

Effect on External Trade

Tanzania's maize production is, at best, only imperfectly correlated with that in other parts of southern and eastern Africa. Thus, in the first half of the 1990s, there was considerable informal export activity overland from Tanzania to Malawi, Zambia, and Kenya, plus some formalized export through the port of Dar es Salaam to Kenya, the Seychelles, and the Comoros. With better harvests to the south of the country, net informal flows subsequently reversed. Meanwhile, in late 1996 the government, fearing food shortages in the country after poor rains, imposed an indefinite ban on cereals exports. This, apparently, had a dramatic impact on the strength of demand for maize, with lower prices being transmitted right down the supply chain to the farm gate and felt particularly in remote surplus areas, which tend to receive the residual demand from elsewhere in the system. As of mid-1998, this ban was still in force, keeping consumer prices down at the expense of surplus producers.

Impact of Liberalization on Production and Market Performance

Despite some encouraging developments within the marketing system, the country has not experienced a sustained increase in maize production. The late 1980s witnessed several years of good weather, causing a rise in per capita production, but a string of poor years[3] in the 1990s has seen per capita production decline to less than preliberalization levels. Other than the poor weather, the following reasons may be given for this:

- There were problems of input supply. According to World Bank and government of Tanzania (1994), in the late 1980s, before the removal of subsidies, almost 70 percent of all fertilizer consumed in Tanzania was used on maize production within the Southern Highlands. Total fertilizer use increased rapidly during these years, combining with the favorable weather and market liberalization to increase maize production. Seppala (1998) presents data showing national fertilizer consumption to have declined dramatically following the removal of subsidies in 1990–92. This is intuitively plausible and supported by anecdotal evidence, but there is some uncertainty over the figures.[4]
- Sustained price incentives were lacking. Some of Tanzania's most productive areas are 1,000 kilometers or more from Dar es Salaam, and post-liberalization price levels reflect difficulties of access and high transport costs. Other markets have emerged, but demand has been sporadic and relatively unpredictable. Coulter and Golob (1992) suggested that this might be regulated by instituting a public stockpiling function in Dar es Salaam so as to maintain prices at around import parity level. However, they went on to recommend against this approach in the near term, on the grounds that political pressures would cause its cost to escalate, much as had occurred with NMC and the cooperatives.
- High seasonal price fluctuations discourage large-scale production of surpluses, and reduce the competitive position of Tanzania relative to other countries. Farmers using purchased inputs are particularly affected as they are unable to foresee their cash flow position and plan accordingly. At the same time there are no futures or forward markets on which they are able to lock in a price.

In the case of paddy rice, the immediate impact of liberalization was to greatly enhance market incentives. The volume of production grew from around 300,000 tons between 1981 and 1984 to a climate-assisted peak of 740,000 tons in 1990, by which year the country had become virtually self-sufficient. As in the case of maize, production has fluctuated during the 1990s in response to climatic conditions, but reached a new peak of 1 million tons in 1998, as a consequence of El Niño.

Available evidence indicates that liberalization reduced the costs of maize marketing. MDB (1990) noted that the margin in the maize price between the leading surplus and deficit regions had already narrowed, while the massive budgetary burden of supporting the state-controlled marketing system was greatly reduced. Research by Gordon (1988) and Scarborough (1989) indicated that excess profits were uncommon in the incipient private sector, and that competition was not inhibited by ethnic domination.

The efficiency of agricultural resource allocation also appears to have improved, as a result of the ending of panterritorial pricing, which encouraged production in remote locations. Official production estimates do not show a very pronounced redistribution of maize production activity[5], but discussions with private traders and Ministry of Agriculture officials reveal that Dar es Salaam is increasingly supplied by surpluses from Arusha, through assembly markets in the Dodoma Region. Meanwhile, traders from the center of the country (Shinyanga, Tabora, and so forth) and from the Lake Zone (Mwanza) now source maize directly from Rukwa and adjacent parts of the Southern Highlands, using road and rail links. The disadvantage for producers of this source of demand (as compared with the old NMC or even SGR) is its unpredictability. Demand depends critically upon the relative harvests in the destination regions and in the Southern Highlands, which in turn depend on localized rainfall that varies dramatically from season to season. In future, however, maize from the Southern Highlands could increasingly be destined for these inland markets, as well as Zambia and Malawi, which are becoming less self-sufficient in grain production. As noted above, Tanzania's current trade policies do not allow it to fully capitalize on these opportunities.

Annex 6.2
Mali's Consensus-Seeking Approach

Mali's main food-grains are millet and sorghum, while some maize is grown, mainly for local consumption, in the south of the country. However, rice is much consumed in urban areas along with these grains, and there is significant consumption of wheat flour in the form of bread.

Approach to Liberalization of Coarse Grain Marketing

Liberalization started in 1981 with the support of a donor consortium (France, Canada, Germany, the Netherlands, the United States, the European Community, and the World Food Program), which together with the government of Mali formed the Cereals Market Restructuring Program (PRMC). It has been funded by the donors each pledging food aid to be used for free distribution or to be sold locally for the purpose of generating "counterpart funds"; these are used to finance various "accompanying measures" to assist the liberalization process. Liberalization of coarse grain marketing has gone through two very distinct phases.

From 1981 to 1987, private traders were allowed to operate, but the marketing board, OPAM, maintained an important role in regulating price levels through market operations, and an official price scale (*barème*) continued to be used. Emphasis was placed on the objective of raising producer prices to remunerative levels, and PRMC counterpart funds were used to cushion the impact on consumers, who in practice were mainly families of public employees, and to pay for the retrenchment of OPAM staff. The system seemed to work satisfactorily from 1981 to 1985, during which time Mali experienced a series of poor harvests and the PRMC's role was mainly that of providing food aid for distribution and sale by OPAM. However, in 1986 and 1987 the country had unusual surplus harvests; OPAM exhausted its funds and suspended purchases.

From 1987, OPAM's commercial role was drastically reduced to just three functions: managing a food security reserve of 58,000 tons to be used for genuine emergencies identified through the early warning system; distribution of food aid; and the sale of grain in remote deficit areas in danger of market failure. Open tenders were introduced in local procurement and for rotational sales from the reserve. In addition the PRMC funded "accompanying measures" in support of the private sector and the country's food security objectives, notably the creation of a Market Information System managed by OPAM; support to the early warning system; marketing credit to traders and farmer groups called village associations to help them to step into the long-term storage role vacated by OPAM; export promotion and processing initiatives to help dispose of production surpluses.

The change from the first to the second phase was absolutely pivotal. The abandonment of the price support objective stemmed from several factors, particularly:

- The difficulty in financing the stock levels necessary to maintain prices in surplus years.
- Donor frustration about major inefficiencies at OPAM and their consequent desire that its role be cut back to a more manageable level.
- Research findings showing that high producer prices benefited only a small percentage of producers and that the short-term producer response was likely to be weak (succinctly summarized in Staatz and others 1989). Farmers made minimum use of purchased inputs in producing millet and sorghum, and price incentives had a limited impact on production.

Notably, levels of on-farm storage, using traditional granaries, are very significant in surplus-producing areas of Mali, and this mitigates climatically induced variations in supply. In contrast to the situation in the other case study countries, farmers engage in considerable interannual storage and sometimes hold stocks for as much as four years. This is partly due to the ease with which traditional varieties of millet and sorghum can be stored on the head, without insecticide.

It is significant that the first phase of Mali's liberalization took place at a time of major drought. The PRMC had planned for such eventualities, so droughts did not derail the reform process. It did not, however, plan for the production surpluses that have occurred since the mid-1980s. From the second phase, much attention has been devoted to disposal of surplus production.

The PRMC, which is a coordinating mechanism under the Ministry of Finance, played a key role in Mali's reform process by building a dual consensus: on the one hand between the donors; on the other hand, between government and donors. The PRMC controlled its own budget and decisions were reached by the unanimous agreement of the government and the various donors represented. The process of reaching a consensus was slow, and the major reforms of 1987 took place under pressure from the International Monetary Fund (IMF), a body that did not belong to the PRMC. Nevertheless the process appears to have been very beneficial and to have enhanced the quality of, and support for, the decisions reached.

Up to its third phase (1990 to 1993), PRMC has been characterized by a high degree of donor involvement in decisionmaking, but in its fourth phase, (1993 to 1996), Malians had equal representation in a Comité Paritaire, which provides technical briefing to the PRMC. Notably the size of OPAM's food reserve has been reduced to 35,000 tons.

The devaluation of the Malian franc (CFAF) at the end of 1993 caused a major change in Mali's economy, encouraging exports but raising prices to urban consumers whose income has not risen proportionately. Some players increasingly question the virtues of liberalization and the country's new export orientation, and have started to advocate a return to former interventionist policies, including controls on exports. The PRMC recently commissioned a major study to examine the issues.

Approach to Liberalization of Rice Marketing

Rice marketing was not included in the original reforms of 1981, but it continued under the control of parastatals, of which the largest, the Office du Niger (ON) ran an irrigation scheme of 44,000 hectares, providing all necessary support services including input supply, mechanization, credit, and so forth. Liberalization did not start in earnest until 1987, but it brought about a major change in the marketing system, with a proliferation of small private rice mills competing effectively with large parastatal mills. Farmers now had an alternative outlet for their produce, which they could sell individually, or collectively through village associations, as white rice, instead of selling as paddy rice.

However, unlike the case with OPAM, parastatal rice millers remained unreformed and notably inefficient. Ouedraogo and Adoum (1993) described the ON as being by common consensus "fraught with corruption and mismanagement . . . overstaffed and nonfunctional." Moreover, parastatals continued setting official support prices for farmers. Import duties were set at levels that helped the parastatals break even, but well in excess of those needed by the small-scale millers. This situation seems to have prevailed because of widespread public sentiment in favor of protecting Malian rice producers, and therefore maintaining high internal prices; the interests of some government officials who had investments in irrigated rice schemes; and the lack of consensus among the various donors supporting the ON (France, Germany, the Netherlands, and the European Community), some of which resisted reorganization of the rice sector (Ouedraogo and Adoum 1993). Donor consensus, which had promoted reforms in other aspects of cereal marketing, failed when it came to reforming rice parastatals.

At the same time, several authors expressed concern about the transparency of the private wholesale market for rice and considered marketing margins to be excessive (see, for example Thénevin 1989 and Deme 1993). Oligopolistic trade structures characterized the rice trade in many West

African countries, and this appeared to be related to their role in controlling imports from outside Africa.

By 1992, the World Bank and the IMF had grown impatient with the ON, to which donors had given or lent more than CFAF 5 billion (about US$20 million) for commercialization activities and made further assistance conditional upon reform. This time the donors supporting the ON fell in line with the World Bank, and the government of Mali had no choice but to accede. For the second time in six years, the full force of the IFIs' conditionality was brought to bear to ensure that key reforms were carried through.

The ON was put under a major restructuring program in 1994, under the prime minister's office, and with the support of all the major PRMC donors. The results are that ON is now responsible for only water management and extension services, all of the four public rice mills were privatized and bought by a Malian investor, and the tenure regime on irrigated land was reformed to allow Malian and foreign private investors to have access to irrigated land under a long-term lease arrangement.

Key Results

An early study by Mehta (1989) indicated that liberalization of coarse grain marketing had been successful and that the private system was efficient and did not earn excess profits. This general picture is confirmed by Egg (1999), who reports an increased number of market intermediaries working on narrower margins. They have a larger geographical coverage and greater penetration in deficit areas. He also notes greater private investment in storage and transport infrastructure, and that the trade has become more flexible, as regards its ability to deal with "external shocks." All this was achieved at a quite modest cost of CFAF 2 billion per year[6], while at the same time the state was relieved of the large budgetary burden of subsidizing the deficits of the government-controlled system (half the budget deficit by the end of the 1970s). The cost to the state of operating OPAM fell from CFAF 2.4 billion (approximately US$10 million) in 1980–81 to CFAF 1.5 billion (approximately US$2.6 million) in 1997, equivalent to a fall from 3.3 percent to 0.4 percent of public expenditure.

In the case of rice, marketing reform has complemented the rehabilitation of irrigation works and other improvements, resulting in a dramatic rise in yields to over 5 tons per hectare. Total national production for 1998 was expected to be over 700,000 tons, compared with 200,000 tons in 1989. Since the privatization of the large mills, many private investors have been attracted into the ON zone. Mali has been self-sufficient in rice for the last three years and, according to some sources, may even export rice to countries such as Burkina Faso, Mauritania and Côte d'Ivoire (the last being targeted by traders who produce "luxury rice"). Devaluation of the CFAF had a very favorable impact on production. Revenue of farmers on average more than doubled between 1991–92 and 1995–96.

Egg (1999) finds that competition between rice traders has greatly increased, and while the oligopolistic trade structure has not altogether disappeared, the market power is greatly diminished and it now plays a more constructive role in support of local producers.

There have also been major improvements in the marketing of machinery (plows, harrows, and so forth) and agricultural inputs in the rice-producing zones, where village associations have jointly organized their procurement by open tender. Coarse grain producers in cotton zones have similarly benefited from machinery purchases.

Egg finds that the overall price level for cereals has increased, particularly after the devaluation of the CFAF at the end of 1993, and that producer and consumer prices have become more variable. He goes on to indicate that this has had an adverse impact on consuming households, most of which are net consumers (this situation seems to have created some pressure for government to backtrack on earlier reforms, which nevertheless has been resisted). Notwithstanding, price instability does not appear to have had a negative impact on production, which has risen by an average of 4.7 percent per year between 1980 and 1997 relative to population growth of 2 percent.

Mali carried through reforms with a remarkable degree of consensus among the donors, the government, and the population at large. This is evidenced by the fact that liberalization figured in the pronouncements of all the major political parties contesting the 1992 elections to replace the deposed Moussa Traoré's regime. It is also evidenced by the relatively unequivocal way in which decisions have been implemented.

With Mali's strong commitment to market liberalization and economic reforms, and with the democratic and decentralization policies currently being implemented, there is, according to Amadou Camara (of the U.S, Agency for International Development), a thriving national private sector emerging even in the agribusiness sector. Many trade associations are emerging, and they are advocating more reforms to improve the enabling environment.

Annex 6.3
Zimbabwe: Fears of Letting Go

White maize is the staple food of the majority of Zimbabweans, with small grains supplementing maize in the driest production areas and in years of anticipated drought. However, maize production and marketing in Zimbabwe have to overcome several significant problems:

- Rainfall (particularly in the lower-lying parts of the country—so-called natural regions III to V) is extremely unreliable, with the country prone to frequent drought. Cereal yields in southern Africa as a whole are among the most unstable in the world (Byerlee and Heisey 1996).
- These risks are compounded by the fact that Zimbabwe is landlocked. For reasons set out in the chapter under the heading "Key Characteristics of Grain Markets in Africa," maize prices are likely to experience wide price variations in response to changing production conditions, unless prices can be buffered by large public stocks.
- Other countries in southern and eastern Africa also produce white maize. The correlation between production levels in Zimbabwe and, say, Tanzania is not high, so surplus maize could in theory be sent from Tanzania to Zimbabwe when the latter was in deficit. However, in practice commodity flows are impeded by slow and inefficient transport infrastructure, compounded by unsupportive policies regarding intraregional trade, and limited means of contract enforcement.

Colonial policy was designed to protect maize production by European commercial farmers against both climatic uncertainty and competition from lower-cost African smallholders (Jayne and Jones 1997). From the 1950s onward, it also promoted the consumption of a highly refined maize flour processed by large-scale roller mills (Jayne and others 1995).

At independence in 1980, the ZANU PF (Zimbabwe African National Union—Popular Front) government sought to implement its "social contract" with its rural constituencies both by land reform and by extending government services and support from commercial to communal farming areas, so as to expand smallholder maize production (Jayne and Jones 1997). A central feature of the latter was the de facto extension of panterritorial pricing for maize purchases by the Grain Marketing Board (GMB) into "communal" areas (that is, areas inhabited by indigenous smallholders), and this was accomplished through the opening of new crop-buying stations around the country[7]. In addition to this, the extension service was greatly strengthened numerically, and increased government credit was targeted at smallholder producers[8] to encourage the uptake of hybrid maize and fertilizer packages[9].

Given this encouragement, the marketed surplus produced by smallholders rose from 87,000 tons in 1980–81 (11 percent of total sales to GMB) to 390,000 tons in 1984–85 (41 percent of total sales) and a peak of 750,000 tons, or 63 percent of total sales in 1988–89, (GMB figures quoted by Mashingaidze 1994). This success was hailed as a "smallholder Green Revolution." Zimbabwe was a regular exporter of maize during this period. Interestingly, there is some doubt as to how important output price incentives were in achieving this success.[10]

What Prompted Liberalization

The successes of the 1980s were achieved at high cost:

- Even though GMB was well run by the standards of many marketing boards, operating costs were inevitably high because of the highly political process by which prices were set. For example, when faced with a large harvest, GMB management lacked discretion to lower procurement prices to levels that would have made it more feasible to store for long periods. Because of panterritorial policies it could not make outlying smallholder producers bear higher than average transport and handling costs.
- The control over maize marketing exerted by the single-channel system led to a circular movement of grain, from surplus producers to large-scale mills in urban areas, before being sent back to deficit households in (often the same) rural areas in the form of expensive, refined flour. The single-channel marketing system discouraged direct sales from surplus to deficit households within rural areas.[11]
- It also discouraged the establishment of small-scale milling enterprises that could turn out less refined forms of flour (thought to be little in demand even from poor consumers). Thus poor urban consumers, as well as rural ones, paid an unnecessary premium for their staple food item.

The inherently high costs of the controlled marketing system forced the GMB gradually to increase its marketing margin. As the real producer price of maize was squeezed, commercial farmers and smallholders farming closer to urban centers began to switch into uncontrolled crops, such as horticultural produce. Maize production thus began to decline again in the second half of the 1980s.[12]

Other parts of the production support package also came under strain. By 1990 (an election year) almost 80 percent of smallholder recipients of government credit were in arrears (Chimedza 1994), threatening future disbursements. The number of maize collection points was reduced in the second half of the 1980s and the budget allocation for Agritex, the extension service, also began to be squeezed.

How Liberalization Was Implemented

While seeking to address these problems, government retained certain major policy objectives with regard to the maize sector, notably:

- To control prices of maize meal, so as to prevent major fluctuations in, or erosion of, real wages and incomes, particularly in the growing urban areas.
- To protect smallholders—both maize surplus producers and food deficit households, and particularly those in more remote areas—from "exploitation" by private traders.
- To support producers of maize in communal areas, so as to compensate for their competitive disadvantages (poorer soils, more erratic rainfall, and poorer market access) relative to commercial farmers. Of course, the really "hot" political issue here was land reform, but until significant progress was made on that issue, price support was likely to remain a top priority.

The Economic Structural Adjustment Program (ESAP) of 1991 was precipitated primarily by fiscal problems at the macroeconomic level. It contained proposals to remove controls on maize marketing and to move toward a more limited market stabilization role for the GMB.

Implementation started slowly after the 1992 drought, and long-distance grain movement, storage, and wholesaling functions of the GMB were gradually opened up to private traders, but its monopoly on external trade was retained (and has remained ever since). At the local level, traders were allowed to enter as private intermediaries between both surplus and deficit households and GMB depots. Depots could also sell directly to farm households as well as buy from them. GMB continued to set official buying and selling prices to provide an "anchor" to the pricing policies of the private traders (Vaze and others 1998). In view of government's price support objective, prices were still set on a panterritorial and panseasonal basis. The importance of maize-pricing policy to the government is shown by the fact that senior politicians continue to exercise control over the GMB's price setting (Jayne and Jones 1997).

Downstream, the dominant position of the large-scale roller mills was also exposed to competition from small-scale hammer mills, which rapidly appeared in large numbers in urban areas. In 1993 maize meal subsidies were abolished and consumer prices were decontrolled.

Key Results

The removal of maize meal subsidies did not lead to dramatic rises in consumer prices. Poor consumers rapidly switched from highly refined "roller meal" to whole maize meal, which cost only 60 to 75 percent of the price. Jayne and others (1995) reported that whole maize meal accounted for around half of all urban meal consumption within two years after the subsidies on maize meal had been eliminated. The removal of restrictions on private grain trade into urban areas was critically important in driving the shift to whole maize meal produced by unregistered small-scale millers. In rural areas, consumer prices were also assisted by the direct shipment of grain from surplus to deficit areas.

However, the (initial) impact on the GMB budget was adverse, rather than beneficial. As GMB continued to set panterritorial buying and selling prices, private traders overwhelmingly began trading in more accessible areas. The transportation of grain to and from accessible districts rapidly passed into private hands. However, this left GMB to service the more remote, high-cost areas without cross-subsidy from more profitable operations elsewhere. In 1992–93, following the drought, the GMB made an early announcement of producer prices that represented a significant real increase on the previous year. As the 1993 harvest was a good crop, the GMB received huge quantities of grain that it had to store. In eight months it ran up a trading deficit equal to 2.8 percent of GNP (Jayne and Jones 1997).

The fiscal objective regarding pricing and support to communal areas thus pulled in opposite directions. For GMB to support both producers in communal areas and consumers would require squeezing its margins, something that was certainly fiscally undesirable (especially given the costs of operating a panterritorial pricing regime).

In 1995–96 GMB set a purchasing price of Z$1,200 per ton that was too low when compared with supply and demand conditions in the market. Farmers with on-farm storage capacity (including, of course, commercial farmers) withheld supplies from the market and GMB only received enough grain to supply deficit areas for a few months. Once GMB stocks were exhausted, the price rose sharply. The following season, the official purchasing price was doubled—an increase in real terms of some 70 percent.

In January 1998, GMB raised its selling price to adjust to market conditions, and the consequent rise in consumer prices for roller meal resulted in food riots. A poor harvest and localized drought conditions heightened government worries about urban consumer prices and civil unrest. In May 1998, the government moved to reintroduce price controls on refined roller meal for the first time since 1993 and accused millers of taking advantage of conditions of scarcity to reap excessive margins.[13] GMB also started vertically integrating into milling to compete with industrial mills.

Since August 1998, the situation has been further exacerbated by rapid currency devaluation, a result of general economic mismanagement[14], as this has fueled inflation.

Price controls have depressed the price of GMB's supplies of maize to the large mills and subsidized both producers and consumers of roller meal. However, general market prices for maize have not been controlled, and for much of 1998 Harare prices have been 30 percent above GMB's selling price. Hence while rhetorically opposed to the oligopoly of large mills, government's current policies are in fact hurting their competitors, the small hammer mills, which must procure maize on the open market at substantially higher prices. In this way policy seems to have gone full circle and created a situation similar to that which existed prior to reform (Jayne and others 1999). The policy also disproportionately benefits higher-income consumers, who purchase more per head than low-income consumers, who rely more on the unrefined meal from the hammer mills.

At the time of writing, this step back from the partial liberalization of the early 1990s has yet to be properly resolved.

Key Problems Elsewhere in the Economy

The events of the past year emphasize the point that reform of the maize sector cannot be considered in isolation from events elsewhere in the (political) economy of the country. Two main areas stand out:

- *Macroeconomic management.* Sustained budget deficits give rise to inflation, as well as threatening to "crowd out" bank lending to private traders. Inflationary fears make the government even more reluctant than it might otherwise be to finally relinquish controls over maize pricing (either grain or, as recently seen, maize meal). Price controls themselves crowd out private sector activity.
- *Land reform.* There has been a lot of activity on this front during 1998, but little (if any) real progress. Meanwhile credit provision to smallholders was dramatically scaled down in the 1990s and other services were cut back. All this makes it more difficult for the government to be seen to be reducing its support to the one remaining part of the social contract, that is, smallholder maize marketing through GMB. Moreover, the removal of panterritorial pricing would be of benefit to

the very same commercial farmers whose dominance government policy was intended to challenge (and who are thus enthusiastic proponents of further marketing liberalization).

Given government's fiscal constraints and political imperatives, it is far from clear that Zimbabwe's partial liberalization is either sustainable or particularly effective in achieving its aims. A new development platform is needed, particularly for the more remote rural areas, with less emphasis on the production of commercial surpluses of bulky grain crops and more attention to activities in which smallholders can develop a comparative advantage.

Annex 6.4
Ghana: Early to Start but Reluctant to Finish

In Ghana maize is one of several starch staples including cassava, yam, plantain, cocoyam, sorghum, millet, and rice, and about 1 million tons is produced per year. It is the main staple of the Ga and Fante people of the coastal savannah, the Ewe people of Volta Region, and in most parts of the Northern Region, but elsewhere it is not the dominant feature of local diets. Perhaps for this reason it was never subjected to the same degree of state control as it was in much of southern and eastern Africa (Boxall and Bickersteth 1991).

It is important to note that maize production in the southern and central parts of Ghana is distributed across two seasons per year. Notably there is a significant problem in drying grain in the "Major Season," which produces a harvest from July onward, as further rain can be expected at this time. Drying problems and cash requirements force many farmers to sell their maize quickly.

How Liberalization Has Been Implemented

Ghana started from a situation where the private sector enjoyed considerable freedom to trade in grain, though, as indicated in the introduction to this chapter, private storage had at times been stigmatized as "hoarding" and accordingly repressed. Paradoxically, Ghana began its period of structural adjustment by government increasing its involvement in the maize marketing system. Motivated by a major drought in 1982–83, it sought to increase the role of the Ghana Food Distribution Corporation (GFDC) in providing for lean season requirements in the consuming areas of southern Ghana. Working capital was provided by a consortium of banks, and several donors supported a silo-building program. By the mid 1990s, GFDC was left with about 21,000 tons of usable storage capacity at 11 sites equipped with dryers and cleaners, in the main surplus producing area of the country—Brong Ahafo and northern Ashanti Regions. There was additional capacity in the capital, Accra, and elsewhere in the country, but much of this was poorly located to capture market surpluses.

Because of overstaffing and the fact that government required it to fulfil unremunerated functions and pay farmers minimum prices above market rates, GFDC's financial position deteriorated to the point where it became technically insolvent. Because of budgetary limitations, GFDC's market share has never exceeded 10 percent of the total marketable surplus, and by

1992 it had fallen to less than 1 percent (2,500 tons). In an attempt to help GFDC's finances, the policy of paying minimum prices to farmers was suspended in 1990. As with the NMC in Tanzania, there was much reluctance to redefine the role of GFDC in the light of liberalization, and the institution remained heavily overstaffed.

The antitrader campaign of 1982–83 left a climate of mutual suspicion between government and traders, and this lingered up to 1993, at which time the United Kingdom's Natural Resources Institute (NRI) sought to introduce the practice of warehouse receipt financing (inventory credit) as a means of financing private storage. This complemented other efforts to develop inventory credit financing at the level of farm cooperatives, notably one started in 1989 by the nongovernmental organization TechnoServe and financed by the Agricultural Development Bank (ADB). Significantly, NRI's proposals were supported by government, and implemented by two local banks, and this had the incidental effect of legitimizing private storage (Coulter and Shepherd 1995, see Case Study 4).

Other aspects of the new policy and institutional environment included:

- Exchange rate reform, which made local cereals more competitive with imports, and helped open up an export market for maize in neighboring francophone countries;
- Liberalization of fertilizer supplies and elimination of subsidies;
- Financial sector reform, involving the financial restructuring of banks and the ending of controls on interest rates and lending policies;
- Improvement of roads, new wholesale markets in a few locations, regular provision of market information through radio broadcasts and the press, and advice on grain storage and quality control.

The external trade regime has been partly liberalized, particularly as regards cross-border exports to neighboring francophone countries. Such exports have been encouraged, even in 1996, a year when there was a major regional shortage. Imports from outside the region pay duties—10 percent on yellow maize, which is used in animal feed, and around 40 percent (including sales tax) for white maize, which competes more directly with local production. All imports have required permits from the Ministry of Food and Agriculture (MOFA).

Key Results

Official statistics show maize production to have grown at an average rate of 4.5 percent since 1983, well in excess of population growth[15], suggesting that the overall impact of government's increasingly liberal policies has been benign. However, the rate of growth has slowed since the end of the 1980s, and this is at least partly the consequence of the elimination of fertilizer subsidies and the failure of credit programs supporting fertilizer usage. This may also explain the increase in growth rates for cassava and yam production, two crops generally grown without inorganic fertilizer; there has been a notable switch to cassava in northern Ghana. Notwithstanding this, fertilizer usage is well established in high-potential areas of central Ghana where farmers continue purchasing it on cash terms, and national usage now appears to be recovering.[16] The elimination of subsidies has led to greater efficiency in the use of fertilizer, but not to an overall fall in production.

Most available information indicates that the maize marketing system is efficient and well integrated, as regards trading margins and spatial price spreads (Armah 1989, Asante and others 1989, Alderman and Shively 1991, Badiane and Shively 1998), and that average retail prices have declined as a result of liberalization (Badiane 1998). Badiane and others (1997) found that interseasonal price spreads had declined across local markets but that they were still extraordinarily high. In key surplus areas, lean-season wholesale prices in May and June were typically more than 100 percent above those of the previous September or October, both in real terms and after allowing for moisture loss. Coupled with high on-farm storage losses, it is likely that this pattern adversely affects production incentives for many farmers and slows the adoption of high-yielding maize varieties.[17]

Despite attempts to alter its structure through public procurement and inventory credit schemes, the maize post-harvest system has remained remarkably resilient, with most storage being carried out using traditional cribs on the farm, and an estimated 90 percent of the trade is accounted for by very small-scale traditional operators who turn over their stock quickly and who do not store significant quantities. Most change has occurred in the "modern" sector, accounting for the remaining 10 percent of the trade, which involves larger private grain-marketing companies and the mechanical drying and storage of grain (particularly gluts that cannot be handled at the peak of the harvest), and supplying poultry farmers, feed millers, food processors, and food-aid donors. They are also increasingly involved in selling to the public in general and in overland exports.

From 1993, the growth of this modern sector has been facilitated by official encouragement of private entrepreneurs (reversing the previous situation), the rental of GFDC drying and storage facilities to private traders, inventory credit and other forms of financing. GFDC's facilities were effectively turned over from public to private use. Banks also increased their financing of poultry farmers for the purchase of inputs. However, the effect of these factors have been seriously blunted by:

- The country's fiscal deficit and consequently weak monetary situation. With interest rates ranging between 30 percent and 50 percent since

1993, treasury bills have been very attractive to the banks, greatly reducing their interest in lending.

- Delays in restructuring and privatizing GFDC, the banks' lack of confidence in this institution as collateral manager[18], and the consequent underutilization of these facilities. The only bank willing to lend against stocks stored by GFDC was the government-owned ADB. In 1995–96, GFDC dried 20,500 tons of grain and stored 10,000 tons for private clients, much of it financed by inventory credit from ADB. The relevant figures for 1997–98 were similar, but there ensued a period of mismanagement, and by 1999 the corporation had practically collapsed. However, with suitable restructuring, much larger quantities could have been handled by the corporation.
- Discretionary control over imports. government feared a major maize shortage after the 1996–97 harvest and confidentially issued selected traders with permits to import around 30,000 tons of white maize free from the normal 40 percent duty.

The importation of 1997 has had adverse effects on the development of the Ghanaian maize trade, partly annulling previous progress in its modernization. The supply projections proved unduly pessimistic and there was no shortage. Moreover, the maize arrived too late for the 1996–97 season and had to be stored for two more years before it could be sold. The large "overhang" of unsold imported maize upset the normal seasonal price pattern, and many traders who were storing local maize—using either borrowed or their own funds—incurred significant speculative losses.

We postulate that with a more fully supportive policy and institutional framework, bank credit for private storage would have been greater, leading to a sustained reduction in interseasonal price variability (Coulter and Shepherd 1995). Instead of this, government succeeded in bringing temporary stability to price levels, at a cost of long-term incentives to greater private storage.

Government has continued intervening selectively in input and product markets in other ways. For example, it has tried to support producer prices by directing lending to particular traders and has imported fertilizer on its own account, with a view to combating a perceived monopoly position enjoyed by the leading importer. If government exercised less discretionary power, it would encourage local players to plan further ahead in covering their requirements—for example, the poultry industry could purchase options on international commodity markets and thereby cover itself against price spikes.

Badiane (1998) suggests that Ghana's liberalization, along with that of some other countries, has been piecemeal and "partial." As evidence for this he notes the continued existence of a marketing board for maize, quasi-monopolistic control of transportation services by a national transport union (GPRTU)[19], licensing restrictions on fertilizer marketing, and the fact that MOFA endorsement is needed to import maize.

The financial sector is a further source of constraints underlining the need for parallel improvements in other areas of the economy. Government's chronic budgetary deficits—and linked to this a weak financial sector with limited competition in obtaining new business—are a major impediment to the development of grain marketing.

Effect on External Trade

Government's relaxed approach seems to have led to increased exports. Between 1990 and 1994, total registered maize exports were only 924 tons. However, in 1996, the whole of West Africa experienced a major production shortfall, resulting in significant export demand, and 17,070 tons of maize were officially exported to Togo and Burkina Faso. In the following year, 3,915 tons were exported to Niger, according to the Ghanaian Ministry of Trade and Industry. Total exports, including unofficial trade, were much higher than this—research work in progress funded by the U.S. Agency for International Development suggests that the ratio of unofficial to official exports may be as high as 10:1 for some commodities (personal communication from Gayle Morris). Whatever the true level of exports, the important finding is that the government of Ghana now welcomes grain exports even in deficit years and sees surrounding countries as welcome customers for Ghanaian grain.

Annex 6.5
Minimizing the Costs of Producing and Distributing Grain

In the main text we highlighted three categories of costs: transport, transaction, and financing costs.

Minimizing Transport Costs

The most single important determinant of marketing costs is probably the state of roads. As highlighted by Dorward and others (1998), it not only affects transport costs, but also information flows and transaction costs (that is, the costs of searching and contract monitoring and enforcement). Platteau (1996) notes that econometric studies on aggregate supply response regularly show the infrastructure variable to be significant, independent of price variables. In the same vein Coulter (1996) reached the conclusion that road and port improvements were the first priority in improving the performance of the maize marketing system of Mozambique.

Consideration should be given to the cost-effectiveness of different kinds of road improvement. Hine (1993) argues in favor of very low-cost improvements, for example, upgrading non-motorable footpaths to earth tracks, or spot improvements in feeder roads (especially at water crossings and in low-lying areas), rather than, for example, on upgrading an existing motorable earth road to a gravel road.

According to the 1994 *World Development Report* (World Bank 1994), road maintenance is as big a problem as initial construction, particularly in Sub-Saharan Africa. The report argues in favor of maintenance by private sector under contract rather than by public employees, and for maintenance in part by local organizations and communities. "The most successful experiences—combine local control with some government funding or provision of materials. In low-income countries, attention should be directed to promoting cost-effective, labor-based approaches for road maintenance, and to construction." The recently restructured road authorities of Sierra Leone and Tanzania were held up by the report as models of agencies that had amongst other things, introduced "a mechanism for users to influence expenditures on road maintenance."

Other literature shows that freight transport costs are much higher in Sub-Saharan Africa than in Asia, in part because of the lower efficiency of transport services. In contrasting Pakistan with four francophone African countries, Hine and Rizet (1991) note that Pakistan:

- Imports a limited range of cheap, low-specification trucks, in large numbers.
- That these are modified to suit local conditions using locally manufactured parts in informal workshops.
- Drivers are given considerable responsibility for finding new business, for maintenance, and for managing truck accounts.
- Drivers work in pairs to allow 24-hour working, with one sleeping while the other drives.
- Average distances traveled per year are very high, but the proportion of empty trips is low; this is assisted by the services of competitive freight agents (a concept frowned upon in many countries as parasitic).

Hine and others (1997) finds that tariff rates per ton-kilometer were between two and five times higher in Tanzania than they were in Pakistan and Indonesia. The main factors contributing to the difference are capital costs, fuel, maintenance, tires, and overhead costs. He also highlights the degree of remaining state (or other) control over freight transport services, especially in West Africa—see the earlier reference to Ghana by Badiane (1998).

Other studies highlight the cost of unofficial tolls levied at roadblocks and frontier posts in raising transport costs. Anyango (1996) finds that landlocked countries of East Africa (Uganda, Rwanda, and Burundi) seeking to import containerized merchandise with c.i.f (cost, insurance, freight) value of US$250 per ton grain have to pay total transport costs of $225 per ton to get the goods out of Dar es Salaam or Mombasa ports to their final destination. Costs include port charges, clearing and forwarding, freight costs, and various duties and other payments.

Much of the higher transport costs in Africa clearly reflect the low density of economic activity in Africa, and the relative immaturity of private trucking sectors after years of domination by parastatal freight organizations (for example, RETCOs in Tanzania). However, other elements may be more amenable to policy intervention, for instance, the oligopolistic nature of importation and dealerships, and GPTRU control over tariff rates in Ghana, and unofficial tolls.

Minimizing Transaction Costs

Transaction costs are high because there is a lack of institutional arrangements for price discovery, for finding trade partners, for evaluating their creditworthiness, and for enforcing contracts.

Market Information Systems

Over the past three decades, there has been considerable donor support for the creation of government-run market information services (MISs), and it has been widely held that these will increase the level of price transparency for agricultural commodities, and put competitive pressure on trading margins. Recent literature indicates that these have not produced their expected benefits. Shepherd (1997), drawing on an FAO (Food and Agriculture Organization of the United Nations) survey of 53 functioning MISs disseminating price information, finds that the majority are under-resourced and that they tend to be operated by officials lacking a commercial approach. Frequently set up by donors, they have often proved unsustainable once donor support has been withdrawn. Shepherd observes that many MISs have been "over-designed," attempting to cover too many crops and markets. The quality of information collected has been poor, and its value to market participants is reduced by delays in dissemination. Some MISs have generated a great deal of data that have been neither analyzed nor disseminated.

Despite these findings, Shepherd believes that market information services are still desirable. Galtier and Egg (1998) expand on many of Shepherd's criticisms, but they go on to question the basic value of price-based MISs. In Mali, they find that private information networks are much more efficient in delivering desired price information to marketing participants than is the MIS, and they question the relevance of price information provided in situations where transactions are not standardized with regard to quality, delivery, payment conditions, and other aspects. For countries like Mali, they argue for a kind of market support service involving a range of interventions to overcome specific information-related problems; these include, for example:

- The establishment of fairs and local markets
- "Small ads broadcasts," enabling players to specify quantity, terms of payment and delivery conditions, as well as quality and price
- Standardization of contracts and contract bidding
- Random monitoring of scales to reduce trader opportunism
- Collection and publication of production and price forecasts for the coming season and year
- Development of forward markets
- Greater transparency on the part of the state regarding its proposed interventions in food and agricultural markets.

On a more positive note, a survey by Asante (personal communication from E. Asante) in Ghana found that 81 percent of producers listened regularly to crop prices announced on the radio and that 65 percent said that these broadcasts were "very helpful" to them.

Jayne and others (1999) recommend strengthening regional market information systems. This will involve reporting local currency prices for grains and the direction of trade flows, and developing better telecommunications and internet infrastructure between market reporting services. In the case of Zambia, they also recommend full reporting on maize imports, so as to reduce losses to traders through the unforeseen actions of competitors.

More research is needed to reach any final conclusions about the usefulness of MISs. However, the above findings suggest that if efforts to improve such systems are continued, target beneficiaries should be clearly identified and their data needs defined through participatory methods. Without prejudging the responses, it is likely that accurate and timely crop forecasts and greater transparency regarding government interventions (with regard to food aid distribution or importation) will be important wherever traders or farmers are being encouraged to undertake speculative storage of grain. Better arrangements are also needed to ensure operational autonomy relative to the government and self-financing.

Bulking Up and Interlocking

For financiers, input suppliers, and marketers, per unit transaction costs are much larger when dealing with small farmers than with commercial farmers. Costs can be greatly reduced by the interlocking of services, so that together with technical assistance, they are simultaneously provided by a single agribusiness company that can share the related overheads over several activities. However, as earlier indicated, such outgrower schemes have not so far had a good record in Africa.

Another approach, which has proved successful in a various countries, is for farmers to form group enterprises that can "bulk up" their members' demands, and thereby prove themselves attractive customers to commercial parties and banks. This approach is much used in Mali, where village associations in cotton- and rice-producing areas deal directly with the banks and regularly procure inputs and agricultural equipment through open tenders. The main limitation on such bulking-up initiatives is the strength and coherence of the group enterprises involved, often formed hurriedly under donor or nongovernmental organization auspices.

Research carried out by NRI (Stringfellow and others 1996 and 1997) reviews experience in five countries and suggests guidelines for the successful organization of group enterprises.

Contract Enforcement and Inspection Services

In industrial countries, speedy settlement of contractual disputes is normally accomplished by writing arbitration clauses into contracts, and by the fact that the courts uphold arbitrators' decisions. In most African countries, there are no local arbitration bodies, and there is little trust in the legal system. Hence the range of feasible contractual arrangements is greatly reduced, particularly contracts for forward delivery, where risk of nonperformance is particularly large. In Ghana, most commodity trade in the "modern" sector takes place under local purchase orders, where the buyer simply pays against delivery. Work is needed to establish the scope for local arbitration services, and for increasing the use of international arbitration services, such as those of the Grain and Feeds Trade Association (GAFTA), which are written under English law. Notably a GAFTA arbitration judgment was recently upheld by Zambian courts.

One way of reducing transaction costs is by having an independent party, such as an inspection company or a warehouse operator, independently verify the physical existence and the quality of the commodity—at a warehouse or in transit. By contracting the services of such companies, trading houses are able to satisfy the requirements of their customers or their lenders. International inspection companies or their African subsidiaries are increasingly providing such services, but given that their customers are restricted to international trading companies, the largest local companies, and food aid donors, the benefits are not being spread very widely.

Commodity Exchanges

Another way of reducing transactions costs is by organizing commodity exchanges, as these reduce the costs of finding a trading partner for volume deals, reduce or eliminate risks of non-performance, and serve as a mechanism of price discovery. The most successful such initiative in Africa is the successful launching of futures contracts for white and yellow maize on the South African Futures Exchange (SAFEX), where contract performance is fully underwritten by the exchange clearing house, SAFCOM, whose members are the country's main clearing banks. Other African countries lack preconditions for the organization of futures and options exchanges, including a large domestic grain market, well-functioning transport and logistics (and consequently low "basis risk"), an efficient and trusted storage sector, and a strong and dynamic banking sector[20]. There is also in Zimbabwe a viable "cash" commodity exchange dealing mainly in spot contracts in grains, and its establishment has been greatly aided by the existence of a major commercial farming sector. In most other African countries, organization of any sort of commodity exchange is likely to prove a difficult venture, given the thinness of most markets and the diverse interests that need to cooperate (Coulter forthcoming). An initiative currently being promoted in Uganda may, if successful, provide a model applicable in some of Africa's more dynamic agricultural economies. As presently designed, the project is highly dependent on donor support, and it remains to be seen whether there will be sufficient local patronage to ensure takeoff.

In some countries, "lower-tech" improvements are appropriate. Market efficiency can be enhanced simply by the institution of weekly fairs or markets; they attract buyers and give farmers an outlet for surplus production. In some countries (for example, Mozambique) they hardly exist, because previous governments have discouraged the development of informal trading networks. However, with the new policy framework they offer a cheap way of enhancing market efficiency. The key to establishing such markets will be for the authorities, or a group of people with sufficient charisma, to encourage a critical mass of farmers and traders to meet on the specified days.

Minimizing Financing Costs

As indicated above, the reform and improvement of financial sectors is a vital concomitant to agricultural market liberalization. Thoroughgoing financial sector reform may take decades, but in the meantime, steps are needed to enhance access to trade and investment credit, and to reduce financing costs.

Agricultural development banks have often performed poorly, but the experiences of Ghana and Mali show that in the absence of adequate alternatives they may perform a valuable function. There may be scope for new banks of this kind jointly financed by IFIs, governments, and private investors. However, Mali's experience also illustrates a danger with agricultural development banks: they sometimes crowd out private sector competitors that do not enjoy access to subsidized credits in hard currency.

One of the fastest ways in which credit can be expanded is by turning stock-in-trade into eligible collateral, through warehouse receipt financing, otherwise known as inventory credit. This topic is discussed at length by Coulter and Shepherd (1995) and UNCTAD (1996). The main precondition for organizing such schemes is the presence of really reliable and trusted warehousing companies in grain-producing areas, which can act as "collateral managers" on behalf of the banks. In the Republic of South Africa such a system has been provided by cooperatives that were nurtured under decades of state control, which have quickly found that liberalization allows them to sell storage services to a range of players including farmers, traders, and millers (see Coulter forthcoming). Outside of South Africa, there are few if any local companies providing these services, so international inspection companies try to fill the gap. However, their services are accessible only to a small number of companies with resources to fill large warehouses. Outside of port areas, there are few "public warehouses" open to multiple depositors.

By organizing such services, it should be possible to smooth interseasonal price fluctuations afflicting many African countries and, as indicated above, standardize grain quality and reduce transaction costs. Alternative approaches are discussed by Coulter and Norvell (1998).

Notes

1. Treasury bill rates now stand at 16 percent, whilst bank lending rates have remained in the low 20s for 18 months or more (compared with 31 percent in late 1996).

2. NMC's lack of access to capital has, in recent years, reduced some of its facilities to offering milling services or to buying maize grain on credit, paying only once it has been milled and sold. The government's intention was to complete sale of all NMC facilities by the end of 1998.

3. Interestingly, whilst El Niño had major impacts on regional production figures in 1997–98, its overall impact on cereal production is thought to have been positive. Maize producers in the central part of the country sustained major crop losses through waterlogging. However, rice production fared exceptionally well under the same circumstances. This created political pressure for a lifting of the export ban on rice, as these producers wished to sell their rice so as to buy maize. It also posed a dilemma for the SGR, which is only mandated to buy maize (Kabyemera, personal communication.).

4. Seppala's cited source is the FAOSAT database. However, figures contained in the database at the time of writing do not show either the significant rise in fertilizer consumption in the late 1980s or the same dramatic fall after 1990–92.

5. Figures from the Marketing Development Bureau and Food Security Department, quoted in Wangwe and others 1997, show the share of the "Big Four" regions in total national production declining from 44 percent in 1989–91 to 36 percent in 1994–96. Over the same period, the share of Arusha and Dodoma is said to have fallen from 10 percent to 9 percent, whilst the main increases have occurred in Mwanza (up from 5 percent to 9 percent) and Shinyanga (up from 11 percent to 14 percent).

6. This figure applies to the period 1981 to 1999.

7. Prior to independence, an official policy of panterritorial pricing was in operation for maize brought into GMB buying stations. However, as the network of buying stations only covered the commercial farming areas, the majority of farmers in communal areas were unable to benefit from this. Instead, the GMB appointed private traders to act as buying agents on its behalf. These agents received a fixed into-store price, but the farmgate prices received by communal farmers reflected the traders' own margins, which were obviously higher in more remote areas.

8. The main vehicle for this lending was the Agricultural Finance Corporation (AFC), which increased its loans to communal farmers from 18,000 with a total value of Z$4.2 million in 1980–81 to a peak of 77,384 with a total value of Z$60.0 million in 1986–87 (AFC figures, quoted in Chimedza 1994).

9. Commercial farmers had been using locally developed hybrids since the 1950s (Rukuni and Eicher 1994).

10. Jayne and Jones (1997) claim that the GMB maintained its buying prices above the export parity price in the main producing regions, even though these prices declined in real terms after 1987. By contrast, Jayne and Rukuni (1994) show the GMB producer price declining in constant 1991 prices throughout the period 1980–91.

11. The increase in smallholder production, it turned out, was generated by a relatively small proportion of better-endowed households, and many poorer households remained net buyers of maize. Jayne and Chisvo (1991) found that 70 percent or more of households in drier parts of the country remained net grain buyers even whilst the country as a whole was exporting.

12. Aggregate figures and the disaggregated figures for smallholder and commercial farming sectors all show pronounced fluctuations during the 1980s, with troughs in 1983 and 1987. However, the post-1987 peak was lower than the two previous highs, particularly in the smallholder sector.

13. A comparison of milling margins in five countries in the region show that margins are lowest in Zimbabwe (Jayne and others 1999).

14. The devaluation came in the wake of the spread of "Asian flu" to South Africa. The onset of a costly intervention in the war in the Democratic Republic of Congo only served to convince speculators even further that the Zimbabwe dollar was ripe for attack.

15. Among the private trade there is widespread apprehension about the accuracy of production figures at the regional level, but there is a consensus that the overall picture is reasonably accurate.

16. In 1996 imports returned to around their 1990 level (over 40,000 tons) after running at around half this level from 1992 to 1995 (source: Statistical Office, Ministry of Finance). The 1997 figure was around 30,000 tons.

17. A recent World Bank/FAO mission (unpublished) calculated that farmers who sell their crop in the immediate post-harvest period get value-to-cost ratios (VCRs) of 1.15 for local maize varieties and 1.85 for improved varieties. According to the accepted rule of thumb that VCR$\geq$ 2, these figures indicate that fertilizer use is not profitable. Only those farmers able to store for several months can obtain reasonable returns.

18. GFDC has outstanding debts to the Ghanaian banking system and is technically insolvent.

19. GPRTU sets the tariff for all major routes, enforced by a system of truck licensing by route and queuing for customers at lorry parks. Hence there is insufficient competition between drivers/owners for business.

20. Prior to the launching of contracts for white and yellow maize in 1996, SAFEX was already trading financial futures, and the banks had established a clearing mechanism (SAFCOM) to underwrite transactions.

References

Abdulwahid, Y. 1995. *Institutional Constraints Affecting Cereals Marketing in Chad.* Master's Thesis, Department of Agricultural Economics, Michigan State University, East Lansing.

Ackello-Ogutu, C., and P. Echessah. 1997. *Unrecorded Cross-Border Trade between Kenya and Uganda: Implications for Food Security.* Africa Bureau, Office of Sustainable Development Publication Series, Technical Paper 59, Washington, D.C.

Alderman, H., and G. Shively. 1991. *Prices and Markets in Ghana.* Working Paper 28. Food and Nutrition Working Program, Cornell University, Ithaca, New York.

Anyango, G. (1996) *Comparative Transportation Cost Analysis in East Africa, Executive Summary.* Africa Bureau, Office of Sustainable Development Publications Series, Technical Paper 21, Washington, D.C.

Armah, P. 1989. *Post-Harvest Maize Marketing Efficiency: The Ghanaian Experience.* Ph.D. Dissertation, Department of Economics and Agricultural Economics, University College of Wales, Aberystwyth.

Asante, E., S. Asuming-Brempong, and P. Bruce. 1989. *Ghana: Grain Marketing Study.* Report prepared for the Ministry of Agriculture and the World Bank.

Badiane, O., F. Goletti, M. Kherallah, P. Berry, K. Govindan, P. Gruhn, and M. Mendoza. 1997. *Agricultural Input and Output Marketing Reforms in African Countries: Final Report.* Washington, D.C.: International Food Policy Research Institute.

Badiane, O. 1998. "The Effects of Liberalization on Food Markets in Africa." Paper presented at the 57th Seminar of the European Association of Agricultural Economists, Wageningen, Germany, September 9, 1998.

Badiane, O., and G. Shively. 1998. "Spatial Integration, Transport Costs, and the Response of Local Prices to Policy Changes in Ghana." *Journal of Development Economics* 56 (August):411–31.

Baris, P., J. Coste, A. Coulibaly, and M. Deme. 1996. *Analyse de la Filière Rizicole de la Zone de l'Office du Niger et des Perspectives à Moyen et Long Termes.* Report by IRAM (L'Institute de Recherches et d'Applications de Developpement) to the Ministry of Rural Development and the Environment, Mali.

Barrett, C. 1997. "Food Marketing Liberalization and Trader Entry: Evidence from Madagascar." *World Development* 25(5):763–77.

Bates, R. 1981. *Markets and States in Tropical Africa.* Berkeley: University of California Press.

———. 1989. *Beyond the Miracle of the Market: The Political Economy of Agrarian Development in Kenya.* Cambridge, UK: Cambridge University Press.

Boughton, D., and T. Reardon. 1997 "Will Promotion of Coarse Grain Processing Turn the Tide for Traditional Cereals in the Sahel? Recent Empirical Evidence from Mali." *Food Policy* 22(4):307–16.

Boxall, R., and S. Bickersteth. 1991 "Liberalization of Cereals Marketing in Sub-Saharan Africa: Implementation Issues." Report 2: Ghana, A Case Study. Natural Resources Institute, Chatham.

Bryceson, D. 1993. *Liberalizing Tanzania's Food Trade.* London: UNRISD (United Nations Research Institute for Social Development).

Byerlee D., and P. Heisey. 1996. "Past and Potential Impacts of Maize Research in Sub-Saharan Africa: A Critical Assessment." *Food Policy* 21(3):255–77.

Chimedza, R. 1994. "Rural Financial Markets." In M. Rukuni and C. Eicher, eds., *Zimbabwe's Agricultural Revolution.* Harare: University of Zimbabwe Publications.

Coste, J., J. Egg, N. Bricas, D. Benoit, P. Diaz-Corvalan, D. Gentil, B. Hibou, J. Igue, A. Lambert. and V. Olivier. 1991. *Cereals Trade and Agricultural Policies in the Western Sub-Market, Regional Processes and the Prospects for Integration. Summary Report.* Paris: OECD/Permanent Interstates Committee for Drought/Club du Sahel.

Coulter, J. 1994. *Liberalization of Cereals Marketing in Sub-Saharan Africa: Lessons from Experience.* Marketing Series, Vol.9. Chatham, U.K.: Natural Resources Institute.

_____. 1996. *Maize Marketing and Pricing Study: Mozambique.* NRI Consultancy Report R2247C (for the World Bank). Chatham, U.K.: Natural Resources Institute.

_____. Forthcoming. "Commodity Exchanges and Warehouse Receipts—Can They Improve the Performance of African Grain Markets?" In the proceedings of the African Food Marketing Agencies/FAO Meeting on Grain Commodity Trading and Commodity Exchanges, Pretoria, November 3–5, 1998.

Coulter, J., and P. Golob. 1991. *Liberalization of Cereals Marketing in Sub-Saharan Africa: Implementation Issues. Report 2: Tanzania, a Case Study.* Chatham, U.K.: Natural Resources Institute. Mimeo.

_____. 1992. "Cereal Marketing Liberalization in Tanzania." *Food Policy* 420–30. December.

Coulter, J., and N. Norvell. 1998. "The Role of Warehousing in Africa: Lessons for Implementation from Four Continents." In *New Strategies for a Changing Commodity Economy: The Use of Modern Financial Instruments.* Ed: UNCTAD, Selected papers from the Partners for Development Summit organized by United Nations Committee on Trade and Development and the City of Lyon, France. UNCTAD, Geneva.

Coulter, J., and A. Shepherd. 1995. *Inventory Credit: An Approach to Developing Agricultural Markets.* FAO Agricultural Services Bulletin 120. Rome: Food and Agriculture Organization.

Coulter, J., and P. Tyler. 1993. *Liberalization of Cereals Marketing in Sub-Saharan Africa: Implementation Issues. Report 4: Mali, a Case Study.* Chatham, U.K.: Natural Resources Institute. Mimeo

Deme, M. 1993. *Etude Sur la Filière Riz au Mali.* Report to the Program for Restructuring the Cereals Market (PRMC), Bamako.

Dorward, A., J. Kydd, and C. Poulton. 1998. "Conclusions: New Institutional Economics, Policy Debates and the Research Agenda." In A. Dorward, J. Kydd, and C. Poulton, eds., *Smallholder Cash Crop Production under Market Liberalization: A New Institutional Economics Perspective.* Wallingford, U.K.: CAB International.

Egg, J. 1999. *Etude de l'Impact de la Libéralisation sur le Fonctionnement des Filières Céréalières au Mali.* Rapport de synthèse. Montpellier: Institut National de la Recherche Agronomique.

Galtier, F., and J. Egg. 1998. "From Price Reporting Systems to Variable Geometry-Oriented Market Information Services." Paper presented at the 57th seminar of the European Association of Agricultural Economists, Wageningen, Germany, September 23–26, 1998.

Golob, P., R. Stringfellow, and E. Asante. 1996. *A Review of the Storage and Marketing Systems of Major Food Grains in Northern Ghana.* Chatham, U.K.: Natural Resources Institute. Mimeo.

Gordon, H. 1988. *Open Markets for Maize and Rice in Urban Tanzania: Current Issues and Evidence.* Ph.D. Dissertation, Fletcher School, Tufts University, Medford, Mass.

Hine J. 1993. "Transport and Marketing Priorities to Improve Food Security in Ghana and the Rest of Africa." In H. U. Thimm, ed., *Regional Food Security and Rural Infrastructure: Linkages, Shortcomings, Needs. Proceedings of the International Symposium on Regional Food Security and Rural Infrastructure.* Vol. 1. Justus-Liebig University, Giessen, Germany.

Hine, J., and C. Rizet. 1991. "Halving Africa's Freight Transport Costs: Could It Be Done?" Paper presented at the International Symposium on Transport and Communications in Africa, Brussels, 1991.

Hine J. L., J. H. Ebden, and P. Swan. 1997. *A Comparison of Freight Transport Operations in Tanzania and Indonesia.* TRL Report 267. Crowthorne, Berks., U.K.: Transport Research Laboratory.

Howard, J., and C. Mungoma. 1997. "Zambia's Stop-and-Go Maize Revolution." In D. Byerlee and C. Eicher, eds. *Africa's Emerging Maize Revolution.* Colorado: Lynn Reinner.

Ikiara, G. 1998. "Rising to the Challenge: The Private Sector Response in Kenya." In P. Seppälä, ed., *Liberalized and Neglected? Food Marketing Policies in Eastern Africa.* World Development Studies 12. Helsinki: UNU/WIDER (United Nations University/World Institute for Development Economics Research).

Jayne, T., and M. Chisvo. 1991. "Unravelling Zimbabwe's Food Security Paradox." *Food Policy* 16(5):319–29.

Jayne T., and S. Jones. 1997. "Food Marketing and Pricing Policy in Eastern and Southern Africa: A Survey." *World Development* 25(9):1505–27.

Jayne T., and M Rukuni. 1994. "Managing the food economy in the 1990s." In M. Rukuni and C. Eicher (eds), *Zimbabwe's Agricultural Revolution.* University of Zimbabwe Publications, Harare.

Jayne, T., A. Negassa, and R. Myers. 1998. *The Effect of Liberalization on Grain Prices and Marketing Margins in Ethiopia.* International Development Working Paper 68, Department of Agricultural Economics, Michigan State University, East Lansing.

Jayne, T., L. Rubey, D. Tschirley, M. Mukumbu, M. Chisvo, A. Santos, M. Weber, and P. Diskin. 1995. *Effects of Food Market Reform on Household Access to Food in*

Four Countries in Eastern and Southern Africa. International Development Paper 19, Department of Agricultural Economics, Michigan State University, East Lansing.

Jayne, T., M. Mukumbu, M. Chisvo, D. Tschirley, M. Weber, B. Zulu, R. Johansson, P. Santos, and D. Soroko. 1999. "Successes and Challenges of Food Market Reform: Experiences from Kenya, Mozambique, Zambia, and Zimbabwe." International Development Working Paper 72, Department of Agricultural Economics, Michigan State University, East Lansing.

Jayne, T., M. Mukumbu, J. Duncan, J. Staatz, J. Howard, M. Lundberg, K. Aldridge, B. Nakaponda, J. Ferris, F. Keita, and A. Sanankoua. 1996. "Trends in Real Food Prices in Six Sub-Saharan African Countries." International Development Working Paper 55, Department of Agricultural Economics, Michigan State University, East Lansing.

Jenkins, C. 1997. "The Politics of Economic Policymaking in Zimbabwe." *Journal of Modern African Economies* 35(4):575–602.

Jones, S. 1998. *Liberalised Food Marketing in Developing Countries: Key Policy Problems*. Oxford Policy Management, Oxford, U.K..

MAFF (Ministry of Agriculture, Food, and Fisheries). 1995. *A Review of Maize Marketing Liberalization during 1994: The Transition Programme 1995–96*. Food Security Division, Lusaka, Zambia.

Mashingaidze, K. 1994. "Maize Research and Development." In M. Rukuni and C. Eicher, eds., *Zimbabwe's Agricultural Revolution*. Harare: University of Zimbabwe Publications.

Mdadila, J. and Associates. 1995. *Maize Milling Industry in Tanzania: Present Position and Prospects*. Marketing Development Bureau, Ministry of Agriculture and Cooperatives, Dar es Salaam.

MDB (Marketing Development Bureau). 1990. *Aspects of the Open Market for Maize and Rice*. Ministry of Agriculture and Cooperatives, Dar es Salaam.

_____. 1997. *Marketing of Maize and Rice in Tanzania*. Ministry of Agriculture and Cooperatives, Dar es Salaam.

Mehta, M. 1989. *An Analysis of the Structure of the Cereals Market in Mali*. Secrétariat Technique de la CESA (Centre d'Enseignement Superieur des Affaires), Bamako.

Newbery, D. 1989. The Theory of Food Price Stabilization. *Economic Journal* 99(398): 1065–82.

Norvell, N. 1998. *The Role of Warehousing in Africa: Lessons for Warehouse Receipt Financing from South Africa, Tanzania and Uganda*. Research Report R2387. Chatham, U.K.: Natural Resources Institute.

OECD (Organisation for Economic Co-operation and Development). 2000. *Agricultural Policies in OECD Countries: Monitoring and Evaluation*. Paris.

Ouedraogo, I., and C. Adoum. 1993. *Improving the Effectiveness of Policy Reform in Africa: Cereals Market Policy Reform in Mali*. Abt Associates, Inc., Washington, D.C.

Pinkney, T. 1993. "Is Market Liberalization Compatible with Food Security? Storage, Trade and Price Policies for Maize in Southern Africa." In A. Valdes and K. Muir-Leresche, eds., *Agricultural Policy Reforms and Regional Market Integration in*

Malawi, Zambia and Zimbabwe. Washington: International Food Policy Research Institute.

Platteau, J-P. 1996. "Physical Infrastructure as a Constraint on Agriculture Growth: The Case of Sub-Saharan Africa." *Oxford Development Studies* 24(3):189–219.

Poulton, C., A. Dorward, and J. Kydd. 1998 "The Revival of Smallholder Cash Crops in Africa: Public and Private Roles in the Provision of Finance." *Journal of International Development* 10(1):85–103.

Risopoulos, J., R. Al-Hassan, S. Clark, A. Dorward, C. Poulton, and K. Wilkin. 1998. *Improving Smallholder Access to Maize Marketing Opportunities in Southern Africa: A Literature Review*. Report submitted under UK Department for International Development (DFID) project ZB0123, Wye College.

Rukuni, M., and C. Eicher, eds. 1994. *Zimbabwe's Agricultural Revolution*. Harare: University of Zimbabwe Publications.

Santorum, A., and A. Tibaijuka. 1992. "Trading Responses to Food Market Liberalization in Tanzania." *Food Policy* 17(6):431–42.

Scarborough, V. 1989. *The Current Status of Food Marketing in Tanzania*. Wye College, University of London, UK.

Seppälä, P. 1998 "Tanzania–Decisive Liberalization Path. In P. Seppälä, ed., *Liberalized and Neglected? Food Marketing Policies in Eastern Africa*. World Development Studies 12. UNU/WIDER, Helsinki.

Shepherd, A. 1997. *Market Information Services: Theory and Practice*. Rome: Food and Agriculture Organization.

Staatz, J., J. Dione, and N. Dembele. 1989. "Cereals Market Liberalization in Mali." *World Development* 17(5):703–18.

Stringfellow, R., J. Coulter, T. Lucey, C. McKone, and A. Hussain. 1996. *The Provision of Agricultural Services through Self-help in Sub-Saharan Africa*. Research report R6117CA Natural Resources Institute, Chatham, U.K.

Stringfellow, R., J. Coulter, A. Hussain, T. Lucey, and C. McKone. 1997. Improving the Access of Smallholders to Agricultural Services in Sub-Saharan Africa." *Small Enterprise Development* 8(3):35–41.

UNCTAD (United Nations Conference on Trade and Development). 1996. *Collateralised Commodity Financing, with Special Reference to the Use of Warehouse Receipts*. UNCTAD/COM/84. Geneva: UNCTAD

Vaze P., J. Wright, G. Mudimu, and S. Gundry. 1998. "Anchoring the Liberalized Market: Zimbabwe's Grain Marketing Board in Rural Deficit Areas." Paper presented at the 57th seminar of the European Association of Agricultural Economists, Wageningen, Germany, September 23–26, 1998.

Wangwe, S., H. Amani, H. Semboja, and W. Mbowe. 1997. *Agricultural Marketing of Cotton and Maize in Tanzania*. Dar es Salaam: Economic and Social Research Foundation .

World Bank. 1981. *Accelerated Development in Sub-Saharan Africa*. Washington, D.C.

_____. 1994. *World Development Report*. Washington, D.C.: World Bank.

World Bank and Government of Tanzania. 1994. *Tanzania: Agriculture*. Washington, D.C.

Data Appendix

To provide a perspective on conditions in the commodity markets covered in this book, this annex presents historic production, trade, and price statistics. In some instances, market conditions rendered existing policies ineffective and unsustainable, triggering reform. In other instances, price movements unrelated to reform worked for or against reformers. However, differences in existing policy approaches among the commodities meant the size and frequency of external market shocks differed among commodity markets. Differences in approach also meant that similar market events had different domestic outcomes. Some key factors for each of the commodity markets are given below.

Cocoa. Real cocoa prices fell every year from 1984 to 1992. This decline rendered the cocoa agreement ineffective and contributed to its demise. Governments sought to stem losses incurred by parastatals and provide relief to producers. Market reforms and a realignment of overvalued exchange rates were introduced.

Coffee. Between 1986 and 1988, arabica prices fell by 46 percent, putting added pressure on a shaky coffee agreement. After the agreement collapsed, prices continued to fall as pent-up inventories were released. Parastatals charged with stabilizing domestic prices were ineffective and incurred losses that strained government budgets. During the next 10 years, nearly all producers introduced sector reforms.

Sugar. Unlike interventions in other markets, most domestic sugar market interventions transfer costs to consumers. Consequently, the two significant price declines—one in the early 1980s and a second in the early 1990s—did not trigger budgetary problems for sugar policy managers or significant pressure for trade policy reform. Market events, however, did affect the profitability of government-owned industries and triggered privatization in several countries.

Cotton. Cotton markets did not experience the persistent price declines that characterized cocoa and coffee markets of the late 1980s and early 1990s. For this and other reasons, reforms have come late. The countries that have undertaken cotton reforms are small producers, while the large producers have yet to reform their subsectors. Between 1995 and 1999, prices steadily declined, a factor that may have triggered recent reforms.

Grains. International markets always provided incentives for domestic traders to circumvent the numerous restrictions countries place on domestic markets. But unlike other commodity market reforms covered in this volume, the grain market reforms discussed were largely independent of events in global grain markets.

Annual Cocoa Prices

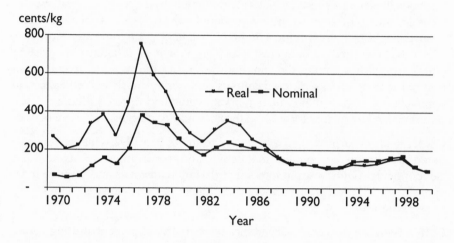

Monthly Cocoa Prices

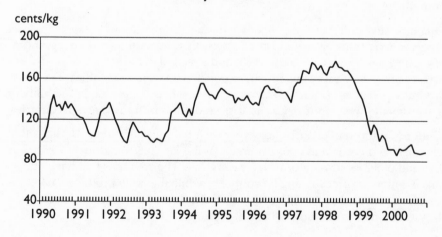

Prices are from the International Cocoa Organization (ICCO) daily price, average of the first three positions on the terminal markets of New York and London, nearest three future trading months. Quantities are also from ICCO and World Bank estimates for 1999.

Table 1. World Cocoa Bean Balance (thousands of tons)

	1970–71	1980–81	1990–91	1995–96	1996–97	1997–98	1998–99	1999-2000
PRODUCTION								
Côte d'Ivoire	180	417	805	1,200	1,108	1,113	1,176	1,250
Ghana	406	258	293	404	323	409	398	410
Indonesia	2	7	145	285	325	331	365	410
Nigeria	305	155	155	158	160	165	195	170
Brazil	182	353	368	231	185	170	133	135
Cameroon	112	117	·115	135	126	115	125	125
Malaysia	4	47	221	115	100	65	70	80
Ecuador	72	87	102	103	103	35	75	95
Dominican Republic	27	35	42	55	52	60	26	47
Colombia	21	38	52	50	50	45	38	40
Mexico	25	30	43	42	45	35	35	35
Papua New Guinea	28	32	33	36	29	29	30	33
World	**1,554**	**1,695**	**2,506**	**2,916**	**2,713**	**2,683**	**2,777**	**2,939**
GRINDINGS								
Netherlands	121	140	267	385	402	425	435	—
United States	279	186	268	342	394	399	395	—
Côte d'Ivoire	38	60	110	140	160	205	225	—
Germany	133	160	306	266	240	226	205	—
Brazil	70	191	260	205	180	188	195	—
United Kingdom	84	80	152	191	172	174	165	—
France	42	48	70	113	106	103	107	—
Malaysia	—	7	85	95	95	100	100	—
World	**1,418**	**1,556**	**2,335**	**2,713**	**2,736**	**2,795**	**2,764**	**2,860**
EXPORTS								
Côte d'Ivoire	145	418	688	1,038	929	964	977	—
Ghana	314	382	245	331	267	326	308	—
Indonesia	1	5	113	224	264	148	212	—
Nigeria	272	76	142	147	137	143	142	—
Cameroon	80	96	90	93	95	84	91	—
Dominican Republic	28	27	36	50	41	54	48	—
Papua New Guinea	32	26	33	35	28	29	30	—
World	**1,186**	**1,114**	**1,732**	**2,116**	**1,932**	**1,941**	**1,990**	
IMPORTS								
United States	321	246	320	445	353	427	408	—
Netherlands	120	167	267	105	464	320	396	—
Germany	144	167	299	299	327	309	312	—
United Kingdom	85	92	173	248	176	193	206	—
France	40	59	74	117	111	108	112	—
Singapore	2	20	121	88	86	89	88	—
Russian Federation	138	114	83+	75	85	75	78	—
Italy	40	32	56	71	71	72	71	—
Belgium-Luxembourg	20	28	50	45	54	82	60	—
Spain	23	37	45	50	49	66	55	—
Estonia	—	—	—	5	65	78	49	—
Japan	39	31	52	49	54	43	49	—
Canada	18	14	25	39	34	53	42	—
World	**1,215**	**1,202**	**1,765**	**2,229**	**2,219**	**2,218**	**2,222**	**—**

— Not available.

Note: Crop year begins October 1.

Source: ICCO and World Bank.

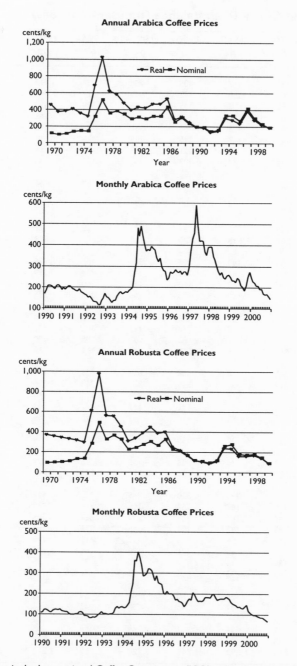

Annual Arabica Coffee Prices

Monthly Arabica Coffee Prices

Annual Robusta Coffee Prices

Monthly Robusta Coffee Prices

The arabica price is the International Coffee Organization (ICO) indicator price—other mild arabicas, average New York and Bremen/Hamburg markets, ex-dock. The robusta price is the ICO indicator price—robustas, average New York and Le Havre/Marseilles markets, ex-dock. Quantities are from ICO, the U.S. Department of Agriculture, and the World Bank.

Table 2. World Coffee Balance (thousands of bags)

	1970– 71	1980– 81	1990– 91	1995– 96	1996– 97	1997– 98	1998– 99	1999– 2000p
PRODUCTION								
Brazil	11,000	21,500	31,000	16,800	27,663	22,756	34,547	26,500
Colombia	8,000	13,500	14,500	12,939	10,876	12,211	11,500	12,000
Vietnam		77	1,200	3,917	5,705	6,893	6,200	7,500
Indonesia	2,330	5,365	7,250	5,800	8,296	7,756	7,589	7,200
Côte d'Ivoire	—	—	—	2,900	4,528	3,682	2,742	5,300
Mexico	3,200	3,862	4,550	5,400	5,324	5,116	4,400	5,200
Guatemala	1,965	2,702	3,282	2,827	4,524	4,218	3,400	4,900
India	1,914	1,977	2,970	3,717	3,469	4,718	3,833	4,700
Uganda	2,667	2,133	2,700	4,200	4,297	3,032	3,600	4,000
Ethiopia	2,589	3,264	3,500	3,800	3,270	2,916	3,867	3,500
Honduras	545	1265	1,685	2,254	2,004	2,564	2,300	2,776
Costa Rica	1,295	2,140	2,565	2,595	2,126	2,489	2,376	2,550
El Salvador	2,054	2,940	2,402	2,325	2,534	2,157	1,840	2,221
Peru	1114	1,170	1,150	1,811	1,802	1,916	2,066	2,150
Ecuador	1,255	1,517	1,850	—	1,993	1,191	1,260	1,800
Thailand	N/A	201	900	1,317	1,403	1,293	993	1,370
Kenya	999	1,568	1,502	—	1,246	882	1,133	1,330
Cameroon	1,180	1,860	1,365	—	1,432	889	1,333	1,300
Venezuela, R. B. de	936	1,109	843	1,067	1,200	975	1,400	1,250
Papua New Guinea	—	—	—	1,002	1,089	1,076	1,340	1,250
Nicaragua	648	971	454		793	1,086	1,044	1,100
World	—	—	—	88,749	102,411	96,438	105,140	107,215
ENDING STOCKS								
Brazil	31,904	6,180	10,372	16,000	14,128	11,278	12,075	7,362
Colombia	5,074	6339	9,351	6,328	4,420	3,929	2,669	2,447
Côte d'Ivoire	1,687	3,696	3,563	1,499	2,915	1,885	1,693	1,517
Costa Rica	337	465	905	1,149	1,212	1,212	1,052	1,122
Ethiopia	1,149	1,088	1,310	—	660	360	1,077	1,102
World	54,126	32,013	4,7251	—	29,185	24,500	24,028	20,039
CONSUMPTION								
United States	—	—	—	17,600	17,847	18,194	18,290	18,110
Brazil	—	—	—	10,230	10,880	10,880	12,500	12,800
Germany	—	—	—	9,480	9,709	9,038	9,300	9,349
Japan	—	—	—	5,750	6,369	5,900	5,710	5,993
France	—	—	—	5,230	5,623	5,317	5,300	5,413
Italy	—	—	—	4,640	4,857	4,843	4,700	4,800
Spain	—	—	—	—	3,029	2,968	2,999	2,999
Canada	—	—	—	2,800	2,960	2,920	2,291	2,724
United Kingdom	—	—	—	2,300	2,296	2,565	2,419	2,427
World	—	—	—	96,300	99,500	99,400	98,000	98,967

— Not available.

Notes The crop year begins April 1 or October 1. Ending stocks refer to producing countries only.
Source: ICO, U.S. Department of Agriculture, and World Bank.

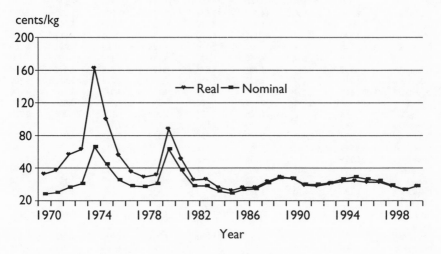

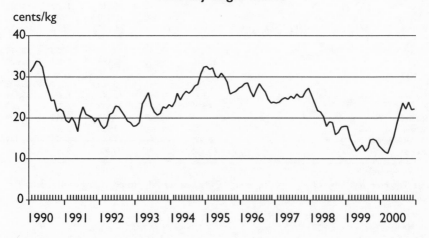

The price is world, International Sugar Agreement (ISA) daily price, raw, f.o.b. and stowed at greater Caribbean ports. Quantities are from the International Sugar Organization.

Table 3. World Sugar Balance (thousands of tons)

	1970–71	1980–81	1990–91	1995–96	1996–97	1997–98	1998–99	1999–2000
PRODUCTION								
Brazil	5,019	8,270	8,007	14,625	15,269	18,134	21,604	19,450
European Union	7,705	13,347	17,175	16,950	18,756	18,900	17,900	19,400
India	4,634	4,528	12,068	17,665	13,898	13,859	16,879	18,000
United States	5,734	5,313	5,740	6,685	6,537	7,274	7,555	8,085
China	2,900	2,800	6,250	6,790	7,323	8,747	9,702	7,975
Thailand	495	778	3,542	6,379	6,099	4,325	5,478	5,700
Australia	2,507	3,415	3,612	5,350	5,793	5,395	5,200	5,400
Mexico	2,402	2,179	3,384	4,750	4,822	5,492	5,025	5,275
Cuba	7,559	6,805	8,445	4,635	4,316	3,284	3,780	4,100
Pakistan	770	686	1,989	2,675	2,460	3,800	3,775	3,000
World	**7,2891**	**83,946**	**11,0894**	**123,949**	**123,698**	**127,501**	**134,573**	**134,175**
CONSUMPTION								
India	3,767	5,042	11,075	14,325	15,195	16,026	16,225	16,600
European Union	7,035	10,608	13,067	13,950	14,605	14,100	14,300	14,600
Brazil	3,495	6,264	6,615	8,475	8,800	9,150	9,250	9,425
United States	10,550	9,330	7,848	8,685	8,838	8,923	9,140	9,300
China	3,150	3,600	7,125	8,100	8,050	8,300	8,630	8,800
Russian Federation	10,247	12,760	13,400	5,300	5,325	5,450	5,975	5,995
Mexico	1,992	3,152	4,424	4,375	4,140	4,416	4,420	4,500
Pakistan	625	781	2,290	3,020	2,910	3,130	3,250	3,300
Indonesia	887	1,550	2,650	3,010	3,280	2,930	3,000	3,025
Japan	3,029	2,982	2,833	2,600	2,478	2,530	2,475	2,525
World	**71,856**	**88,647**	**108,417**	**118,003**	**122,231**	**125,199**	**128,065**	**130,587**
EXPORTS								
Brazil	1,130	2,662	1,640	5,435	5,995	8,483	11,291	10,025
European Union	927	4,325	5,353	4,305	5,064	6,158	5,160	6,325
Australia	1,660	2,411	3,069	4,365	4,415	4,514	4,142	4,322
Thailand	52	460	2,496	4,758	4,129	2,570	3,283	3,510
Cuba	6,906	6,191	7,172	3,810	3,597	2,569	3,121	3,345
South Africa, Republic of	691	785	833	674	939	1,078	1,531	1,180
Guatemala	57	210	549	920	1,047	1,324	1,140	1,130
Colombia	130	280	416	900	808	849	875	850
Mexico	612	0	5	425	742	1,137	605	775
Mauritius	616	655	612	25	600	685	495	500
World	**21,766**	**26,826**	**28,474**	**34,755**	**35,410**	**36,647**	**39,012**	**37,534**
IMPORTS								
Russian Federation	3,005	4,981	4,082	3,200	3,060	4,395	5,750	4,025
European Union	121	1,431	1,719	4,305	1,902	1,896	1,825	1,825
Japan	2,480	2,334	1,752	1,790	1,726	1,660	1,598	1,630
United States	4,807	4,709	2,508	2,525	2,620	2,106	1,680	1,590
Korea, Republic of	221	799	1,097	1,210	1,446	1,376	1,445	1,470
Canada	999	907	2,508	1,105	1,064	1,068	1,140	1,145
Malaysia	382	510	756	1,050	1,122	1,010	1,260	1,135
Egypt	45	469	805	690	1,295	1,210	1,125	1,085
Iran, Islamic Republic of	78,785	606	890	1,390	1,075	1,050	1,075	
Indonesia	129	398	320	735	1,690	1,080	1,850	975
World	**21,238**	**26,692**	**27,622**	**34,024**	**35,425**	**36,631**	**39,029**	**34,435**

— Not available.

Note: Crop year begins October 1.

Source: ISO and World Bank.

Annual Cotton Prices

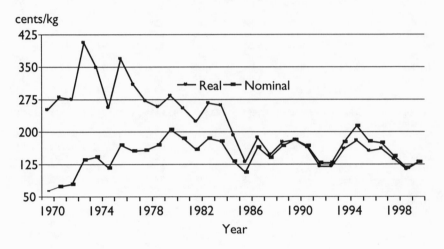

Monthly Cotton Prices

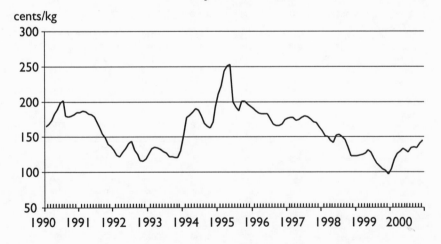

The price is for "Cotton Outlook A Index" middling 1 ¾₂ inch, average of the cheapest 5 of 15 styles traded in Northern Europe, c.i.f. Quantities are from the International Cotton Advisory Committee.

Table 4. World Cotton Balance (thousands of tons)

	1970–71	1980–81	1990–91	1996–97	1997–98	1998–99	1999–2000p	2000–01f
PRODUCTION								
United States	2,219	2,422	3,376	4,803	4,092	3,030	3,700	3,900
China	1,995	2,707	4,508	4,100	4,600	4,501	3,900	3,500
India	909	1,322	1,989	2,351	2,450	2,710	2,800	2,750
Pakistan	543	714	1,638	1,800	1,530	1,480	1,800	1,550
U.S.S.R./ Uzbekistan	2,342	2,661	2,593	1,198	1,150	1,000	1,160	1,100
West Africa	140	224	562	716	956	897	928	901
Turkey	400	500	655	792	795	871	850	816
Australia	19	99	433	552	681	726	700	650
Brazil	549	623	717	368	370	420	569	580
Greece	110	115	213	400	348	405	390	394
Turkmenistan	—	—	—	120	180	200	280	350
Syrian Arab Republic	150	118	145	223	355	335	325	254
World	**11,740**	**13,831**	**18,970**	**19,622**	**20,015**	**18,551**	**19,298**	**18,620**
ENDING STOCKS								
China	412	299	1,550	4,438	4,198	4,124	3,339	2,289
India	376	59	539	760	811	1,011	1,217	1,217
United States	915	653	510	829	844	849	979	1,034
Pakistan	55	204	313	312	323	353	533	598
Turkey	24	129	256	123	100	269	437	413
Australia	13	61	150	310	326	424	432	382
World	**4,605**	**5,152**	**6,653**	**9,419**	**9,825**	**9,699**	**9,702**	**8,696**
EXPORTS								
United States	848	1,290	1,697	1,550	1,695	915	1,400	1,750
U.S.S.R./ Uzbekistan	553	616	397	1,050	950	900	950	1,009
West Africa	137	185	498	690	815	843	866	839
Australia	4	53	329	467	625	650	640	678
China	22	1	202	2	40	147	300	300
Turkmenistan	—	—	—	115	58	210	230	298
Greece	0	13	86	251	200	230	222	274
World	**3,875**	**4,414**	**5,081**	**6,076**	**5,982**	**5,274**	**5,972**	**6,193**
IMPORTS								
Indonesia	36	106	324	475	425	500	555	542
Mexico	1	0	43	161	330	302	390	533
Italy	178	193	336	356	350	330	365	381
Turkey	1	0	46	243	280	250	376	371
Korea, Republic of	121	332	447	284	265	330	360	370
Brazil	4	2	108	493	380	292	284	344
Taiwan, China	160	214	358	300	275	293	322	310
Thailand	46	86	354	298	285	271	295	307
Japan	796	697	634	270	285	270	230	270
India	155	0	0	5	180	136	300	251
U.S.S.R./Russian Federation	238	28	1,190	406	223	179	224	227
World	**4,086**	**4,555**	**5,222**	**6,160**	**5,725**	**5,429**	**5,972**	**6,193**

— Not available.

Note: The crop year begins August 1; Figures in the rows denoted (U.S.S.R./Uzbekistan) and (U.S.S.R./Russian Fed.) refer to the Soviet Union up to 1990–91 and to Uzbekistan, the Russian Federation, respectively, onward.

Source: ICAC.

Annual Wheat Prices

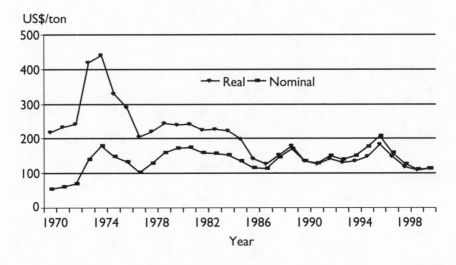

Monthly Wheat Prices

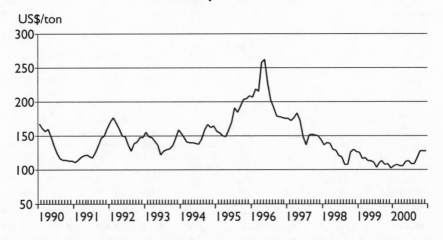

Price is U.S, No. 2, soft red winter, export price delivered at the Gulf port for prompt or 30 days shipment. Quantities are from the U.S. Department of Agriculture.

Table 5. World Wheat Balance (thousands of tons)

	1970–71	1980–81	1990–91	1995–96	1996–97	1997–98	1998–99	1999–2000
PRODUCTION								
China	29,185	55,210	98,229	102,215	110,570	123,389	109,726	—
European Union	45,598	67,390	89,095	86,161	98,506	94,181	103,074	—
India	20,093	31,830	49,850	65,470	62,097	69,350	66,350	—
United States	36,795	64,798	74,292	59,411	61,980	67,534	69,327	—
Russian Federation	—	—	49,596	30,100	34,900	44,200	26,900	—
Canada	9,024	19,291	32,098	25,037	29,801	24,280	24,076	—
Australia	7,890	10,856	15,066	15,504	23,702	19,417	22,108	—
Pakistan	7,294	10,857	14,429	17,002	16,907	16,650	18,694	—
Turkey	8,000	13,000	16,000	15,500	16,000	16,000	18,500	—
Argentina	4,920	7,780	10,900	8,600	15,900	14,800	12,000	—
Ukraine	—	—	30,374	16273	13,550	18,404	14,937	—
Kazakhstan	—	—	16,197	6,490	7,700	8,950	4,700	—
Mexico	2,148	2,650	3,930	3468	3,107	3,639	3,250	—
World	**30,6531**	**436,250**	**588,058**	**538,647**	**582,751**	**609,359**	**588,771**	**585,589**
ENDING STOCKS								
United States	22,398	26919	23627	10,234	12,073	19,663	25,744	27,144
China	7,200	31700	23513	24,252	24,166	33,455	27,921	26,121
European Union	7,177	12580	17936	11,120	13,764	14,500	19,022	15,529
India	5,000	4000	6800	12,000	7,000	10,081	11,081	14,111
Canada	19,980	8510	10285	6,728	9,047	6,009	7,365	7,415
Australia	3,665	2044	2823	1,475	2,395	1,348	2,400	2,825
World	**80,529**	**113788**	**145029**	**106,702**	**113,494**	**138,288**	**135,556**	**126,863**
EXPORTS								
United States	20,167	41,200	29,106	33,681	27,093	28,090	29,035	28,500
Canada	11,846	16,262	21,731	17,066	18,167	21,325	14,455	18,500
Australia	9,145	9,577	11,760	12,131	18,191	15,444	16,000	18,500
European Union	6,249	22,485	35,673	13,250	17,834	14,196	14,589	15,500
Argentina	969	3,845	5,592	4,442	10,079	9,606	8,700	10,000
Kazakhstan	—	—	5,000	4,422	2,320	3,428	2,280	4,500
Turkey	0	530	546	1,178	989	1,274	3,000	1,500
World	**56,479**	**96,911**	**11,7276**	**98,762**	**103,597**	**103,262**	**100,464**	**104,310**
IMPORTS								
Iran, Islamic Republic of	458	1,896	4,000	2,793	7,117	3,587	2,538	7,000
Brazil	1,710	3,910	4,444	5,530	5,724	5,969	7,290	6,700
Egypt	2,835	5,423	5,680	5,932	6,893	7,156	7,430	6,300
Japan	4,834	5,840	5,552	6,101	6,264	6,200	5,883	5,900
Russian Federation	—	—	10,849	5,242	2,629	3,085	2,500	4,800
Algeria	646	2,294	4,360	3,780	3,630	5,221	4,200	4,500
European Union	14,882	12,172	15,508	21505	2,442	3,858	3,761	3,600
Korea, Republic of	1,384	2,095	4,206	2,554	3,465	3,917	4,689	3,500
Indonesia	455	1,233	2,036	3,613	4,201	3,664	3,075	2,800
Mexico	5	1,235	486	1,581	1,940	2,166	2,485	2,700
Morocco	645	1,960	1,954	2,336	1,587	2,565	2,557	2,500
Iraq	156	1,366	124	515	1,136	2,707	2,028	2,500
World	**58,808**	**96,068**	**112,983**	**98,762**	**103,597**	**103,262**	**100,464**	**104,310**

— Not available.

Note: All quantities are in local crop years, except imports, which begin on July 1.

Source: U.S. Department of Agriculture and World Bank.

Annual Rice Prices

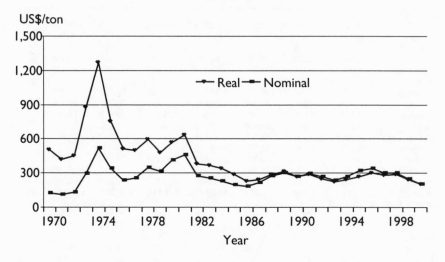

Monthly Rice Prices

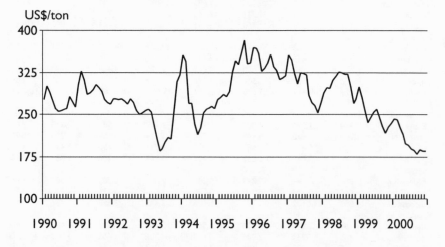

The price is for Thai, 5 percent broken, white rice, milled, indicative price based on weekly surveys of export transactions (indicative survey price), government standard, f.o.b. Bangkok. Quantities are from the U.S. Department of Agriculture.

Table 6. World Rice Balance (thousands of tons)

	1970–71	1980–81	1990–91	1995–96	1996–97	1997–98	1998–99	1999–2000
PRODUCTION								
China	110,003	139,906	189,331	185,214	195,100	200,700	198,714	201,429
India	63,401	80,527	111,448	119,442	121,980	123,822	129,013	126,763
Indonesia	19,324	32,774	44,680	51,100	49,360	49,237	50,791	50,791
Vietnam	9,915	11,842	18,777	26,729	27,277	28,930	30,467	30,455
Bangladesh	16,731	20,844	26,781	26,533	28,326	28,296	29,784	30,378
Thailand	13,570	17,368	17,192	21,800	20,700	23,500	23,000	24,015
Myanmar	8,179	10,680	13,695	17,000	15,517	15,345	16,034	16,466
Philippines	5,235	7,723	9,885	11,174	11,177	9,982	10,268	11,923
Japan	15,861	12,188	13,124	13,435	12,930	12,532	11,201	11,470
Brazil	5,394	8,638	10,000	10,026	9,504	8,551	11,375	10,588
United States	3,801	6,629	7,081	7,887	7,783	8,300	8,530	9,547
Pakistan	3,303	4,689	4,898	5,951	6,461	6,500	7,012	7,651
World	**312,496**	**396,999**	**520,519**	**551,036**	**563,740**	**574,323**	**585,247**	**591,960**
ENDING STOCKS								
China	11,070	25,000	28,220	21,732	25,556	26,723	26,539	27,089
India	6,000	6,500	14,500	11,000	9,500	10,500	12,000	12,500
Indonesia	531	2,252	885	2,615	1,530	3,529	4,025	2,425
Philippines	620	1,470	1,821	1,670	1,590	1,566	2,115	2,165
Thailand	1,232	1,980	941	852	708	1,051	652	2,002
Korea, Republic of	4	1,495	2,151	245	390	805	980	1,330
World	**28,794**	**48,542**	**59,187**	**49,815**	**51,306**	**54,895**	**58,203**	**59,255**
EXPORTS								
Thailand	1,576	3,049	3,988	5,281	5,216	6,367	6,679	5,500
Vietnam	3	5	1,048	3,040	3,327	3,776	4,555	4,000
United States	1,461	3,028	2,292	2,624	2,292	3,165	2,650	3,000
China	1,306	509	689	265	938	3,734	2,708	2,850
Pakistan	182	1,163	1,274	1,677	1,982	1,800	1,850	2,000
India	20	900	500	3,556	1,954	4,491	2,400	1,500
Uruguay	60	184	270	596	640	639	725	600
World	**8,465**	**13,114**	**12,591**	**19,655**	**18,806**	**27,270**	**24,986**	**22,971**
IMPORTS								
Indonesia	516	543	192	1,233	808	6,081	3,900	2,000
Iran, Islamic Republic of	60	636	599	1,294	973	500	1,000	1,200
Bangladesh	347	84	11	655	44	2,499	1,400	900
Nigeria	1	394	224	350	731	900	900	850
Saudi Arabia	202	356	547	786	660	775	750	800
European Union	620	1,142	1,267	895	844	787	775	800
Brazil	1	0	965	786	845	1,457	850	800
Japan	10	75	17	445	546	479	633	750
Iraq	97	350	268	236	684	610	781	700
Malaysia	356	167	298	573	645	593	650	675
South Africa	68	126	295	448	573	525	550	575
World	**7,695**	**12,117**	**11,278**	**19,655**	**18,806**	**27,270**	**24,986**	**22,971**

— Not available.

Note: Production refers to paddy. All quantities are in local crop years.
Source: U.S. Department of Agriculture and World Bank.

Annual Maize Prices

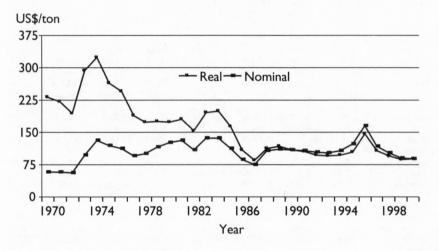

Monthly Maize Prices

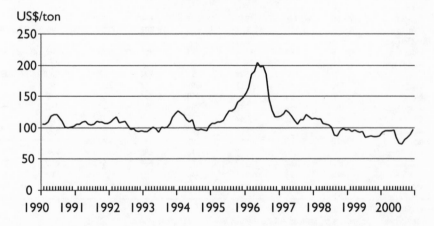

The price is for U.S., No. 2, yellow, f.o.b. U.S. Gulf ports. Quantities are from the U.S. Department of Agriculture.

Table 7. World Maize Balance (thousands of tons)

	1970– 71	1980– 81	1990– 91	1995– 96	1996– 97	1997– 98	1997– 99	1999– 2000
PRODUCTION								
United States	105,472	168,648	201,534	187,970	234,518	233,864	247,882	239,719
China	33,030	62,600	96,820	112,000	127,470	104,300	132,954	128,000
European Union	16,368	21,640	23,523	29,224	34,794	38,522	35,105	37,145
Brazil	14,130	22,555	24,330	32,480	35,700	30,100	32,200	32,000
Mexico	8,900	10,400	14,100	17,780	18,922	16,934	17,600	19,000
Argentina	9,930	12,900	7,600	11,100	15,500	19,360	13,500	15,500
India	7,486	6,957	8,692	9,530	10,612	10,852	10,680	10,500
Romania	6,536	11,153	6,800	9,923	9,610	12,680	8,500	10,500
South Africa, Republic of	8,600	14,872	8,614	10,200	10,136	7,693	7,700	9,500
Canada	2,634	5,753	7,067	7,271	7,380	7,180	8,952	9,096
World	**268,078**	**408,764**	**482,412**	**516,637**	**591,979**	**575,254**	**605,872**	**600,721**
ENDING STOCKS								
United States	16,840	35,361	38,641	10,819	22,433	33,220	45,391	44,181
China	8,875	25,768	23,000	34,700	45,000	26,000	38,616	38,916
European Union	2,230	4,258	1,411	2,311	3,280	4,368	4,468	5,168
South Africa, Republic of	1,625	4,500	1,000	1,200	2,450	1,599	1,449	1,749
Brazil	1,993	1,348	751	3,222	2,633	1,109	1,034	1,034
Argentina	620	210	385	400	750	1,540	741	742
Thailand	245	103	288	297	222	134	284	284
World	**36,148**	**85,451**	**81,130**	**68,776**	**92,870**	**6,856**	**109,254**	**108,628**
EXPORTS								
United States	12,854	60,737	43,858	52,681	46,633	37,697	51,886	48,000
Argentina	6,441	9,098	4,000	6,952	10,210	12,756	7,849	8,500
China	33	125	6,880	168	3,892	6,173	3,338	8,000
Hungary	49	300	0	122	1,122	1,289	1,766	1,700
South Africa, Republic of	2,555	4,955	900	1,541	2,200	1,041	1,000	1,100
World	**32,156**	**84,851**	**64,463**	**64,906**	**67,138**	**62,887**	**68,832**	**70,420**
IMPORTS								
Japan	5,173	13,989	16,345	15,976	15,963	16,422	16,336	16,250
Korea, Republic of	315	2,355	5,571	8,963	8,336	7,528	7,517	9,000
Mexico	139	3,833	1,939	6,379	3,141	4,376	5,612	5,000
Taiwan, China	556	2,703	5,289	5,733	5,741	4,474	4,575	4,700
Egypt, Arab Republic of	76	984	1,943	2,223	3,196	3,259	3,700	4,000
Malaysia	169	77	1,370	2,444	2,485	2,145	2,500	2,600
European Union	17,969	25,347	8,680	2,966	2,595	2,065	3,000	2,500
Colombia	40	140	38	1,495	1,674	1,694	1,570	1,700
Brazil	1	0	700	160	513	1,324	968	1,600
Saudi Arabia	0	280	800	923	1,272	1,234	1,500	1,500
Venezuela, R. B. de	82	1,060	321	1,205	1,494	1,161	1,500	1,250
Iran, Islamic Republic of	22	400	796	822	1,503	900	750	1,200
World	**28,392**	**79,110**	**61,335**	**64,906**	**67,138**	**62,887**	**68,832**	**70,420**

— Not available.

Note: All quantities are in local crop years.

Source: U.S. Department of Agriculture and World Bank.

Index